CONSTRUCTIONIST
CONTROVERSIES

SOCIAL PROBLEMS AND SOCIAL ISSUES

An Aldine de Gruyter Series of Texts and Monographs

SERIES EDITOR
Joel Best
University of Southern Illinois, Carbondale

CONSTRUCTIONIST CONTROVERSIES
Issues in Social Problems Theory

Gale Miller and James A. Holstein
EDITORS

ALDINE DE GRUYTER

New York

About the Editors

Gale Miller is Professor of Sociology at Marquette University. His recent research focuses on social problems theory and the social organization and use of language in everyday life, particularly in human service organizations. His study of a Work Incentive Program (*Enforcing the Work Ethic*) analyzes how human service work is rhetorically organized and accomplished. He and James Holstein coedit the research annual, *Perspectives on Social Problems*.

James A. Holstein is Associate Professor of Sociology at Marquette University. His research brings an ethnomethodologically-informed constructionist perspective to a variety of topics including mental illness, social problems, family, the life course, and dispute processing. His recent publications include *Court-Ordered Insanity* (Aldine de Gruyter 1993) and *Constructing the Life Course* (1993) and *What Is Family?*, co-authored with J. Gubrium.

Copyright © 1993 Walter de Gruyter, Inc., New York

ALDINE DE GRUYTER
A division of Walter de Gruyter, Inc.
200 Saw Mill River Road
Hawthorne, New York 10532

This publication is printed on acid-free paper ∞

Library of Congress Cataloging-in-Publication Data
Miller, Gale.
   Constructionist controversies : issues in social problems theory /
Gale Miller and James A. Holstein.
     p. cm. — (Social problems and social issues)
   Includes bibliographical references and index.
   ISBN 0-202-30457-4 (pbk. : alk. paper)
   1. Social problems. 2. Sociology–Philosophy. I. Holstein.
James A. II. Title. III. Series.
HN28.M55 1993
361.1—dc20   92-36979
                                                CIP

Manufactured in the United States of America

10 9 8 7 6 5 4 3 2 1

Contents

v

List of Contributors

Joel Best

Department of Sociology
Southern Illinois University
Carbondale

David Bogen

Humanities and Social Sciences
Emerson College

Herman Gray

Sociology Board
University of California
Santa Cruz

Jaber F. Gubrium

Department of Sociology
University of Florida

James A. Holstein

Department of Social and
        Cultural Sciences
Marquette University

Peter R. Ibarra

Sociology Board
University of California
Santa Cruz

John I. Kitsuse

Sociology Board
University of California
Santa Cruz

Donileen Loseke

Department of Sociology,
        Anthropology and Social Work
Skidmore College

Michael Lynch

Department of Sociology
Boston College

Michal M. McCall

Department of Sociology
Macalester College

Gale Miller   Department of Social and
                                       Cultural Sciences
                                   Marquette University

Leslie J. Miller   Department of Sociology
                                   University of Calgary

Melvin Pollner   Department of Sociology
                                   University of California
                                   Los Angeles

Preface

This book rekindles some of the controversies that have animated the study of social problems for the past twenty years. The social constructionist approach to social problems theory has been both provocative and controversial since its introduction by John Kitsuse and Malcolm Spector during the 1970s. This volume reexamines constructionist theorizing and considers a variety of arguments it has generated. The cornerstone of the book is a paper by John Kitsuse and Peter Ibarra which addresses some of the major controversies that have emerged in recent years. The paper is a point of departure for further consideration of some of the disputes that continue to flourish.

This is a unique group of essays. The authors of this collection—and its companion volume, *Reconsidering Social Constructionism: Debates in Social Problems Theory* (Aldine de Gruyter 1993), represent diverse perspectives, but they share an interest in what the constructionist perspective on social problems has to offer. While the essays present a wide range of opinions, each offers a healthy dose of constructive criticism. Consequently, we hold little hope for resolving disputes, but rather hope to animate further debates and discussions.

This volume is organized around several recent controversies relating to the constructionist perspective. Part I offers a diverse set of commentaries on the perspective, beginning with Ibarra and Kitsuse's bold pronouncement on the state of constructionism and the directions it should pursue in the future. Other essays in the section raise a set of important issues that constructionists must engage if the perspective is to continue to be a productive source of social problems scholarship and research. Part II offers some provocative suggestions for expanding the constructionist program. Some of the essays call for extensions of familiar constructionist themes, while others bring ethnomethodological, poststructural, feminist, and critical perspectives into the constructionist picture.

Throughout the volume, our intent is to articulate alternative points of view on the constructionist project, using the arising tensions as opportunities for theoretical clarification and growth. Some of the perspectives represented here are not generally associated with the constructionist program, but we hope that bringing disparate approaches to bear on a common theme might provoke new ways of looking at, and doing, the sociology of social problems.

John Kitsuse has been at the forefront of the sociology of deviance and social problems since he arrived at Northwestern University in 1958. There, and later at the University of California at Santa Cruz, Kitsuse pursued a consistently radical program of constructionist studies that has transformed American sociology. While his work has clear affinities for what has come to be known as "labeling theory," Kitsuse's analysis has been distinguished by its uncompromising constitutive emphasis. His early collaborations with Aaron Cicourel and, later, with Malcolm Spector, represent foundational pieces in the constructionist program that challenged the dominant sociological paradigms of the mid-twentieth century. Generations of sociologists are indebted to his clear and forceful articulations of the approach.

We are very much indebted to John for his work over the years, and for his contribution to this collection. Perhaps no higher tribute can be paid to a scholar than for his friends, colleagues, and detractors to get riled up over what he has to say. We think this collection is evidence that John Kitsuse can still provoke a good argument.

We have many people besides John and his coauthor, Peter Ibarra, to thank for making this project possible. Ron Troyer organized a social problems colloquium at the meetings of the Society for the Study of Social Problems in 1989 that sparked many of the debates that we have pursued in this collection. Some of the papers in the volume got their start at that session. We are deeply indebted to all the contributors to this book for their superb essays.

Getting a project of this magnitude into print is not an easy task. Joel Best, editor of Aldine de Gruyter's series in "Social Problems and Social Issues" was enthusiastic about the project from the start. Executive Editor Richard Koffler has been a tremendous help in working out the details and making it possible to publish the two volume set. They deserve our special thanks. Finally, Arlene Perazzini and Mike Sola have done a superbly professional job in pulling this difficult project together into a final product.

Introduction

1

Constructing Social Problems: Context and Legacy

Gale Miller and James A. Holstein

This book is concerned with recent developments in and challenges to the social constructionist perspective on social problems. The perspective has been the most controversial—if not the most influential—development in social problems theory in the past twenty-five years. *Constructing Social Problems* ([1977] 1987) offered what is generally regarded as the quintessential statement of the approach, both transforming and revitalizing the sociology of social problems. In the book and a series of articles published in *Social Problems* (Kitsuse and Spector 1973, 1975; Spector and Kitsuse 1974), Kitsuse and Spector challenged conventional approaches to the field with their vision of social problems as social constructions, that is, as the products of claims-making and constitutive definitional processes.

While the constructionist approach quickly produced a torrent of empirical studies (see Schneider 1985a; Maynard 1988; Best 1989), it just as quickly became the focus of a variety of controversies. Objections from the more conventional or "realist" orientations insisted that there is an objective reality to social problems that should be the topic of sociological studies and that constructionists stubbornly deny. Charges of unacknowledged objectivism and "ontological gerrymandering" (Woolgar and Pawluch 1985) resounded from the opposite direction. Most recently, the constructionist camp finds itself divided, some arguing for the "strict" constitutive reading of *Constructing Social Problems*, while others argue for a "contextual" constructionism that focuses on the claims-making process, but acknowledges assumptions about objective conditions (Best 1989).

The purpose of this book is to reconsider the social constructionist perspective in light of new developments and emerging controversies in social problems theory. Although they all express appreciation for the constructionist approach, the essays that follow offer a variety of orientations to the study of social problems. They critique previous constructionist formulations, make suggestions for advancing, expanding, or diversifying the constructionist agenda, and challenge the perspective and agenda.

The book's focal point is the essay by Ibarra and Kitsuse, which refocuses and redefines Spector and Kitsuse's original programmatic position. Subsequent essays include constructionist responses to the revised position and discuss how ethnomethodological concerns relate to the construction of social problems. Other essays offer new challenges to social constructionism that emanate from a variety of related, though not wholly sympathetic perspectives. Critical and poststructural challenges provide the basis for wide-ranging discussions of the prospects and possibilities for the constructionist approach and social problems theory. We provide a background for subsequent discussions in this essay, which reviews the major issues at stake in current debates about social constructionism.

The Challenge of Social Constructionism

The social constructionist perspective has been controversial since its inception. Most notably, the approach breaks with conventional and commonsensical conceptions of social problems by analyzing them as a *social process* of definition. In their seminal paper, Kitsuse and Spector define social problems as "the activities of groups making assertions of grievances and claims with respect to some putative conditions" (1973, p. 415). Construed in this fashion, social problems are not objective conditions to be studied and corrected; rather, they are the interpretive processes that constitute what come to be seen as oppressive, intolerable, or unjust conditions like crime, poverty, and homelessness.

From this point of view, social problems are not distinctive and inherently immoral conditions; they are definitions of and orientations to *putative* conditions that are *argued* to be inherently immoral or unjust (Spector and Kitsuse [1977] 1987). The constructionist position emphasizes that the activities through which social problems are constructed are both implicitly and intentionally rhetorical. Public rhetoric and the politics of claims-making are analyzed in the myriad circumstances in which social problems construction takes place, including "demanding services, filling out forms, lodging complaints, filing lawsuits, calling press conferences, writing letters of protest, passing resolutions, publishing exposes, placing ads in newspapers, supporting or opposing governmental practice or policy, setting up picket lines or boycotts" (p. 79). The result is a constructionist sociology of social problems that attempts to "account for the emergence and maintenance of claims-making and responding activities" (Kitsuse and Spector 1973, p. 415).

Initially, the constructionist approach was a response and alternative to the structural functionalist approach to social problems. Structural functionalists assume that social conditions exist separately from persons' interpretations of them. They believe that objective knowledge of social conditions is obtainable through the scientific method and that the scientific study of social conditions will demonstrate that some social conditions are truly social problems. Sociologists use the assumptions as a warrant for defining problems as real and observable social conditions, portraying their studies as objective analyses, and describing themselves as experts on social problems.

Spector and Kitsuse's claims-making approach undercuts these fundamental assumptions by questioning the possibility of knowing the objective status of conditions. Indeed, their challenge is almost ironic because they take structural functionalists' definitions of social problems seriously, even as they undermine them. For example, in a classic functionalist statement, Merton contends that *"a social problem exists when there is a sizeable discrepancy between what is and what people think ought to be"* (1976, p. 7). Spector and Kitsuse appreciate several questions implicit in this definition by asking, how do people know what is, and what ought to be? They also ask, How do persons know that there is a sizeable discrepancy between what is and what ought to be? Spector and Kitsuse's answers to the questions emphasize the ways in which social conditions, cultural ideals, and discrepancies between them are socially constructed.

Spector and Kitsuse also challenge structural functionalists by analyzing how professional sociologists' conventional theories of social problems involve claims-making about putative social conditions. Like Merton, authors of social problems texts use their portrayals of "real" aspects of everyday life to justify their interest in analyzing the pervasiveness, social organization, and consequences of the conditions that they describe as manifest and latent social problems. Sociologists also act as expert consultants to policymakers, who assume that social problems exist as objective conditions and that sociologists are experts on them.

Thus, Spector and Kitsuse use the social constructionist perspective to subvert other sociologists' claims to objective knowledge about social problems and expert status. They also point to the theoretical advantages of studying sociologists as claims-makers by arguing that constructionism provides the basis for developing a distinctively sociological approach that focuses on the social processes through which social problems are constructed. Such a sociology would examine the diverse claims-making groups and activities, and avoid its own claims-making activities. Specifically, Spector and Kitsuse's ([1977] 1987) approach to constructionism would avoid defining "real" social problems, or distinguishing between "real" and "spurious" social problems.

Contemporary Controversies

Some contemporary controversies surrounding social constructionism recast old issues raised in Spector and Kitsuse's debate with structural functionalists. Questions still arise concerning sociologists' responsibilities to point out "real" social problems that are ignored by political leaders and the public. Some critics argue that definitions of social problems are important, but there is a "reality" behind them that is paramount (Eitzen 1984; Collins 1989). There are also debates that raise new questions about the fundamental assumptions and goals of social constructionism.

Many of the new critics argue that the constructionist perspective actually invokes a selective "objectivism" because it assumes that social construction processes are observable aspects of social worlds that exist separately from social constructionists' descriptions of them. Social constructionists, then, act as "objective" analysts of and experts on the "real" social processes through which social problems are constructed. Perhaps the most influential of the new critics are Woolgar and Pawluch (1985), who analyze social constructionist theorizing as ontological gerrymandering.

Woolgar and Pawluch suggest that social constructionist arguments can generally be broken out into three parts: First, the analyst identifies particular conditions or behaviors. Then he or she identifies various definitions or claims made about these conditions or behaviors. Finally, the analyst highlights the variability of the definitions or claims relative to the constancy of the conditions to which they relate. The implication is that since the condition is invariant, changes in the definition of the conditions must result from the social circumstances of the definers rather than from the condition itself.

Woolgar and Pawluch note that this sort of analysis depends upon the "objective" statement about the constancy of the condition under consideration in order to justify claims about the shifting definitional process. Assumptions must be made regarding the actual existence and status of the condition if apparent change in the condition or problem is to be considered a definitional artifact. Woolgar and Pawluch argue that this selective "objectivism" represents a theoretical inconsistency in the definitional approach since it manipulates an analytic boundary to make certain phenomena problematic while leaving others unquestioned. Ontological gerrymandering, then, glosses over the ways in which constructionist analysts' descriptions of conditions are themselves definitional claims.

Woolgar and Pawluch draw two very different implications from their analysis: First, they suggest that ontological gerrymandering may be a necessary aspect of the social constructionist project. It is not a practice that can be avoided; rather, it sets constructionist theorizing apart from other interpretive approaches to social problems. The response justifies the theoretical status quo, even taking an appreciative stance toward social constructionists' writing practices. A second and very different implication is that social constructionists should examine and reconsider their own writing and rhetorical practices. Woolgar and Pawluch suggest that constructionists "search for forms of argument which go beyond the current impasse between proponents of objectivism and of relativism" (p. 224). The suggestion assumes that it is possible to write about social life and experience in ways that do not objectify the phenomena under discussion.

Responses to the Ontological Gerrymandering Critique

Woolgar and Pawluch's critique has raised a variety of responses among social constructionists concerning the essential claims and assumptions of the perspective, and the purposes of their studies. These involve both assessments of and responses to Woolgar and Pawluch's critique, and portrayals of social constructionism as a complex intellectual movement that includes diverse and somewhat opposed orientations to social problems theory. For example, in this volume, Ibarra and Kitsuse react to Woolgar and Pawluch by distinguishing between the assumptions and claims of the social constructionist perspective—as it was initially formulated by Spector and Kitsuse—and the ways in which it has been explained and applied by other social constructionists (see Schneider 1985b).

Ibarra and Kitsuse state that while Woolgar and Pawluch's critique is appropriate for much contemporary research on social problems that is called social constructionist, it is an inappropriate description of Spector and Kitsuse's formulation of the perspective because they express little interest in the sociohistorical circumstances associated with social problems definitions. Rather, they focus on how claims-making activities are organized and accomplished. Thus, Spector and Kitsuse analyze social problems as real to the extent that claims-makers are able to convince others to honor their claims, and state that it is sociologically counterproductive to ask whether claims-makers' definitions are accurate or warranted.

Other social constructionists, however, have responded to the ontological gerrymandering critique by emphasizing the implications noted by Woolgar and Pawluch. Specifically, contextual constructionists argue that Woolgar and Pawluch's critique is counterproductive to the development of an adequate social constructionist theory of social problems

(Best 1989). They state that the critique diverts attention away from the study of the social worlds within which and social processes through which social problems are constructed. For example, Gusfield (1985) rejects the critique because it only focuses on the logic of social constructionists' theorizing and writing. It does not consider what it is that social constructionists are theorizing and writing about or, as Gusfield states, the substance of the social constructionist project.

The contextual constructionists' position derives from their orientation to sociological research and analysis. They argue that the object of research and theory should be to offer information about and insights into the organization and workings of social problems movements, and the social conditions that claims-makers describe as social problems. While not denying that their analyses are social constructions, contextual constructionists argue that a *primary* focus on such matters makes sociologists' studies of social problems irrelevant to most audiences within and outside the field.

Contextual constructionists also emphasize the theoretical usefulness of ontological gerrymandering in explaining why and how social problems claims emerge within sociohistorical contexts. Best (1989) justifies the practice in two major ways. First, he states that it may be impossible for social constructionists to avoid ontological gerrymandering, no matter how hard they try. It is a necessary aspect of writing about social worlds and definitional processes as existing separately from writers' portrayals of them. Second, efforts to avoid ontological gerrymandering may undermine the social constructionist project because social constructionists may quit asking important questions about claims-making activities.

Finally, where strict constructionists try to avoid ontological gerrymandering by refusing to evaluate the accuracy of claims-makers' claims, contextual constructionists treat the evaluation of social problems claims as an important part of their analyses. It is one way in which they contribute to public and academic debates about social problems. According to Best, any social problems claim can be evaluated with reasonable confidence by using available statistical and other information about the condition that the claim describes. It is irrelevant that the information used to make the evaluation is itself a social construction and rhetorical claim. As Best states, "calling a statement a claim does not discredit it" (1989, p. 247).

The second implication Woolgar and Pawluch (1985) draw from their critique involves developing new ways of writing social problems texts. They state that the purpose of the new writing forms is to get beyond the fruitless debates between advocates for objectivist and relativist positions. Such debates are fruitless because they are unresolvable within the writing forms typically used by sociologists to formulate and express their positions. An example of how new writing forms might be developed is Hughes's (1961) study of a drug addict. The research is based on extensive, tape-recorded conversations between Janet (a drug addict) and Howard S. Becker.

Hughes edited the tapes to produce a story that might be read as Janet's autobiography. Thus, Hughes's study gets beyond the objectivist-relativist debate by allowing Janet to tell her story without submitting it to external, sociological analysis. Similar concerns and themes are central to McCall and Becker's (1990) experiment with performance science, which is intended to show how the "findings" of field studies may be recast as theatrical performances. Among the advantages of such a mode of presentation are the organization of the findings as dialogues between actors, and opportunities to show the complexities of others' orientations to and responses to diverse situations and issues.

Other social constructionists have experimented with reflexive writing forms. Such texts are organized to remind readers that authors are aware of the rhetorical devices that they use to construct textual realities, and that they offer understandings that are partisan and potentially contestable by others. While social constructionists' interest in developing reflexive writing practices may be seen as an attempt to become more self-aware and sophisticated theorists and writers, it promises more than this. It is a possible bridge between social constructionism and related, but very different poststructuralist perspectives.

Ethnomethodology and Social Problems

While it remained for Woolgar and Pawluch to point out some of the major theoretical inconsistencies in the application of Spector and Kitsuse's initial formulations, ethnomethodologists anticipated Woolgar and Pawluch's argument, most specifically in early critiques of labeling theory. For example, in commenting on Becker's (1963) theory of deviance, Pollner (1974, 1978) distinguishes between "mundane" and "constitutive" versions of labeling theory. He states that mundane labeling theorists, like Becker, analyze the labeling process by assessing whether persons and/or acts have been accurately labeled as deviant. Making such assessments necessarily involves making privileged judgments about the "real" or "factual" character of the phenomena in question, and the objective character of acts and/or conditions retains its importance as the determinant of the accuracy of the labeling process.

For example, Becker takes this position when he suggests that "the degree to which an act will be treated as deviant depends on who commits the act" (1963, p. 12), then illustrates the point by documenting the differential fates of middle-class versus lower-class boys, or white versus black youth when confronted by the criminal justice system for committing the "same" act. Establishing the "sameness" of the act, Pollner argues, requires reference to a criterion other that the actual disposition of and reaction to the cases under consideration. The independent criterion is necessary to establish that similar acts have elicited differential responses. Thus, some inherent feature of the act, not societal reaction or the labeling process itself, is treated as defining the act's character.

Pollner contrasts mundane labeling theory with an ethnomethodological or constitutive version, which assumes that the labeling process *constitutes* the phenomenon. There is no need to assess the "objective" characteristics of persons or events labeled as deviant because their deviant status is an interpretive accomplishment. Labelers accomplish deviance by applying deviant labels to themselves, others, activities, and/or events. Thus, the ethnomethodological approach is radically different from mundane labeling theory.

The Ethnomethodological Focus

Ethnomethodology attends to the commonsense practices, procedures, and resources that persons use to produce and recognize mutually intelligible objects and actions in the life world (Garfinkel 1967; Heritage 1984). It emphasizes locally managed, ongoing practices of reality construction and maintenance, and treats the social construction of social realities as an ongoing accomplishment. Talk and interaction are the focus of ethnomethodological studies of social problems. Aspects of the ethnomethodological perspective are clearly evident in Spector and Kitsuse's initial formulation of the social constructionist project. As Troyer states, Spector and Kitsuse emphasized ethnomethodological assumptions and concerns when they argued for

> suspending the issue of whether or not there is an external world and argued that social problems researchers should look at how the agreement arises that there is a "social problem." . . . . Spector and Kitsuse ask that researchers examine the methods people use in creating a sense that there is a bad condition. The definition itself is secondary: the primary concern is the methods (activities) used to create the "problem." (1989, p. 44)

Aspects of ethnomethodology resonate with Wittgenstein's (1953, 1969) analysis of language games and forms of life. For Wittgenstein, language games are the diverse, concrete, and culturally shared ways in which actors use language to organize situations and achieve practical ends. They include asking questions, telling stories, giving orders, and describing objects. Further, each of these language games is related to other activities in everyday life, including other language games. For example, asking questions is typically associated with the language game of answering questions, telling stories with laughter, and describing objects with questions about them. In associating language games with other activities, actors construct social contexts for assigning meaning to their own and others' actions (Wittgenstein 1967). Thus, language games are aspects of forms of life, i.e., patterns of behavior and relationship to which actors orient.

Ethnomethodology complements Wittgenstein's analysis of language games and forms of life in at least two major ways. First, it is a radically social approach to everyday life that focuses on the ways in which actors descriptively construct and assign meanings (including intentions). Ethnomethodologists analyze actors' interpretive practices as reflexively implicated in situations; that is, they are constitutive aspects of the situations in which they occur. Meaning construction and assignment is a multifaceted process that simultaneously involves defining the events, objects, or issues under consideration, as well as the situations in which the considerations are made. The analyses may be further extended to consider the methods used by ethnomethodologists to describe and analyze situations (Mehan and Wood 1975; Pollner 1991; Wieder 1988).

Ethnomethodology also complements Wittgenstein's analysis in its concern for the practical assumptions and practices associated with meaning construction and assignment. Ethnomethodologists often express the concern as a problem of analyzing the taken-for-granted and "seen but unnoticed" aspects of everyday life (Garfinkel 1967). This partly involves analyzing the assumptions that underlie the natural attitude (Schutz 1970) and mundane reasoning (Pollner 1987) through which everyday life is organized.

Ethnomethodology and Social Problems Theory

Ethnomethodology is a diverse mode of inquiry, composed of a variety of research methodologies and analytic techniques (Holstein and Gubrium forthcoming; Maynard and Clayman 1991). Ethnomethodological studies include in-depth, ethnographic studies of interaction in social institutions, highly detailed analyses of transcripts of conversations, and abstract studies of such issues as the natural attitude, the documentary method of interpretation, and reflexivity. One way in which the ethnomethodological perspective has been applied within social problems theory is by analyzing the situated interactional and interpretive procedures used by claims-makers to describe aspects of everyday life as social problems.

Such analyses are central to studies of the micropolitics of trouble in institutional settings (Emerson and Messinger 1977), which focus on the concrete ways in which interactants describe and orient to aspects of their own and others lives as troublesome (Emerson 1969; Gubrium and Holstein 1990; Holstein 1993; Loseke 1989, 1992; Miller 1983, 1991). The studies differ from those criticized by Woolgar and Pawluch because the analysts do not assume that troublesome conditions exist separately from interactants' descriptions of them. Both the trouble categories used by interactants and conditions that they describe as troublesome are analyzed as social constructions.

Where Spector and Kitsuse specified the processes by which social problems categories are made culturally prominent, ethnomethodologically informed analyses have attempted to describe the practices by which the categories are assigned to concrete cases. The reality-assigning practices that link public interpretive structures to aspects of everyday life can be called social problems work (Miller and Holstein 1989; Miller 1992). Studies of social problems work consider the culturally available labeling resources while maintaining the ethnomethodological focus on the ways that actors apply labels in relation to commonsense methods for handling experiences that come to be portrayed as troubles or problems (Maynard and Clayman 1991).

Many of the pioneering ethnomethodological studies of achieved social order involve social problems categorization. For example, Bittner's (1967a, 1967b) studies of police work and peacekeeping describe the variegated and complex interpretive practices used to establish and maintain order in the community. Integral to the process is police officers' use of social problems categories like crime and mental illness as both definitional and practical resources. Similarly, Sudnow (1965) shows how attorneys employ commonsense models of typical offenders, offenses, problems, and solutions to make plea bargaining arrangements that assign persons to social problems and criminal categories. Unofficial categorization practices have also been analyzed.

Cicourel's (1968) study of the policing of juveniles also elucidates several important aspects of social problems work. He analyzes the processes involved in classifying "juvenile delinquents" and the reflexivity of the categorization process. The study demonstrates how police activities were informed by commonsense theories of delinquency. For example, offenses by juveniles from "broken homes" were treated more seriously by officers than were actions by juveniles from stable families. As a consequence, offenders from broken homes were more likely to be officially apprehended and processed as delinquents—made formal occupants of the category. This practice, in turn, provided concrete documentary evidence in the form of crime statistics that verified the commonsense theory. Thus, the officers' commonsense theories reflexively produced and reproduced the evidence of their own validity.

Another provocative ethnomethodological theme is an ongoing concern for reflexivity. Pollner (1991) argues that as ethnomethodology has settled down in the "suburbs" of sociological inquiry, it has become increasingly committed to interactional, conversational, and scientific practices of reality construction. The emphasis on radical reflexivity—the appreciation of all analysis as constitutive activity—has been set aside. Woolgar and Pawluch's (1985) critique of social constructionism highlights aspects of the neglect. Pollner (1991) has gone further in calling for the resurrection of ethnomethodology's early emphasis on reflexivity. He states that studies of reflexive processes reveal to "epistemologically settled communities" the grounds on which their claims about social reality are built, including those underlying social constructionist and ethnomethodological studies.

A final set of ethnomethodological concerns involves Garfinkel and his close associates' studies of doing science (Heritage 1987). Conceived as "studies of work," their examinations focus on the embodied conceptualizations and practices that practitioners within a particular domain of work activities recognize as belonging to that domain (Garfinkel 1988; Garfinkel, Lynch, and Livingston 1981; Livingston 1986; Lynch, Livingston, and Garfinkel 1983). The studies show how scientists' competencies are reflexively described *in situ*, the competencies being recognized and acted on in locally reasoned and temporally organized sites of the activity. The major implication of this program for social problems theory and research is the recommendation that social problems analysts generate detailed descriptions of highly localized, temporally bound practices through which social problems are accomplished in specific and historical circumstances.

Recent Challenges to Social Constructionism

While several points of contention persist, contemporary challenges to social constructionism differ in several respects from those offered by structural functionalists. Some of the differences are related to the elaboration of diverse feminist perspectives since the publication of *Constructing Social Problems* (Spector and Kitsuse [1977] 1987), while others relate to movements within Marxism and other international intellectual communities concerned with social critique and change. The movements are often discussed under the rubrics of postmodernism and poststructuralism. Three aspects of recent challenges to social construction-ism are particularly relevant to this book.

First, whereas previous challenges to social constructionism tended to disallow any possibility that social problems are social constructions, many contemporary critics acknowledge that social problems are, at least, partly constructed. For example, many critical-feminist theorists and other social critics treat public understandings of and orientations to everyday life as social constructions, but they also emphasize how the understandings and orientations are constructed within gendered and/or capitalist social institutions and relationships. Thus, contempo-rary criticisms are not organized as outright rejections of the construc-tionist perspective, but as attempts to relocate social constructionists' concerns and studies within perspectives that the critics argue are more comprehensive.

A second set of challengers emphasizes the realist and elitist assump-tions of social constructionism. They argue that while social construction-ists state that social problems conditions only exist as claims-making activities, social constructionists' analyses actually treat social problems conditions and claims as observable and objective (Hazelrigg 1985; Pfohl 1985). Recent critics also accuse social constructionists of being elitists who wish to produce a "pure" theory of social problems, which is uncon-taminated by any moral and political assumptions and concerns (Rafter 1992). They add that social constructionists' pursuit of such a theory is impossible and, in pursuing it, social constructionists gloss over the values underlying, and political implications of, their perspective.

A third challenge involves the ways in which social interests are re-lated to social problems claims-making. While contemporary critics of social constructionism state that political, economic, and other social interests are aspects of social problems claims-making movements, they also argue that persons' knowledge about social reality and their social problems claims are related to conditions that are largely unrecognized by them. From their perspective, social problems claims-making in-volves assumptions, desires, and concerns that are so fundamental that claims-makers and others are unlikely to recognize the conditions as anything other than facts. So viewed, the conditions are not matters for conscious reflection, public debate, or social constructionist analysis.

For example, feminist theory assumes that persons' gender status shapes their experiences and understandings of social reality. Not only is gender a master status, but women and men orient to social relation-ships and practical issues in different ways. The differences are related to their positions within social relationships and institutions, including the ways in which they are socialized as children, expectations associ-ated with their adult roles, and practical opportunities made available to them. Thus, differences in female and male orientations to practical issues (including their definitions of social problems) may not be reduced to simple differences of political and economic interest. The differences are also related to the unrecognized ways in which modern social existence is gendered.

Organization of the Book

The rest of the book is organized as two sections. The first, "Contemporary Issues in Social Constructionism," includes Ibarra and Kitsuse's important clarification and expansion of Spector and Kitsuse's constructionist theory of social problems. They assert that their revised approach answers the most significant questions raised in Woolgar and Pawluch's critique. In the following essay, Gubrium notes that the focus of much constructionist theorizing and research on social problems (including Ibarra and Kitsuse's paper) has been on large-scale claims-making— "publicity" as he calls it. He recommends a similar emphasis on mundane interpretive practice in everyday interaction.

Next, Pollner discusses the ethnomethodological concern for reflexivity by reflecting on issues central to the ontological gerrymandering debate. He challenges constructionists to make reflexivity into a topic for analysis, rather than simply treating it as a problem to be managed. Best takes a very different position on the issue in his paper. He argues that the "strict constructionist" concern with epistemological consistency is both misguided and counterproductive. Best encourages constructionists to "worry a little less about how we know what we know, and worry a little more about what, if anything, we do know about the construction of social problems." Finally, Bogen and Lynch question the desirability of a general theory of social problems. As an alternative, they suggest that researchers aim to produce rich, detailed, and interesting descriptions of unique ensembles of discursive routines and practices.

The essays in the second section offer "New Directions for Social Constructionism." Holstein and Miller argue for the development of a research program that focuses on social problems work, the ways in which social problems categories are invoked, articulated, and applied to concrete events and persons in the life world. Leslie Miller's essay is a feminist, poststructural analysis of gender, silence, and claims-making. She argues that social constructionism's emphasis on public claims-making leads to incomplete understandings of social problems construction. For Miller, a more comprehensive approach considers how the contemporary organization of power, knowledge, and discourse precludes the conceptualization and expression of some social problems claims.

McCall's essay also argues for a feminist approach to social problems, although it differs substantially from Miller's approach. Specifically, Mc-Call calls for a critical-feminist social problems theory that treats some social conditions as real social problems. She also encourages social problems theorists to advocate for policies that will change social problems conditions. Gray wishes to extend the social constructionist program to include recent developments in cultural studies, feminism, and minority discourses. He "encourages social constructionists to take a more reflexive and political stance" toward their own writing and theorizing.

Finally, Loseke suggests that social constructionism be extended to take account of the ways in which putative people—as well as putative conditions—are constructed within social problems discourses. She stresses that one way in which social constructionists may do so is by analyzing the folk universes of morality and emotion associated with the discourses.

References

Becker, Howard S. 1963. *Outsiders.* New York: Free Press.

Best, Joel. 1989. "Afterward." Pp. 243–54 in *Images of Issues,* edited by Joel Best. Hawthorne, NY: Aldine de Gruyter.

Bittner, Egon. 1967a. "Police Discretion in Emergency Apprehension of Mentally Ill Persons." *Social Problems* 14:278–92.

———. 1967b. "The Police on Skid Row." *American Sociological Review* 32:699–715.

Cicourel, Aaron V. 1968. *The Social Organization of Juvenile Justice.* New York: Wiley.

Collins, Patricia Hill. 1989. "The Social Construction of Invisibility." Pp. 77–93 in *Perspectives on Social Problems,* Vol. 1, edited by James A. Holstein and Gale Miller. Greenwich, CT: JAI Press.

Eitzen, D. Stanley. 1984. "Teaching Social Problems." *SSSP Newsletter* 16:10–12.

Emerson, Robert M. 1969. *Judging Delinquents.* Chicago: Aldine.

Emerson, Robert M. and Sheldon L. Messinger. 1977. "The Micro-Politics of Trouble." *Social Problems* 25:121–35.

Garfinkel, Harold. 1967. *Studies in Ethnomethodology.* Englewood Cliffs, NJ: Prentice-Hall.

———. 1988. "Evidence for Locally Produced, Naturally Accountable Phenomena of Order, Logic, Reason, Meaning, Method, etc. in and as of the Essential Quiddity of Immortal Ordinary Society." *Sociological Theory* 6:103–9.

Garfinkel, Harold, Michael Lynch, and Eric Livingston. 1981. "The Work of a Discovering Science Construed with Materials from the Optically Discovered Pulsar." *Philosophy of Social Science* 11:131–58.

Gubrium, Jaber F. and James A. Holstein. 1990. *What Is Family?* Mountain View, CA: Mayfield.

Gusfield, Joseph R. 1985. "Theories and Hobgoblins." *SSSP Newsletter* 17:16–18.

Hazelrigg, Lawrence E. 1985. "Were it Not for Words." *Social Problems* 32:234–37.

Heritage, John. 1984. *Garfinkel and Ethnomethodology.* Cambridge: Polity Press.
———. 1987. "Ethnomethodology." Pp. 224–72 in *Social Theory Today*, edited by Anthony Giddens and Jonathan H. Turner. Stanford, CA: Stanford University Press.

Holstein, James A. 1993. *Court-Ordered Insanity.* Hawthorne, NY: Aldine de Gruyter.

Holstein, James A. and Jaber F. Gubrium. Forthcoming. "Phenomenology, Ethnomethodology, and Interpretive Practice." In *Handbook of Qualitative Research*, edited by Norman Denzin and Yvonna Lincoln. Newbury Park, CA: Sage.

Hughes, Helen MacGill. 1961. *The Fantastic Lodge.* Greenwich, CT: Fawcett.

Kitsuse, John I. and Malcolm Spector. 1973. "Toward a Sociology of Social Problems." *Social Problems* 20:407–19.
———. 1975. "Social Problems and Deviance." *Social Problems* 22:584–94.

Livingston, Eric. 1986. *The Ethnomethodological Foundations of Mathematics.* London: Routledge and Kegan Paul.

Loseke, Donileen R. 1989. "Creating Clients." Pp. 173–93 in *Perspectives on Social Problems*, Vol. 1, edited by James A. Holstein and Gale Miller. Greenwich, CT: JAI Press.
———. 1992. *The Battered Woman and Shelters.* Albany, NY: SUNY Press.

Lynch, Michael, Eric Livingston, and Harold Garfinkel. 1983. "Temporal Order in Laboratory Work. Pp. 205–38 in *Science Observed*, edited by Karin Knorr-Cetina and Michael Mulkay. Beverly Hills: Sage.

Maynard, Douglas W. 1988. "Language, Interaction, and Social Problems." *Social Problems* 35:311–34.

Maynard, Douglas W. and Steven E. Clayman. 1991. "The Diversity of Ethnomethodology." *Annual Review of Sociology* 17:385–418.

McCall, Michal and Howard S. Becker. 1990. "Performance Science." *Social Problems* 37:117–32.

Mehan, Hugh and Houston Wood. 1975. *The Reality of Ethnomethodology.* New York: Wiley.

Merton, Robert K. 1976. "The Sociology of Social Problems." Pp. 3–43 in *Contemporary Social Problems*, 4th ed., edited by Robert K. Merton and Robert Nisbet. New York: Harcourt Brace Jovanovich.

Miller, Gale. 1983. "Holding Clients Accountable." *Social Problems* 31:139–51.
———. 1991. *Enforcing the Work Ethic.* Albany, NY: SUNY Press.
———. 1992. "Human Service Practice as Social Problems Work." Pp. 3–21 in *Current Research on Occupations and Professions*, Vol. 7, edited by Gale Miller. Greenwich, CT: JAI Press.

Miller, Gale and James A. Holstein. 1989. "On the Sociology of Social Problems." Pp. 1–16 in *Perspectives on Social Problems*, Vol. 1, edited by James A. Holstein and Gale Miller. Greenwich, CT: JAI Press.

Pfohl, Stephen. 1985. "Toward a Sociological Deconstruction of Social Problems." *Social Problems* 32:228–31.

Pollner, Melvin. 1974. "Sociological and Common Sense Models of the Labeling Process. Pp. 27–40 in *Ethnomethodology*, edited by Roy Turner. Middlesex, England: Penguin.

———. 1978. "Constitutive and Mundane Versions of Labeling Theory." *Human Studies* 31:285–304.

———. 1987. *Mundane Reason*. Cambridge: Cambridge University Press.

———. 1991. "Left of Ethnomethodology." *American Sociological Review* 56:370–80.

Rafter, Nicole H. 1992. "Some Consequences of Strict Constructionism." *Social Problems* 39:38–39.

Schneider, Joseph W. 1985a. "Social Problems Theory." *Annual Review of Sociology* 11:209–29.

———. 1985b. "Defining the Definitional Perspective on Social Problems." *Social Problems* 32:232–34.

Schutz, Alfred. 1970. *On Phenomenology and Social Relations*. Chicago: University of Chicago Press.

Spector, Malcolm and Kitsuse, John I. 1974. "Social Problems." *Social Problems* 21:145–58.

———. [1977] 1987. *Constructing Social Problems*. Hawthorne, NY: Aldine de Gruyter.

Sudnow, David. 1965. "Normal Crimes." *Social Problems* 12:255–76.

Troyer, Ronald J. 1989. "Are Social Problems and Social Movements the Same Things?" Pp. 41–58 in *Perspectives on Social Problems*, Vol. 1, edited by James A. Holstein and Gale Miller. Greenwich, CT: JAI Press.

Wieder, D. Lawrence. 1988. *Language and Social Reality*. Landham, MD: University Press of America.

Wittgenstein, Ludwig. 1953. *Philosophical Investigations*. Translated by G. Anscombe. Oxford: Basil Blackwell.

———. 1967. *Zettel*. Edited by G. Anscombe and G. von Wright. Translated by G. Anscombe. Oxford: Basil Blackwell.

———. 1969. *The Blue and Brown Books*. Oxford: Basil Blackwell.

Woolgar, Steve and Dorothy Pawluch. 1985. "Ontological Gerrymandering." *Social Problems* 32:214–27.

PART I

Contemporary Issues in Social Constructionism

2

Vernacular Constituents of Moral Discourse: An Interactionist Proposal for the Study of Social Problems

Peter R. Ibarra and John I. Kitsuse

Introduction

As a preface to this paper, we would like review the ongoing commentaries and critiques that bear upon the constructionist formulation of social problems, especially as presented in Spector and Kitsuse's *Constructing Social Problems* ([1977] 1987, hereafter *CSP*), suggest how some of the conceptual problems might be resolved, and identify some central issues worth clarifying for the further development of a sociological theory of social problems.

The statement in *CSP* was directed toward the consolidation of a particular perspective, to encourage research oriented by a set of theoretical questions, and to suggest that such work might appropriately be called studies in the sociology of social problems. A fundamental point was made with regard to the ambiguous and often logically inconsistent use of "social problems" as an analytical category in sociology. Major statements on the part of the "objectivist" perspectives were reviewed and were found to typically group various social conditions (e.g., prostitution, crime) under the rubric *social problems* in an ad hoc manner. In the process the concept of social problems was rendered without theoretical precision or scope. Indeed,

> the concept *social problems* was never made to refer to a distinctive set of conditions, processes or activities. The application of the term to conditions identified as [for example] dysfunctional is simply redundant. For is anything added to the study of deviant behavior by calling it a social problem? Do we increase our understanding of crime or poverty by calling it a social problem? (pp. 38–39)

What Spector and Kitsuse proposed instead of a normative-functionalist conception of social problems was one oriented toward figuring out "what it is that people seem to know and use" (Sacks, quoted in Heritage 1984, p. 233) in discerning the objectionable amid their lives. In distancing themselves from normative formulations, Spector and Kitsuse noted that their "formulation will not offer a rival explanation for a commonly defined subject matter. We argue for a different subject matter for the sociology of social problems" (*CSP*, p. 39). In our reading, *CSP* pointed the way to an *interactionist-based* program concerned with explicating social problems as constituted by claims-making activities. Theoretical work would be concerned with elucidating the abstract features of the conventional presuppositions, interpretive practices, rhetorical devices, joint activities, and variety of forums involved in the discursive production of social problems.

The shift from the normative to the interpretive paradigm (Wilson 1971) entails sustaining the distinction between the sociologist's perspective and the member's—especially for coherently translating the theoretical statement in *CSP* to an empirical site. According to Spector and Kitsuse, the member's perspective is employed whenever *anyone* engages in *proposing or contesting* the designation of a category of putative behaviors, expressions, or processes as "offensive," about which something of a remedial nature should be done, i.e., "claims-making and responding activities" (p. 76). Now, in the normative conception, sociologists can "objectively" (and independently of members) view "social conditions" and designate them social problems—by virtue of their recognition of a disjunction between a norm-based conception of society and a state of affairs presumably antithetical to those norms and values. For these sociologists, definitional processes are marginal to the "more important" questions regarding the scope, magnitude, causes and consequences of the social problem itself. By contrast, in the constructionist perspective the sociologist observes/interprets members as perceiving subjects actively engaged in constructing social conditions (or "putative conditions") as moral objects. In this conception, definitional activities are central to the subject matter, and precedence should be given to members' interpretive practices inasmuch as social problems are possible strictly as assemblages of the member's perspective.

The conventional formulation is ironic to the extent that it attempts to display members perceiving a social problem where "in fact" there is none, or not perceiving a social problem where "in fact" there is one, as in Merton's (1974) concepts of "manifest" and "latent" social problems (cf. Pollner 1975, pp. 422–26). The constructionist perspective is ironic by virtue of bracketing the "natural attitude" that enables the analyst to discern and describe "the ways in which [members'] praxis and perception organizes and constitute a world while simultaneously masking the organizational work so as to provide for the appearance of determinate and objective or absolute entities" (Pollner 1978, p. 284), where those entities are social problems.[1] But while both analytics are ironic in their attitudes toward members' commonsense experiences and activities (albeit in different senses), this should in no way conceal the crucial difference between them. This difference rests in how the two formulations address the *warrant* members have for assuming the sensible character of their experiences and actions. Whereas conventional sociologists adopt the "expert" role in passing judgment on the "rationality," "value," "sensibleness," etc., of members' formulations of social problems or lack thereof, the constructionist examines *how* members produce determinations of warrant among themselves while flatly refusing any such privilege for him-/herself. This is not to imply that sociologists have no right to their evaluations about those they study as well as a right to consider this or that morally offensive. But we fail to see the *theoretical rationale* for employing or embedding such judgments in our analytical renditions of the member's perspective.

It is a source of endless interest that executing and maintaining a "rationality from within" stance (Garfinkel 1967, pp. 31–34) proves to be difficult for those expressing sympathy with the constructionist perspective. In our view the persistence of the so-called objective-subjective debate that dominated commentary in the mid-1980s (Woolgar and Pawluch 1985a, 1985b; Hazelrigg 1986; Schneider 1985) on the constructionist formulation is an indication of the obdurate character of this difficulty. Moreover, this focus deflected attention from the development of an empirically based theory of social problems, which was clearly the impetus for Spector and Kitsuse's formulation. More recently the theoretical significance of the objective/subjective issue has been further diffused by Best (1989), who, as a constructionist, proposes that a distinction be made between what he terms "contextual" and "strict" constructionism.[2]

This unfortunate state of affairs may reflect an absence of clear directives for theoretical development in Spector and Kitsuse's original statement. Their studied rejection of a positivist conception of social conditions, in favor of the term *putative conditions,* as well as the absence of a systematic presentation of the theoretical bases and implications of the constructionist perspective have in part contributed to these controversies. Thus Hazelrigg (1986) has criticized the constructionist formulation as "internally inconsistent" and Woolgar and Pawluch (1985a) have charged that practitioners of constructionism lapse into an objectivism at odds with their stated premises for analysis. We agree that constructionists have compromised the perspective on more than a few occasions by engaging in the "analytic" moves described by the critics. We believe, however, that an attentive reading of *CSP*, and Chapter 6 in particular, would make clear that explaining "the variability of the definitions vis-à-vis the constancy of the conditions to which they relate" (Woolgar and Pawluch 1985a, p. 215) is *not* the focus of the theory. Rather the theory directs attention to the claims-making process, *accepting as given and beginning with* the participants' descriptions of the putative conditions and their assertions about their problematic character (i.e., the definitions). From this methodological stance the research questions concern not how those definitions are produced by the sociohistorical circumstances in which they emerged, but rather how those definitions express the members' conceptions of "the problem," how they are pressed as claims, to whom, mobilizing what resources, and so forth. The constructionist conception of the claims-making process *accepts the members' constructions of putative conditions as "objects in the world,"* which thus meet the definitional requirements of social problems as subject matter for empirical investigation.

If the difficulties the field is confronting are fostered by the conceptual ambiguities in the social constructionist approach, then any act of theoretical clarification must attend to imprecisions in the language that we as sociologists use to describe, analyze, and interpret our subject matter. Especially at issue here is the ambiguous status of the concept *social problem*: Is it a technical or a vernacular term? In the constructionist formulation, the term *social problem* does double service: It is now a member's then a sociologist's concept. But when a sociologist presumes to oversee the propriety or rationality of members' usage of the term, a rigorous constructionist is obliged to consider the stance implicit in such a handling of the vernacular as a display of the sociologist's own membership. Analysis consists of reconstructing the vernacular, not downgrading it or leaving it unexplicated. Thus, the importance of the member/sociological analyst distinction rests on the constructionist's view that members provide the linguistic productions and activities (the first-order constructs in Schutz's terminology), which the sociologist can in turn subject to theoretical (as opposed to practical) scrutiny (i.e., the second-order constructs). *Social problems* points to *that class of social interactions* consisting of members' analytically paraphraseable means for formulating, describing, interpreting, and evaluating a symbolically constructed and morally charged intersubjective existence. For members, claims are "readable at a glance" (Goffman 1979), symbolic acts, and it is the sociologist's task to specify the configuration of premises, conventions, categories, and sensibilities constitutive of social problems as idiomatic productions.

If then we change our perspective and assume the gaze of members, *social problems* appears in a different light. For members, social problems do not *typically* refer to their own acts of definition and evaluation; they are not "talked into being." Rather social problems are what elicit their acts of judgment.[3] Membership is thus predicated upon what Pollner (1978) has called "mundane ontology," which entails a strict demarcation between the objects in the world, including the moral objects studied by sociologists, and persons' perceptions, beliefs, and ideas regarding those objects. What authorizes, idiomatically, the social problems process is the mundane claim that objects and their qualities have an existence independent of their apprehension. Thus, Spector and Kitsuse's proposal that we study claims "about" putative social conditions can easily be construed as a mundane directive, still grounded in an ontology where words and things are separable, that is, a correspondence theory of meaning. This view of constructionist inquiry has lent itself to research on what claims-making is "about" instead of the *conventional features of the claims-making process itself,* thus producing case studies of smoking, child abuse, wife battering, obesity, and so on. Since the members' claims are grounded in a folk version of the correspondence theory of meaning that is shared by the positivist sociologists (indeed, because members are fundamentally required to make claims *about* something), constructionist case studies of social problems are considered and critically evaluated by such sociologists as competing explanatory versions of the social conditions that the studies are "about." By entering into this dialogue, the constructionist is unwittingly drawn into assuming a stance that violates the methodological commitment to refrain from privileging or honoring certain mundane versions of the condition over others.

The recognition of the distinction between the members' *practical* project in contrast to the sociologist's *theoretical* project is fundamental in the constructionist methodological stance. The former are engaged in efforts to alter or defend some aspect of social life, and can therefore include sociologists on occasion, while the latter—insofar as s/he transforms members' practically based resources into researchable topics—is engaged in the theoretical reconstruction of the vernacular features of social problems as moral discourse. If sociologists are to be in the position of examining social problems as members' constructions, we must be willing to refrain from tacitly privileging the status of, say, scientists' versions of the condition in question and instead treat those accounts, and the sensibility they express, as items in our explications of the social problems language game (cf. Aronson 1984). Similarly, instead of incorporating interest- and value-based "explanations" in our theorizing, we should, after Mills (1940), recognize them as vernacular displays and thereby study them in their own right—for the ways in which the associations drawn by counterclaimants regarding claimants' motives can contribute to the shifting trajectories of social problems discourse. Proper consideration of the claims-making process entails attention to both how claims are licensed and acted upon as well as how they are displaced or discredited; the status of claimants' motives apparently can have something to do with both processes.

To summarize this part of our argument, Spector and Kitsuse's central distinction between putative condition and social condition may have amplified the confusion between the different layers of theoretical and mundane discourse, and seduced constructionists into making statements reflecting members' idioms instead of discerning them, thus inhibiting the development of an interpretive theory of the social problems process. Contextualist practice is both a narrow construal of the constructionist project and too bound up in a sociological discourse in which constructionists need to "score points" against the objectivists' notion that conditions can in and of themselves be harmful. We consider this practice to be fostered by the ambiguous ontological burden placed on *putative* conditions in Spector and Kitsuse's presentation. This language has been taken by constructionists to entail treating the perspective's axiom ("claims-making constitutes social problems") *as a proposition* (Woolgar and Pawluch, 1985a), thus formulating research that in one way or another focuses on social conditions. This in turn has deflected attention from the conventional features of the claims-making process that are available to participants qua participants for elaborating the social problems process. Thus, theoretical development has stalled while the perspective has been embroiled in a competitive dialogue with members' claims and those of positivist sociologists. Further, "selective relativism" or "ontological gerrymandering" (which in our reading is an act of according privileged status to apparently more respectable accounts and claims by reifying them) has generated a flat contradiction. We propose, therefore, to replace *putative condition* with the term *condition-category* as a means of eliminating the contradiction and to suggest new lines of theoretical development.

Categories, Not Conditions

Condition-categories are typifications of socially circumscribed activities and processes—the "society's" classifications of its own contents—used in practical contexts to generate meaningful descriptions and evaluations of social reality. They vary in their level of abstraction and specificity (e.g., "antismoking" in contrast to "smoke-free public spaces"), but they are the terms used by members to propose what the social problem is "about." As parts of a classification system, condition-categories are first and foremost units of language. The initial analytic topic is thus how practical accounts of these vernacular terms are situated and elaborated upon in the making of moral objects. We intend *condition-categories*, then, to highlight the symbol- and language-bound character of claims-making, as well as *how* members' facility with certain discursive strategies—including rhetorical and reasoning idioms—initiate and constitute the social problems process.

Commonsense understandings of both idiomatic competence and the function of language invite the analyst to "go native," that is, implicitly assimilate the object-subject distinction and treat the members' language of condition-categories as referents for independently documentable social conditions. But this is seductive: First, because the strict constructionist never leaves language. Whether s/he is paraphrasing members' arguments or recording their deeds, s/he is always in the realm of the textual. Protests, for example, are dramatizations of certain meanings, which make them linguistic-expressive. Lodging a complaint is an action that implies an analysis on the member's part about effective action, and thus a set of meanings. It also conveys something about him-/herself and other categories of people. In other words, the process we are studying is a language game into which actions are translated as publicly (and variously) readable expressions.

Second, "going native" can lead the analyst into the tacit use of the very vernacular resources that s/he should be assembling as data for theoretical reconstruction. In other words, it has proved difficult for constructionists to avoid making moves in the social problems language game. But, theoretically, it is unclear to us what the coding rules or even the point of the games are when analysts engage in such activities. If such activities are intended as correctives for the defective or inadequate character of members' claims-making, neither the efficacy of those correctives nor the standards by which they might be judged are evident.

The increased flexibility of *condition-categories* is important for how it alerts us to attend to the ways in which the denotations and connotations of the term become the subject of a kind of articulation contest on the part of members to establish what the social problem is "really about." In the case of the so-called abortion issue, for example, one side dramatizes abortion's status as a symbol of sexual permissiveness and murder. Legalized abortion becomes, in turn, a signifier of a more diffuse sense of moral decay. Is the social condition (or the social problem for that matter) abortion, murder, licentiousness, or moral decay? It is *semantically* ambiguous, perhaps even, as deconstructionists would say, "undecidable." It certainly cannot be said, analytically, that the social condition, putative or otherwise, is abortion as such, for to say that is to miss the subtexts and symbolic ramifications growing out of the "pro-life" group's moves in the social problems process. Similarly, the "pro-choice" side sees legalized abortion as a symbol of women's struggle to acquire "reproductive rights," which is itself a signifier of a long-fought battle to overcome men's domination of their "bodies and selves." Is the problem then *about* gender inequality, Christian intolerance, right-wing fanaticism, or anticonstitutionalism? To speak as an analyst of "the social condition of abortion" is to try arbitrarily to contain the evolution and change of meanings and subtexts as members press their claims, redefine their concerns, make alliances with some groups, collide with others, assess their political strategy, and so forth. We consider that dynamism to be the process that theorists of social problems must describe and comprehend.

The term *social conditions,* with its connotations of objective and recurrent properties, misdirects our attention, leading us to miss the central question of how there can be social problems discourse in the first place. When viewed in general terms, the social problems process resembles a kind of game whose moves are perennially subject to interpretation and reinterpretation, whose aims are subject to dispute, whose players are ever shifting, whose settings are diverse, and whose nominal topics stretch as far as the society's classification system can provide members with typifications of activities and processes. Indeed, the classification system is itself subject to transformations as new semantic distinctions and equivalences are made. Even though the process, conceived in its most general terms, is so unstable, members will nevertheless describe the social problems language game as a "controversy over the issue of X" precisely because members' participation is predicated on mundane ontology. In other words, claims-making activities reflect substantive concerns on the part of participants, but analytically we take those claims to be reflective of the interplay between their moral sensibilities and the dynamics of the process itself.

In sum, social problems discourse is open-ended, its "aboutness" being contingent upon the courses taken by members' practical theorizing on moral order, including one another's claims-making activities. These communicative activities are conceived as "language games" to indicate the sense in which our field is fundamentally concerned with understanding the constitutive ("world-making") and strategic dimensions of claimants' discursive practices in demarcating moral objects of relevance to a "public." We conceive of social problems as "idiomatic productions" to accentuate their status as members' accomplishments as well as to emphasize the sense in which scientific standards of rationality (Garfinkel 1967) cannot be used by the analyst to coherently describe the features of claims-making activities.

If pressed for a summary description of the phenomena in need of identification and theoretical reconstruction, we would name those "vernacular resources" drawn upon in claims-making activities. Vernacular resources are the conventional means by which members can realize the signifying processes called claims. Thus, they can refer to forms of talk, frames of interpretation, and contexts for articulation inasmuch as these effectively organize and circumscribe members' social problems discourse. To state the matter in still another way, vernacular resources include those rhetorical idioms, interpretive practices, and features of settings that distinguish claims-making activities as a class of phenomena while also differentiating instances of claims-making from one another.

We are thus confronted with the relationship between the general and the specific, an issue that has often remained unstated by social constructionists, yet is of central importance to the project. That is, what are the formal features of social problems theory to be about? We take the question to be basic to the enterprise, and our position is that the project of developing a theory of *social problems discourse* is a much more coherent way of proceeding with constructionism than, for example, the development of a series of discrete theories on the social construction of X, Y, and Z. To develop a theory about condition X when the ontological status of X is suspended results in "ontological gerrymandering" and "conceptual knots" (Pollner, 1978), which is to say flawed theory. It is much more exact to declare our approach to be concerned with the very discourse by which moral objects are created as objects of *address* even as the moral objects are treated by members as existing independently of their claims-making activities about them. In that sense, social constructionism studies members' distinctive ways of perceiving, describing, evaluating, and acting upon *symbolically demarcated social realities*—what we have termed condition-categories.

We believe that our conception is suited to addressing the relationship between the *specific* features of various condition-categories and their exposition in the social problems language game. This conception explicitly counters the specious objectification of the condition-category because the specificity of the "condition" is understood to be a matter of its having been situated within a network of signs, i.e., language. Nor is the social problems process itself reified, for its features are conceived to be *conventional*, not invariant. Analytically, the development of social problems is conceived to be up for grabs.

The Rhetoric of Social Problems Discourse

When constructionist theorizing blurs the basic distinction between vernacular resources and analytic constructs, it invites an indiscriminate fusion of mundane and theoretical perspectives that, among other things, leads to a retreat from the distinctive task of description posed by

Spector and Kitsuse's formulation. Now, bracketing has always been a recommended policy for executing constructionist-style inquiry, and the difficulty that analysts have in sustaining that methodological attitude has provided much of the impetus for our current thinking. We wish to highlight the centrality of bracketing in our proposed clarification of the research agenda by explicitly identifying *rhetoric* as an area of study for a project that seeks to develop a theory of the vernacular constituents of social problems. *Rhetoric* brings to the fore the sense in which the task for constructionism lies less with the *referential aspects of claims* than with the constitutive techniques and processes that are entailed in claims-making as such. That is, the issues posed for us by the maxim "claims-making constitutes social problems" are clarified because rhetoric focuses our attention on the distinctive but conventional ways of speaking and reasoning that obtain whenever persons qualify as participants in social problems discourse.

To speak of the rhetoric of social problems discourse is not to limit our domain to techniques of persuasion. The concept of rhetoric is useful for providing a framework for discerning patterns in phenomena that appear "from the outside" to be incoherent and in a constant state of flux, even as participants assert their claims to be intelligible concerns about conditions. That is, it allows us to move from single social condition–centered analyses to a more comparative approach by seeking and identifying commonalities at the level of members' discursive practices.

In our view, constructionist studies of social problems discourse can profitably proceed by distinguishing four overlapping but analytically distinct rhetorical dimensions: rhetorical idioms, counterrhetorics, motifs, and claims-making styles. The last of these leads us into the study of settings. The inventory of specific idioms, styles, and so forth that we offer is composed of ideal types and thus stands to be refined, reformulated, and elaborated upon through empirical observation and further theoretical reflection.

Rhetorical idioms are definitional complexes, utilizing language that situates condition-categories in moral universes. Several operations occur in that process of signification; suffice it to say that idiomatic application of the theme to the condition-category results in its acquiring problematic status. Each rhetorical idiom calls forth or draws upon a cluster of images. The *rhetoric of loss*, for example, evokes symbols of purity and tends toward nostalgic tonalities. The *rhetoric of unreason* evokes images of manipulation and conspiracy. The *rhetoric of calamity* situates condition-categories amid narratives of widespread devastation, and so on.

The *counterrhetorics* are discursive strategies for countering characterizations made by claimants. They tend to be less synoptic or thematic: For example, instead of arguing for ozone layer destruction, it is the claimant's description, proposed remedies, or something other than the candidate problem that is rebutted. These counterrhetorics tend not to counter the "values" conveyed in the rhetorical idioms so much as they address their current application or relevance.

Motifs refer to figures of speech operating as shorthand descriptions/evaluations of condition-categories. They are probably independent of rhetorical idioms, though certain motifs may have affinities with particular idioms. *Plague,* for example, has close and obvious affinities with the rhetoric of calamity, as does *crisis. Tragedy* may, on the other hand, be closely tied to the rhetoric of loss, though it is not difficult to think of applications in other formats. Thus, the relationship between idioms and motifs is one that requires empirical delineation. Our task is to explicate the presuppositions and indexical considerations that go into applications of motifs, idioms, and counterrhetorics. Instead of being disappointed or frustrated by the lack of easy correspondence between our analytic reconstructions, we should marvel at the artfulness with which claimants continuously innovate new meanings, associations, and implications, stretching the conventions underlying the coherence and intelligibility in social problems discourse.

The fourth rhetorical dimension that stands to provide material for a theory of social problems is what we term *claims-making styles.* By thinking of claims-making activities as possessing style, a shift in our attention is encouraged—from the language in which the claims are cast to the bearing and tone with which the claims are made. For example, claimants (and counterclaimants) may deliver their claims in legalistic fashion or comic fashion, in a scientific way or a theatrical way, in a journalistic ("objective") manner or an "involved citizen" (or "civic") manner. All of these modes are styles insofar as they inform the texture of and structure the reception accorded to claims. What each style entails and encourages, the way each style combines with different condition-categories, rhetorical idioms, and so forth—these become investigable topics.

Rhetorical Idioms

Claims-making activities are directed at problematizing specific condition-categories; rhetorical idioms refer to the distinctive ways in which their problematic status is elaborated. They are not, however, mainly concerned with documenting the *existence* or *magnitude* of the condition-categories. Instead, their domain is that of moral reasoning. Hence they function as moral vocabularies, providing participants with sets or clusters of themes or "sacred" symbols capable of endowing claims with significance. As we shall observe, each rhetorical idiom encourages participants to structure their claims along particular lines and not others.

Rhetorical idioms are also commonsense constructions of "moral competence" in the sense that their deployment tends to presume that auditors are obliged to acknowledge the import of the values expressed and consequently the claimant's current application of the idiom. Thus, the rhetorical idioms locate and account for the claimant's participation in the social problems language game by reference to moral competence (instead of strict self-interest). On the other hand, rhetorical idioms are useful in either enlisting another to make "sympathetic moves" in the social problems language game or at sustaining such moves by the already converted. In each case, what is distinctive about rhetorical idioms is their capacity to clarify and evoke the ethos implicit in the claim. This is especially facilitated by each idiom's characteristic set of positive and negative terms, that is, the idiom's preferred objects of praise and scorn.

There are several general issues that are delineated when social constructionism takes as one of its tasks the elucidation of claimants' applications of rhetorical idioms, moving investigation toward a general, comparative level of theoretical inquiry. Hence, the questions that are raised concern not specific conditions but the varieties of claims that the idioms are good for expressing. For example, what makes a claim "idiomatic" in the first place would appear to involve a certain kind of "readability," a usage of the language that is both symbolically coherent and morally competent. Given that premise, we can inquire as to what it is that members "know" when they hear a claim as especially edifying, moving, or insightful, on the one hand, or far out, incomprehensible, or mistaken, on the other. The utility of the rhetorical idioms derives from the discursive materials they provide to claimants to structure and lend urgency to their claims, but presumably those materials cannot be applied in merely any old way. The conventions underlying the idiomatic elaboration of condition-categories constitute one aspect of our subject matter. Artfulness consists of stretching and moving the boundaries of what can be construed as idiomatic.

What kinds of semiotic operations does a condition-category undergo as it is moved from one rhetorical idiom to another? Are some kinds of condition-categories more versatile or adaptable in this regard than are others? How might the idioms be variously combined? What are the distinctive kinds of vulnerabilities that each idiom poses for claimants and claims? What kinds of "atrocity tales" (Best 1987) do the various idioms accommodate? Does sponsorship (or disallowance) of a given claim under one rhetorical idiom entail sponsoring (or disallowing) other claims directed at other condition-categories that are drawing upon the same rhetorical idiom? What are the ways in which this is managed?

To what extent is intractability in social problems discourse contingent on participants' usage of different rhetorical idioms? What vernacular resources do members have access to for countering an idiomatic claim while retaining moral standing?

The *rhetoric of loss* is not concerned with mourning the extinction of something but rather inveighing against its devaluation. One of its central images is that of humans as custodians or guardians of some unique and sacred thing or quality. It is by virtue of the loss of prestige or value accorded to the sacred object that its existence is threatened, with the concomitant implication that such negligence is deeply revealing of our character in the eyes of some future judge(s). The *present* is given an all-embracing context: Situated between an "enchanted" or quasi-divine moment in the past and a still to be realized judgment in the future, our actions are situated to seem *historical*.

This rhetoric works most idiomatically with objects (i.e., condition-categories) that can be construed to qualify as forms of perfection in some sense or other. The positive terms composing the idiom's moral vocabulary are *innocence, beauty, purity, nature, clarity, culture* (in the sense of civilization), *cleanliness*, and so forth. Negative terms would consequently locate types of contamination and imperilment culminating in devaluation: *sin, pollution, decadence, chaos*, etc.

Rhetorical idioms can cut across ideological divisions like liberal and socialist and conservative, inter alia. In the case of the rhetoric of loss, claims-making campaigns on ideologically incompatible fronts reflect idiomatically compatible rhetorics. Political conservatives may be pre-eminent in the antiabortion movement, for example, and political liberals may constitute the strongest supporters for strict environmental controls, but both groups of claimants are relying upon a common rhetorical format, one that posits clear-cut opposition between such terms as the priceless or irreplaceable character of life and nature respectively, and the selfish disregard for those objects by women and industry.

The concept of *protection* assumes a central position in this rhetorical idiom's remedial discourse, suggesting the sense in which it is well-suited to evoking the *heroism* of the *rescuer*. Indeed, although Operation Rescue is the name chosen by the now well-publicized antiabortion organization, it is a name that is paradigmatic of the idiom's characteristic rhetoric and could probably be applied or adjusted to "fit" other condition-categories by claimants who use the rhetoric of loss. (Think of the "save the planet" slogan of the environmentalists and the "save the schools" cry of antibusing parents.) When articulated idiomatically, the rhetoric of loss suggests a defensive posture that is heroic rather than merely "reactionary." Such an impression is assisted by the premise that the sacred objects or beings cannot save or help themselves and so must

have the claimants acting on their behalf to protect their elevated symbolic positions and interests. (The rhetoric is wholly unidiomatic when
the concern at issue is revealed to be for the loss of "white male privilege" rather than "great books," or the "profit motive" rather than the
extinction of spotted owls or dolphins.) The rhetoric of loss elaborates
features of condition-categories that can be likened to precious positions
or presences that something or someone/group is threatening to either
appropriate, displace, extinguish, or lower in prestige or value. The
claimants' identification of the practices contributing to that devaluation
generates the targets that remedial activities seek to eradicate ("legalized
abortion" to counter the "devaluation of the gift of life," "clear-cutting"
to counter the "despoiling of virgin forests").

Whereas the rhetoric of loss is rooted in a language of altruism and
social responsibility to something other than the claimant's own interests, the *rhetoric of entitlement* emphasizes the virtue of securing for all
persons equal institutional access as well as the unhampered freedom to
exercise choice of self-expression. The sensibility expressed by this idiom is egalitarian and relativistic. It is egalitarian in its aversion to forms
of discrimination against categories of people. Thus, its negative terms
are emblematic of forms of discrimination: *intolerance, oppression, sexism,
racism, ageism,* and even *speciesism.* The idiom's positive terms stem from
its relativist philosophy: *lifestyle, diversity, choice, tolerance, empowerment,*
and so forth. *Liberation* evokes the value of having the freedom to choose
how one might realize one's life.

The concept of *expansion* is central to this idiom's remedial vocabulary
(whereas *conservation* is the most apparent connotation of "protection"
as it is inflected by the rhetoric of loss); claimants seek to expand the
distribution or scope of a good, service, or right. The notion is that
the greater the extension of *fair play, tolerance, justice, equality before the
law, respect for human dignity,* etc., into greater spheres of social life, the
greater the benefits for all members of the society. Claims cast in this
rhetorical idiom are often phrased in terms that evoke the image of an
inexorable march of history in a "progressive" direction toward the de-
mocratization of society (generating the idiom's preferred pejorative:
reactionary). Condition-categories generated by typifications of gender-,
race-, class-, and disability-based inequality are the most obvious candidates for exposition within the rhetoric of entitlement, but it can be
applied to abstract concepts like privacy. Entitlement claims have also
been extended to animals, trees, and cultural objects (such as films about
to be "colorized") on the argument that they have their right to exist as
"created."

Whereas the rhetoric of entitlement is applied most idiomatically
when the condition-category can be rendered an instance of injustice or

the inhibition of freedom, the *rhetoric of endangerment* is applied to condition-categories that can be expressed as threats to the health and safety of the human body. Thus, this rhetorical idiom is a relative of entitlement discourse inasmuch as the presumption is that individuals have the *right* to be safe from harm, to have good health, and to be shielded from preventable or reducible types of bodily risk. But the rhetoric of endangerment is composed of a cluster of themes and symbols distinct from those associated with the rhetoric of entitlement. Consequently, the urgency of its moral discourse is due less to issues regarding obstacles to freedom and equality than to optimal bodily function and health care.

In the rhetorical idiom of endangerment, condition-categories are problematic not because they are immoral per se, but because they pose intolerable risks to one's health or safety. This idiom's hallmark is a kind of moral minimalism: Claims that reflect or conceal "value judgments" have a decidedly negative valence because they don't possess the impersonality required to ensure that the claimant is not *really* attacking or seeking to undermine another's right to choose how to live. Claims are most idiomatic, i.e., suasive, when it is evident that medical judgment has taken precedence over moral judgment since the understanding of the body that is grounded in scientific knowledge is presumed to be both impartial and more factual, hence demonstrably superior to views generated by moral beliefs.

The rhetoric of endangerment shifts the site to which urgent action must attend. Where the rhetoric of loss evokes the image of transitory yet custodial human beings entrusted with an irreplaceable legacy, and where the rhetoric of entitlement evokes the fundamental importance of expressivity, the rhetoric of endangerment evokes the possibility that the transitory status of the person might be extended and the fear that it is being further curtailed. Such concerns recommend weighing the value of expressivity against the risks posed by expressive practices and beliefs. The issue is fundamentally instrumental: How might life be extended, and what might shorten it? Positive terms address the hope that has been evoked: *hygiene, prevention, nutritiousness, fitness,* and so on. Negative terms pinpoint the processes that warrant fear: *disease, pathology, epidemic, risk, contamination, health threat,* etc.

While claims employing the rhetoric of endangerment are most idiomatic when delivered in scientific style, language, and reasoning, or when endorsed by medical testimony, they are not immune to being answered. The counterrhetoric of the telling anecdote (q.v.) is a characteristically vernacular way of responding to endangerment claims. In addition, this idiom is circumscribed by being applied to condition-categories that can be shown to impinge on secondary parties (e.g., "bystanders," "the general population," "innocent victims"), precisely because of its bodily centered individualism: In the absence of an analysis linking a private act to a public consequence, the person who insists that the pleasures derivable from the problematic practice (for example, smoking) outweigh the extended lifespan attendant upon cessation is understood to be making a personal valuation that must finally be respected, though not necessarily admired.

Of course, "self-destructive" or "reckless" behavior may in and of itself become the problematic category, a sign of a less than total mastery of one's powers of the intellect. This type of claim draws upon another rhetorical idiom, what we call the *rhetoric of unreason*. Idiomatic usage is contingent upon a condition-category's describability in terms that highlight concerns about being taken advantage of, manipulated, "brainwashed," or transformed into a "dupe" or "fool." The spectre of subliminal messages, conspiracies, hidden forces, and the mesmerizing powers of advertising are common evocations in this rhetoric's lexicon.

The rhetoric of unreason posits an idealized relationship between the self and the state of knowing, and then locates an instance where that proper relationship is being distorted, undermined, and even destroyed. The assumption is that in the absence of the pernicious influence, the combined force of being fully informed and in complete control of one's cognitive powers would result in preferable courses of action. A wide range of claims-making activities reflects the logic of this rhetorical idiom: Rational (and equitable) administration of government is hampered under the influence of large campaign contributors; teenagers adopt the destructive habit of cigarette smoking because of the way advertisers "glamorize" it in targeted promotional campaigns; claims directed at the absence of full disclosure regarding the chemical contents in food are evoking the importance of making "informed decisions" regarding one's health. Given the logic of the idiom, "education," as a means of solving the social problem, acquires a particularly powerful resonance since the presumption is that knowledge leads to wiser action.

Certain categories of persons are understood to require greater vigilance in regard to the issues encapsulated by this kind of discourse. Those who can be said to be *trusting, naive, innocent, uneducated, uninformed, desperate*, and so forth can be "taken advantage of" as *easy prey, vulnerable* to being manipulated by persons or institutions of greater power or authority. Children provides a paradigmatic vernacular resource for articulating this rhetorical idiom. Playing off the understanding that they are as yet "unformed," interjecting into social problems discourse the suggestive question, What about the children? directs auditors to extrapolate the worst-case scenario: What a child would "end up like" were s/he to mature under the tutelage or influence of the pernicious agent(s).

Unlike the four rhetorical idioms we have so far discussed, the *rhetoric of calamity* is distinguished by being composed of metaphors and reasoning practices that evoke the unimaginability of utter disaster. Its way of articulating claims may be most significant when the social problems language game is especially crowded with a panoply of claims-making movements vying for attention. Claimants using this idiom will recognize the existence of other claims-making activities directed at nominally unrelated condition-categories, yet cast things into perspective by demonstrating how those other moral objects are contingent upon the existence of "their" condition-category. The one is either symptom, effect, or logically subordinate to the other. Thus, it is poverty that generates urban crime, drug abuse, poor schools, teenage pregnancies, and so on; it is the problem of the greenhouse effect that stands to create disasters of every imaginable kind; it is AIDS that threatens to create disease on an epidemic scale, an overburdened medical system, explosive insurance premiums, gay-bashing, etc.

This type of rhetoric can be conceived as a way of countering the centrifugal tendencies apparent when claims-making activities are considered across the board: It brings a variety of claimants under a kind of symbolic umbrella, hence providing the basis for coalition building. The rhetoric of calamity does not advocate a specific kind of moral system, as do the other idioms. It recognizes that moral reasoning may differ between allies, but the implication of the rhetoric of calamity is that now is not the time for sorting out ethical grounds: There will be time enough later for "mere" talk; now is the time for action. Thus, the idiomatic expression "the crisis of X" will be understood to mean that inaction on the condition will result in creating other social problems at an exponential rate, or exacerbate existing ones to the point of intractability. A claim expressed in this rhetorical idiom may lend itself to garnering high degrees of serious and prolonged attention in the public press (because of the various angles it delineates), as well as summary dismissals because of what may be seen as the hysterical or obsessive cast of mind of claimants using the calamitous imagery. Furthermore, the habit of linking several ostensibly unrelated conditions to the megacondition can be easily parodied, such as when an absurdist counterclaimant draws linkages that lack any "face validity" whatsoever, thereby alluding to the sense in which those kinds of claims are "merely" claims and nothing more.

The thematic complexes we have termed rhetorical idioms are vernacular resources, each serving as a kind of narrative kit through which is articulated a condition-category's socially problematic and justifiably treatable status. Analytically, they locate one area in which the central insight of social constructionism—that claims-making activities constitute social problems—can be investigated.

Counterrhetorical Strategies

If rhetorical idioms render claims both symbolically coherent and morally competent, then auditors are obliged, as members of the same cultural community the claimant has invoked, to either convey sympathy or else have "good reasons" for refraining from doing so. Rhetorical idioms usually posit hierarchies of value (e.g., freedom over oppression) with which it is difficult to disagree without discrediting oneself; to invert the hierarchy is to marginalize oneself as a social problems participant. Countering claims entails an artfulness that comes with being versed in the uses of certain vernacular resources, especially since counterclaimants can be told, "If you're not part of the solution, then you're part of the problem."

Before describing what we identify as the counterrhetorical strategies, we should note the service that alternative rhetorical idioms can perform in countering claims. Idioms other than the one implicit in a claim are useful in shifting the focus of discourse from the condition-category the claimant has singled out to the meaning of the claimant's claims-making itself. An example: The "war on drugs" initiated under the Reagan and Bush administrations was itself rendered problematic when civil libertarians cited the intrusiveness of such measures as drug testing in the workplace (Staudenmeier 1989). In this case the rhetoric of entitlement (viz., the right to privacy) was evoked to counter a claim arguably rooted in a rhetoric of endangerment. A similar discursive move was made by critics of antiabortion claimants, the charge being that one kind of moral belief (itself not disputed) was taking precedence over another to the point of usurpation (e.g., the blocking of entrances to abortion facilities by protestors).

Whereas the rhetorical idioms are drawn upon in amplifying and justifying one's claims while seeking to sway others to sympathetic stances, counterrhetorics block either the attempted characterization of the condition-category or the call to action, or both. These rhetorical strategies are generalized ways of speaking as morally competent counterclaimants, and thus can be articulated with reference to a variety of provisionally problematized condition-categories. The strategies fall into two classes: (1) sympathetic counterrhetorics, which accept, in part or whole, the problematic status of the condition-category, but which in effect block the request for remedial activities; and (2) unsympathetic counterrhetorics, which countenance neither the proposed characterization and evaluation nor the suggested remedies.

First the sympathetic counterrhetorical moves: *Naturalizing* is a move that accepts the assessment proposed while rejecting the call for action by making inevitable the very condition-category that claimants seek to render problematic and contingent (i.e., eradicable). The claimant may be met with the response, "Well, what did you expect? *Of course* society is violent, the world has always been, and always will be, a hostile place." If the condition-category is an instance of how the world "naturally" is, then calls for remedies are hopelessly naive. Yet the user of this gambit runs the risk of being labelled a "cynic" or "pessimist," labels that acquire negative connotations when applied to certain categories of persons in certain settings, such as politicians during reelection campaign debates.

Second, one might use the counterrhetoric of *the costs involved*. The upshot of this technique is to say that the problematic condition-category must be lived with rather than remedied through the claimant's specific measures, either because "two wrongs don't make a right," or because the claimed "benefits" do not outweigh their "costs." "Saving" the spotted owl might result in "costing" thirty thousand logging jobs; implementing civil rights legislation to eradicate racism in the workplace might involve "reverse discrimination"; pornography is the "price" of free speech. A term that often indicates the use of this counterrhetoric is *draconian measures,* a figure of social problems speech that equates the remedy with either imprudent short-sightedness or heartless punishment, or both. While the counterrhetoric of *naturalizing* is fairly unequivocal about the inevitability of our suffering the condition-category, there is some imprecision in the costs involved gambit: Adapting to a preexistent condition is implied in the first; contemplating a "trade-off" is encouraged in the second, meaning that one might well find that the costs involved are not very "costly" after all.

A third way to accept the claimants' complaint or dissatisfaction with a condition-category while withholding support for remedial action lies in *declaring impotence,* which entails registering one's moral sympathy while pointing to an impoverishment of resources at hand for dealing with the issue. In personal terms, this may mean not having enough time, energy, or authority for countering the problem in question. Or it may involve constructing a calculus of priorities: Yes, racism is a problem, but it is futile to try and do away with it until class oppression is countered. At an institutional level, budgets may be declared to be too tight to allow deployment of clean-up agents, as when a police chief, in response to demands that something be done about the problem of crime in the ghettos, contends that there simply aren't enough men and women on the force to eradicate the condition. Those who declare impotence, in either personal or institutional capacities, may be subject to charges of merely giving "lip service" to the problem and become objects of dis-

trust. Indeed, officials may in turn become the object of claims-making
activities for their very declared impotence. This occurred when miss-
ing-children advocates turned their attention to the government itself
for its inept, confusing, or unresponsive styles of bureaucratic record-
keeping: Thus the FBI became part of the problem of missing children
(Best, 1987).

The fourth sympathetic counterrhetorical strategy we call *perspectivizing*. This form of talk is possible because the social problems process is
premised on the object-subject distinction (Pollner 1978). That is, it consists of observing that the claimant's account is a "take" on a state of
affairs that is distinct from the state of affairs itself: The claim is characterized as an opinion. In the locution, "You're entitled to your opinion,"
the counterclaimant avers the right of the claimant to participate in the
social problems process while simultaneously placing a check on that
participation by implying the counterclaimant need not, as a matter of
opinion, subscribe to either the same view or the call for remedies. The
significance of this move can vary: It may express anything from an
indication of cool disinterest to an assertion of a competing definition of
the condition-category that indicates the issue to be precisely that it is a
matter of perspective or personal philosophy. In the case of abortion, for
example, for a prochoice activist to say to a prolife demonstrator that she
is merely expressing a personal preference is in effect to substantiate the
former's stand that abortions should be left legalized: The latter can
refrain from having an abortion if she so desires, but she does not have
the authority to deny the right of the prochoice woman to an abortion,
inasmuch as the personhood of the "fetus" is contingent on personal
philosophy. At this point then, the strategy moves from being sympathetic to being actively hostile, from the claimant's perspective. Perspectivizing is in effect a mundane form of relativism. And claimants who
proceed to insist that such a relativizing characterization reflects a lack of
moral competence may open themselves up to being considered intolerant of differing opinions. (In this way, this strategy has an affinity with
the rhetorical idiom of entitlement noted above.) Thus, this rhetoric is
being employed whenever counterclaimants make reference to "life-
style" as a legitimation of a series of activities: That the condition in
question is a life-style is supposed to guarantee its propriety.

A fifth counterrhetorical style in this category we call *tactical criticism*.
Tactical critics accept the characterization of the condition-category being
proffered, but demur in the means claimants employ. "Yes, women are
oppressed, but do those feminists have to be so militant and strident
about publicizing the fact?" is an example here. Tactical critics can either
imply their status as a potentially supportive group of fellow travelers,
or suggest that the means claimants are employing might themselves be

viewed and treated as a social problem (as when prolifers who engage in the bombing of abortion clinics are characterized by fellow travelers as a "fringe element" that is potentially dangerous, both to society and to the cause). Of all sympathetic counterrhetorical moves, this one carries the possibility of being seen as the least hostile by claimants, for the "counterclaimant" is both sympathetic with the effort to problematize *and* is willing to discuss tactics.

Then there are the *unsympathetic* counterrhetorical strategies. These oppose the condition-category's candidacy as a social problem and therefore also reject the call for remedial activities. First, *antipatterning* holds that the claim has not in fact characterized a full-scale social problem at all, but rather is focused on something akin to "isolated incidents." This was a characteristic response to charges of racial harassment on college campuses, in the 1980s. Or, it might be held that "victims of magnetic radiation" were merely "unlucky" in developing cancer (Brodeur 1990). Claimants may interpret the gist of the counterclaim as suggesting that the incidence of the phenomenon has been exaggerated or its nature misunderstood. In this usage, antipatterning serves in effect as a challenge for the claimant to verify the magnitude of the condition-category, or specify the meaning of the terms being used to link instances of the condition-category into a social pattern worthy of attention. This can thus engender "hair-splitting" debates over the meaning of a key term employed by claimants ("What counts as sexual harassment?" or "How should one define racism?") or a kind of numbers game ("Are there three hundred thousand or three million homeless persons?").

In a related form, the counterrhetoric of the *telling anecdote* presumes to invalidate a claim by virtue of citing an instance, for example, a personal instance or one that the media has treated as a novel case, illustrating that the generality of the analysis offered by claimants is suspect. To a charge that "the streets are unsafe to walk at night," the anecdotal response can be, "Oh, I've been doing just that for many years with no difficulty." To the charge that smoking is a problem since it causes cancer can come the response, "My grandfather smoked two packs a day and lived to be a good eighty years and then some." The telling anecdote thus holds the claims-maker's characterization accountable to invariability instead of likelihood. Therefore, claims couched in the language of scientific generalization are particularly susceptible to the usage of this strategy.

In using the *counterrhetoric of insincerity* the counterclaimant either suggests or declares that the claimant's characterization is suspect because of a "hidden agenda" on his part: namely that he is either participating in the social problems process as a means of advancing or guaranteeing his career, or as a means of securing or gaining power, status, or wealth. The successful use of this device is premised on the notion that claims forwarded by self-interested parties are by definition or tendency more reflective of the claimants' designs than of what is "best for society." Thus, prolife men are involved in the movement to reassert masculine privilege; social workers trumpet poverty programs because it further solidifies their source of income; civil rights leaders aren't really interested in ending racism because, should they realize that goal, their political power and leadership positions would be undermined (Steele 1988), and so forth. (A variant of this rhetorical gambit emphasizes the exploitation of rank and file participants by careerist leaders.) This form of talk can have an accusatory, ad hominem tone, and it often is delivered in the shape of "sincerity tests": If prolifers really cared about children, then why don't they do something about malnutrition or children in poverty? If antivivisectionists really cared about animal rights, then why don't they wear synthetic fibers on an exclusive basis? and so forth.

A fourth unsympathetic strategy is the *counterrhetoric of hysteria*, a way of speaking commonly involved in efforts at deproblematizing condition-categories. It is unsympathetic insofar as its usage implies that the moral judgment of the claimants is not based in a "sound" assessment of the condition but is under the influence of "irrational" or "emotional" factors. Thus, the U.S. economy is not really in a recession, though the nervous perceptions of panicky stockholders might ironically induce one; the involvement of "Hollywood liberals" in efforts to "save the Amazon rain forest" is yet another demonstration of their susceptibility to "faddish causes"; Evangelical Fundamentalists are on a "crusade" against pornography because of a "suspicious" obsession with sexuality nurtured by their leaders. The counterrhetoric of hysteria characterizes the claimants as members of a social category, and then dismisses their claims as "typical" expressions of "bleeding heart liberals," "narrow-minded religious fundamentalists," "crazy environmentalists," and so forth. In other words, auditors are instructed to note that the claims display (cultlike) features of the claimants' subcultures, rather than matters of concern to the "mainstream" of society.

Whether the counterrhetorics be sympathetic or not, the format that they have in common is, "yes, but . . . . " Yet each counterrhetoric carries its own shadings of meaning, and therefore conceivably preferable and less preferable uses. Theoretical reconstruction of social problems discourse can proceed by investigating the kinds of uses the strategies are good for, and the kinds for which they fall flat. How are they adapted to different condition-categories, rhetorical idioms, settings, and claims-making styles? What do participants know when they read a counterclaim as an indication of the speaker's being morally incompetent? The matter of marginality in social problems discourse is a subject that greatly interests us; here we would just note that counterclaimants always skirt having their moral standing questioned, and thus their capacity for being participants in social problems discourse in the first place. By studying counterrhetorics we can discern how credibility is sustained by virtue of being well-versed in the vernacular.

Motifs

Motifs are recurrent thematic elements and figures of speech that encapsulate or highlight some aspect of a social problem. They are not complexes of moral discourse in the same sense as rhetorical idioms; rather, they are a kind of generic vocabulary conventionally used in claims-making, each term or phrase acquiring distinctive connotations in being situated in one kind of context instead of another. The study of motifs in social problems discourse ought to focus our attention on how morally imbued metaphors and phrases can be intelligibly applied in claims-making.

Some examples of motifs: *epidemic, menace, scourge, crisis, blight, casualties, tip of the iceberg, the war on* (drugs, poverty, crime, gangs, etc.), *abuse, hidden costs, scandal.* Some of these terms refer to kinds of moral agents, others to practices, and still others to magnitudes. What is entailed in using these terms in one's moral discourse? For example, what variety of descriptive requirements is associated with applications of a motif like *scandal,* as opposed to *crisis*?

More specifically, one set of issues involves the versatility of members' vocabularies given the constraints imposed by their vernacular origins and standards of idiomatic articulation. As an example, consider the metaphor of the *ticking time bomb.* Now, it is common to hear that phrase employed in a range of claims-making contexts, with respect to diverse condition-categories, and under the auspices of different rhetorical idioms. Urban poverty, depletion of the ozone layer, and AIDS are often spoken of as ticking time bombs, but why would it be unusual to find "abortion" spoken of or associated with that metaphor, and not, say, "the politics of abortion'? What do condition-categories have to be presumed to share such that they can be said to involve a common motif? What features are shared by those to which no such motif can be applied? What would be an innovative usage of a motif? What do such innovative applications and adaptations involve as symbolic operations? When is freshness a consideration in motif usage, as opposed to clichéd application? What mixtures of revelation and confirmation seem to be preferred by claimants?

The study of motifs also calls attention to the need for understanding their *symbolic currency,* that is, why some motifs are prized while others are considered best avoided. In fact, the *identical* motif may undergo such a transformation of value. Consider Holstein and Miller's (1990) study, which provides a reconstruction of members' "victimization practices" that we take to be illustrative of the kind of work that the study of motifs can generate. Working with the motif *victim,* they describe how it is that the victim identity is sometimes considered valuable, and other times pointedly not, because the connotations of the victim motif vary when positioned amid diverse kinds of claims.

Holstein and Miller's study offers an indication that motifs afford us an avenue for reconstructing social problems discourse without succumbing to the ontological gerrymandering that Woolgar and Pawluch addressed (1985a). Research formulated in terms of motifs readily jettisons that single-social-condition emphasis of contextual constructionism (Best 1989) in favor of another emphasis: how the terms of social problems discourse evolve and are fine-tuned, and how their symbolic implications are contained. As we see it, these constraints have more to do with the politics and poetics of description—that is, with articulation—than with the "ontology of the described" that has so dogged social constructionism. Whether studied for their "grammar" or utility, motifs offer us a way to appreciate what claimants make when they make claims.

Broadening the Subject Matter

Joseph Gusfield has observed that "the concept of 'social problems' is not something abstract and separate from social institutions," stating that the "conceptualization of situations as 'social problems' is embedded in the development of the welfare state" (1989, p. 432). His examples of how social agencies, professions, and institutions claim "ownership" of public problems (a term that Gusfield prefers to *social problems*) direct attention to processes of conflict and consensus with regard to such problems, and the language and rhetoric in which those problems are cast. Gusfield's discussion reflects a conceptual tilt in the sociology of social problems, one that neglects social problems discourse formulated in and addressed to *private realms* in favor of a state-centered model. In turn, the focus on ownership leads to assessments of claimants' "successes" or "failures" at inspiring collective redefinition or new legislation and public policies supportive of the claimants' concerns. Such an emphasis inhibits theoretical development inasmuch as it presupposes that members' discourses on social problems are most exhaustively reconstructed for their sociological weight or significance when situated within a unidimensional analytic scheme of success or failure.

In light of these implications for constructionist theorizing we would argue for a reconsideration of the kinds of activities worth attending to as claims-making, extending them beyond the legal-rational and state-centered realms. In the section that follows we would like to indicate how considerations of claimant *style* and *setting* will facilitate such a broadening of constructionism's scope, especially when we theorize our subject matter *comparatively.*

Claims-Making Styles

We introduce the concept of *claims-making styles* in order to suggest a research agenda derived from the central premise of social constructionism—the constitutive character of claims-making activities. That is, if we extend the scope of what counts as claims-making, social constructionists are poised to take inquiry in new directions.

By using the noun *style* in the context of claims-making activities, we are pointing to a neglected but investigable issue within the purview of our subject matter: how various groupings of the claimant's bearing, tenor, sensibility, and membership category can inform both a claim's general appearance and specific content as well as instruct auditors on how the claim should be interpreted. As a transitive verb, *style* refers to the act of fashioning a claim that is consistent with the conventions of claims-making styles, as when one styles, say, a scientific claim. Our task is to specify, first of all, the kinds of styles that are evident across the range of social problems discourses; second, discern the practices constitutive of the various styles; and third, comprehend the range and shadings of meaning that these genres of moral representation are capable of conveying. In other words, how is style useful? What difference does style make?

What is going on when a claimant is described or recognized as speaking in a *scientific style?* The frame of reference being invoked probably includes certain typifications: a bearing that is "disinterested;" a tone that is "sober;" and a vocabulary that is "technical" and "precise." Presumably, anecdotes should serve prefatory or illustrative purposes only, thus "humanizing" or "making accessible" the presentation, but such anecdotes should be incidental to the substance of the claims produced. Similarly, to be "too rhetorical," "political," or "poetic" can be taken to be a liability, a departure from the hallmark of the style. The point of the style is not to fashion emotive imagery or reveal the personal stamp of its authors, but rather be anonymous, even "styleless," while diminishing uncertainty about the "properties" of condition-categories. It is quite

evident that many practitioners of claims-making recognize the importance of scientific style for lending "objectivity" to their claims. Thus,
examining how members communicate "scientifically" is relevant for the
realization of an interactionist understanding of the social problems process. Analytically, "the scientific method" is, subsumed under the concept *scientific style*, and it is not given any greater epistemological significance than any other body of practices associated with a particular kind
of style. Even if some styles seem to carry the day and are more often
"effective" (i.e., accorded credibility by auditors of claims), that does not
detract from the importance of studying alternative or "oppositional"
styles as well in view of the comparative theoretical perspective we
recommend.

Since they are general ways of articulating moral stances, we take
claims-making styles to be as valuable in rendering condition-categories
problematic as in making the categories seem unobjectionable, harmless, or otherwise not warranting attention. Claimants and counterclaimants can both draw upon aspects of the same style even though they
hold opposing views, as when scientists have disagreements over, say,
recognizing the problem of "the greenhouse effect." As Aronson (1984)
and others have argued, scientist's disagreements about "scientific
claims" can also be the disagreements of participants in the social problems process (Spector and Kitsuse [1977] 1987). Now, the significance of
an "intrastylistic" dispute can vary. In the context of scientific-styled
discourse, disagreement over the applicability of the social problem
epithet will be thought indicative of a failure in methodology. Insofar as
the premise of this style assumes that the "facts of the case" are objective, stable, and discoverable (a premise that is also central to legalistic
styles; Pollner 1987), intrastylistic disagreements focus on challenges to
the methods employed to assert "the facts." On the other hand, intrastylistic disputes conducted within other "speech genres," to borrow
Bakhtin's term (1986), such as what we call the civic style, can point to a
different kind of significance altogether. There, intrastylistic disjunc-
tions can be indicative of the very magnitude of the problem with which
participants are contending. That is, the hallmark of civic-styled claims
and claimants—"mad as hell" moral indignation—can itself be taken as
a sign of the extent to which the dispute "touches a raw nerve." The
presence of "citizen anger" on either side of the conflict points to the
intractability of the problem itself.

Aside from concerning ourself with the symbolic interaction that is
activated during intrastylistic disputes, we can obviously inquire into
what trajectories social problems discourse tends to take when disputants draw upon different stylistic options. Claims-making styles em-
body or express a variety of ways of engaging in moral representation

and understanding. The study of interstylistic discourse can attend to the happens when ways of "showing the moral" are framed by participants as being as important to what gets claimed about a condition-category as the category itself. Indeed, in the event of purportedly "subversive" subcultural styles (Hebdige 1979), such as that amalgam of speech and music known as "rapping," a style's alleged implications or politics may themselves be construed as "the issue."

In addition to the scientific style of claims-making, we would like to point to what might count as specific kinds of styles in claims-making. Such a listing is undertaken for illustrative purposes only, to suggest the range of interactional practices that we can concern ourselves with describing more precisely and exhaustively.

Under the term *comic style* we wish to include those practices by which members foreground absurdities in certain positions, highlight the hypocrisies of claimants or counterclaimants, or draw upon some measure of irony or sarcasm to point up a particular moral. Comic styles represent interesting problems of claim-readability inasmuch as the esthetic imperative of making a good joke can come into conflict with the practical goal of building a constituency. Requirements that humor not be "off-color," a "cheap shot," or a "low blow" are apparently conventionally present, even though what counts as being in "poor taste" is itself variable. Another issue is whether there are circumstances under which the comic style seems most pointed or strategic. That is, with respect to what kinds of categories does it make the most difference? Is it a style better suited to claiming or counterclaiming?

Consider how the comic style of caricature might be used to fashion a counterclaim by ad absurdum extension of claims couched in the entitlement idiom. Thus, recent efforts by gay educators in California to include recognition of the contribution of gays in high school history textbooks (as a way of "empowering" gay teens) was countered by such rhetorical questions as "Should we mention the contributions of pedophiles and prostitutes as well?" Implied in this rhetorical gambit are at least two subtexts: first, a moral equivalence between gays and pedophiles that would presumably embarrass proponents of the project, and second, the notion that history textbooks would, by the logic of entitlement, soon take on the character of a perverts' gallery and thus could not be placed in the hands of the impressionable young. This counterclaim charges those who press such entitlement claims with creating a "slippery slope" from which there would be no return—evoking the spectre of nihilism. Thus, the central concept of the entitlement idiom's remedial vocabulary—i.e., expansion—is countered in this instance by "exposing" the absurd, i.e., the unidiomatic lengths to which the rhetoric of entitlement can be taken.

The *theatrical style* encompasses those instances of claims-making that make a point of illustrating the group's moral critique in the very way in which the claim is represented. ACT-UP's various "actions," such as "die-ins," are dramatizations of the issue being contested. "Guerilla theatre" activists also seek to become living illustrations of their claim's substance, such as when an anti–Miss California Pageant demonstrator in Santa Cruz dressed up in a bathing suit consisting of pieces of meat. Theatrical styles seem to have gained wider usage in recent years, so that what might have once been, and probably still is, the preferred style of artists and other cultural workers, has filtered out to other segments of society. Thus, Operation Rescue demonstrations against abortion have featured such actions as symbolic mass funerals. The danger in this style is inscrutability, especially when the symbolic stagings carry the burden of being produced for the edification of both the claimants themselves as well as the larger public (Gamson 1989). When that occurs, we may find literary critics or social scientists brought in to "translate" for the public the allegorical or symbolic meaning embedded in the representation, or vouch for the integrity of the speech style itself, as when Henry Louis Gates, Jr. testified on behalf of rap musicians 2 Live Crew in a 1990 obscenity trial. (However, in our classification scheme, rapping is better considered a subcultural style.)

The *civic style* of claims-making entails making claims that have what we might call "the look of being unpolished." That is, the civic style's distinctive character is based in being "honest," "sincere," "upright," "unstylized." Where premeditation is clearly the rule in the theatrical style, claimants using the civic style should be readable as participating in social problems discourse out of strict moral indignation or outrage. To appear too well organized or "too slick" is to be part of an "interest group." The civic style involves trading off an ideal of the "common, decent folk," and its character is often used as the face of commonsense morality, especially in such popular culture icons as the film "Mr. Smith Goes to Washington." Ross Perot's 1992 presidential campaign exemplified the civic style: Witness his references to his supporters as "volunteers," and his denunciations of "handlers," "spin doctors," etc.

The *legalistic style* is premised on the notion that the claimant is in fact speaking on behalf of another party, a defendant or plaintiff, and that the merits of that party's case are consistent with rights and protections embodied in the law. The reason that the legalistic style is not subsumed under the theatrical style, in spite of the courtroom theatrics of attorneys, is because a legalistic-styled claim is presumably neither allegorical nor symbolic, but rather particular, specific, and analogic, with the full weight and prestige of institutional justice supporting it.

Finally, we would like to point to a category that might provide a linkage between social constructionism and cultural studies: *subcultural style.* Here we have in mind the notion that various segments of society—whether self-defined by class, race, ethnicity, gender, sexual orientation, or geographical location—tend to evolve unique or "local" (Geertz 1983) ways of commenting on the larger social world. Possible connections that might be considered: the relationship between "camp" and moral positioning; the styles of moral discourse evolved in such dialogical situations as "self-help groups," or consciousness-raising sessions; and the claims-making formats nurtured by bilingualism or the use of nonstandard English. The value of including the category of subcultural style is that it reminds us of something easily overlooked: Social problems discourse occurs in all manner of forums and among a wide range of persons. The concerns that these diverse peoples may have in commenting on and their characteristic ways of describing the symbolic order in which they are involved are not necessarily apparent if we take state- or, for that matter, media-sponsored discourse as offering us a privileged point of entry into the sociology of contemporary moralities.[4]

Settings

The issues posed by rhetorical strategies, motifs, and styles are particularly context sensitive; with that in mind, we would like to indicate the importance of *setting* for understanding the articulation of claims-making.

Studies of the settings in which claims are delivered also stand to move research onto a trans-condition-category level of analysis, since the settings we have in mind are not related exclusively to claims regarding one type of condition-category. Indeed, the variety of condition-categories that have been addressed in constructionist-style research using bureaucratic data is proof of this. The ways in which these various settings are constituted such that they can provide us with records of the claims-making process can thereby become an investigable topic. Conceiving of settings as contexts for scrutiny and representation, we can pose the following kinds of questions: How do the formal qualities of particular settings structure the ways in which claims can be formulated, delivered, and received? What kinds of rhetorical forms can be employed because of the imperatives or conventional features constituting the various locations? What are the various categories of persons populating these settings, and how do their characteristics entail accountably interacting with claims and claims-makers?

The media constitute one class of setting in which claims-making occurs, for example, and these can be further broken down into the subclasses of print, radio, television, cinema, and so forth. These can be further distinguished: Television has news programs, talk shows that address social issues, documentaries, etc., each of which has occasion to disseminate claims in presumably distinctive ways. What are the explicit or tacit rules for admissible testimony, fairness, objectivity, and so on? How does the visual component of some of these media alter the claim's sense, reception, and structure? A comparison with radio as a medium would be an instructive contrast in this regard. How are some rhetorical treatments of condition-categories made to possess greater visuality than others; in fiction versus nonfiction presentations? Are the print media able to engage in the depictions of claims in ways that are distinct from the other media? How does the size of the audience, or members' understanding of the viewership, become a consideration for the assertion of claims? What are the modes of address that are commonly employed in mass-mediated claims-making, what are the assumptions made thereby, and what are the implications of such practices for understanding social problems as a language game?

The second type of setting is *legal-political*. The obvious candidates for inclusion are courts, city council meetings, congressional hearings, electoral campaigns, policy think tanks, public interest groups, and so forth. What are the distinctive features of these contexts, and how do these structure social problems discourse? Questions regarding standing, admissible testimony, and dramaturgy might be particularly relevant issues here. This category encompasses a wide range of activities—from the tightly regulated courtroom, to the congressional hearing, to the electoral strategies of political campaigns—and thus requires that we be attuned to the distinctive sensibilities and conventional purposes obtaining in each. What needs to be kept in mind is the project of theorizing each context's particular engagement with claims-making activities.

The third setting in which social problems discourse can be readily observed is in *academia*, including academic conferences and journals. Presumably, Woolgar and Pawluch's call for constructionists to examine their own practice would be included under these auspices. Once again, the general issue here is the distinctive contribution of the setting to the way in which the social problems process proceeds. This can involve taking a sociology of knowledge approach to the various academic disciplines as they have engaged various condition-categories. How does the distinction between the humanities, sciences, and social sciences give distinctive accents to each academic division's participation in the process? What are the understandings of personhood (e.g., professional vs. laypersons) that are operative in the claims offered by each? How does "professional" status entail engaging the social problems process?

Settings may themselves be framed as moral objects, of course. The process of so viewing settings usually involves a *mundane* reflexivity about the social problems language game itself. Consider recent charges of "political correctness." They are usually setting specific: It is not the mass media or the various levels of government that are being invoked but rather the academy. Political correctness refers to a condition of communication: a "climate of opinion" that regulates what can be idiomatically claimed and counterclaimed in academic forums.

The discourse on political correctness plays off an idealization of the university as a freewheeling "marketplace of ideas," one that is being stifled by "liberal orthodoxy" and the "timidity" of professors who avoid critical discussion and examination of that orthodoxy, thus abdicating educational responsibility. The argument is that political correctness trivializes the notion of "diversity," transforming a "legitimate" concern for multiple philosophical perspectives into simple-minded representation of demographic heterogeneity. At a more concrete level, critics of political correctness hold that the kind of condition-category targeted by the politically correct (usually campus-related, such as "date rape," "racism in the humanities curriculum," and "hate speech"), and the ways in which they address them, is reflective of ideological, obscure, frivolous, or otherwise mistaken thinking. In any case, such condition-categories are held to be so ambiguous as to permit "diversity of opinion" about them, which is precisely what political correctness discourages.

Claims about political correctness ordinarily employ the comic style (q.v.). Note the series of ironic reversals that these claimants like to point out: The tolerant are intolerant; the international university is a parochial institution; "freethinkers" spout narrow-minded political dogmas; antiracists are reverse racists; the educated do not educate; and so forth. These ironic reversals carry the tone of discovery—between subject and predicate is the adverb "really."

The study of such varied and specific settings would also enable us to understand how it is that we are able to have a record of the claims-making process. Sociologists of deviance have been sensitized to the distinctive contribution made by bureaucratic organizations to the deviant-making process (Cicourel 1968); there has not yet been a similarly concentrated focus on the importance of settings for the study of the social problems process, even though it would appear to be an elementary task in any effort to understanding claims-making as a general process.

Summary

In this paper, we hope to have demonstrated the fruitfulness of investigating vernacular resources, especially rhetorical forms, in the social
problems process. In proposing the term *condition-category* to rectify the
confusions that have been generated by *putative condition* we have outlined an agenda that directs our attention to research sites consistent
with Spector and Kitsuse's premises that will be productive of an interpretive theory of the social problems process. In particular, the discursive practices through which the claims are constituted attune us to the
richness of language and reasoning that participants are capable of tap-
ping as a continually available resource. Our task as theorists is to note
the differences in meaning and consequence that the strategic uses of
vernacular forms can have for the shape of the social problems process.

In sum we believe that the study of the vernacular constituents of
social problems provides us with new ways of conceiving our project—
an ethnography of moral discourse—as well as indicating to us the
necessity for rethinking or refining the theoretical language we employ
to reconstruct those social interactions we have called "claims-making
activities."

Acknowledgments

Earlier versions of this paper were presented at meetings of the Society for the
Study of Social Problems in 1989 and 1990. The authors express their appreciation to Herman Gray, Melvin Pollner, Joseph Schneider, Carol Ray, Jay Gubrium,
and Doug Maynard for their thoughtful responses to earlier drafts. We wish also
to acknowledge Jim Holstein and Gale Miller for their substantive as well as
generous editorial contributions.

Notes

1.   An illustrative aside: Constructionist irony could have led us to title this
paper "In Appreciation of Social Problems."
2.   The "contextual constructionist," according to Best (1989), would seek to
analytically locate the constructions of members in everyday life in the "social
and historical contexts" in which they are presumably embedded to "account"
for the construction. We consider this analytic maneuver to represent just the
sociology of knowledge rationale that generates the conceptual inconsistencies
noted both in *CSP* and Woolgar and Pawluch (1985a). Instead, our outline reflects an interactionist conception of the social problems research agenda.
3.   Obviously, the member's perspective can self-reflexively comprehend the
social problems process. Such reflexivity seems to be especially encouraged

during strategy sessions, when members compare notes on what modes of presentation work best with what topics before what audiences. The paradigm case is provided by political consultants employed by presidential election campaigns, since such efforts invariably embrace more than one topic, audience, and setting. The difference between member's and analyst's reflexivity is that the former's is practical while the latter's is theoretical. Indeed, there are interesting papers to be written about just this topic: how such reflexivity tends to emerge, the courses it tends to take, the limitations it must respect because of practical considerations, and the ways in which the practice of mundane reflexivity may eventuate in the departure from the member's perspective altogether in favor of a strictly theoretical reflexivity (in which the "natural attitude" is suspended).

4. Tuchman discusses the way in which consciousness raising sessions in the women's movements were not amenable to the conventional formats of news reporting. As she puts it "the reporter could not draw on narrative forms imbedded in the web of facticity to frame seemingly 'formless kind of talk' as a topic—a news story she could tell" (1978, p. 139).

References

Aronson, Naomi. 1984. "Science as a Claims-making Activity: Implications for Social Problems Research." Pp. 1–30 in *Studies in the Sociology of Social Problems,* edited by J. Schneider and J. I. Kitsuse. Norwood, NJ: Ablex.

Bakhtin, Mikhail M. 1986. *Speech Genres and Other Late Essays.* Austin: University of Texas Press.

Best, Joel 1987. "Rhetoric in Claims-Making: Constructing the Missing Children Problem." *Social Problems,* 34:101–21.

_____. 1989. "Afterword: Extending the Constructionist Perspective: A Conclusion and an Introduction." Pp. 243–53 in *Images of Issues: Typifying Contemporary Social Problems,* edited by J. Best. Hawthorne, NY: Aldine de Gruyter.

Brodeur, Paul. 1990. "Annals of Radiation: Calamity on Meadows Street." *The New Yorker,* July 9.

Cicourel, Aaron. 1968. *The Social Organization of Juvenile Justice.* New York: Wiley.

Gamson, Josh. 1989. "Silence, Death, and the Invisible Enemy: AIDS Activism and Social Movement 'Newness.'" *Social Problems* 36:351–67.

Garfinkel, Harold 1967. *Studies in Ethnomethodology.* Englewood Cliffs, NJ: Prentice-Hall.

Geertz, Clifford. 1983. *Local Knowledge: Further Essays in Interpretive Anthropology.* New York: Basic Books.

Goffman, Erving. 1979. *Gender Advertisements.* New York: Harper and Row.

Gusfield, Joseph. 1989. "Constructing the Ownership of Social Problems: Fun and Profit in the Welfare State." *Social Problems* 36:431–41.

Hazelrigg, Lawrence. 1986. "Is There a Choice Between 'Constructionism' and 'Objectivism'?" *Social Problems* 33:S1–13.

Hebdige, Dick. 1979. *Subculture: The Meaning of Style.* London: Methuen.

Heritage, John. 1984. *Garfinkel and Ethnomethodology.* Cambridge: Polity.

Holstein, James A. and Gayle Miller. 1990. "Rethinking Victimization: An Interactional Approach to Victimology." *Symbolic Interaction* 13:103–22.

Merton, Robert K. 1974. "Introduction: The Sociology of Social Problems." *Contemporary Social Problems.*, 4th ed. New York: Harcourt, Brace & World.

Mills, C. Wright. 1940. "Situated Actions and Vocabularies of Motives." *American Sociological Review* 6:904–13.

Pollner, Melvin. 1975. "The Very Coinage of Your Brain: The Anatomy of Reality Disjunctures." *Philosophy of the Social Sciences* 5:411–30.

———. 1978. "Constitutive and Mundane Versions of Labeling Theory." *Human Studies* 1:269–88.

———. 1987. *Mundane Reason: Reality in Everyday and Sociological Discourse.* New York: Cambridge University Press.

Schneider, Joseph. 1985. "Defining the Definitional Perspective on Social Problems." *Social Problems* 32:232–34.

Spector, Malcolm and John I. Kitsuse. [1977] (1987). *Constructing Social Problems.* Hawthorne, NY: Aldine de Gruyter.

Staudenmeier, William J., Jr. 1989. "Urine Testing: The Battle for Privatized Social Control during the 1986 War on Drugs." Pp. 207–21 in *Images of Issues: Typifying Contemporary Social Problems,* edited by J. Best. Hawthorne, NY: Aldine de Gruyter.

Steele, Shelby. 1988. "I'm Black, You're White, Who's Innocent?" *Harpers Magazine,* May.

Tuchman, Gaye. 1978. *Making News: A Study in the Construction of Reality.* New York: Free Press.

Wilson, Thomas. 1971 "Normative and Interpretive Paradigms in Sociology," Pp. 57–79 in *Understanding Everyday Life,* edited by J. Douglas. London: Routledge & Kegan Paul.

Woolgar, Steven and Dorothy Pawluch. 1985a. "Ontological Gerrymandering: the Anatomy of Social Problems Explanations." *Social Problems* 32:214–27.

———. 1985b. "How Shall We Move Beyond Constructionism?" *Social Problems* 33:159–62.

3

For a Cautious Naturalism

Jaber F. Gubrium

My reactions to Peter Ibarra and John Kitsuse's important paper come from one who is sympathetic to the point of view, and who indeed has framed much research in terms of social constructionism. Of course, like other frameworks, there are brands of constructionism and, to that extent, I have highlighted certain topics in my work and proceeded in my own fashion. I have not focused on claims-making activities—publicity—oriented to the state or public agencies, an emphasis that has come to virtually typify constructionist writing in the area. Rather, my instinct has been to consider the cultures of small worlds like support groups, psychiatric units, rehabilitation clinics, counseling centers, and nursing homes as a way of addressing the interactive and discursive features of personal realities (Gubrium 1989, 1991). Still, the analytic thrust of the research aligns with the spirit of Ibarra and Kitsuse's [originally Malcolm Spector and Kitsuse's [1977] (1987)] departure from the conventional position on social problems, one based on the understanding that social problems are accomplishments.

Ibarra and Kitsuse's paper, which is the latest formulation of this significant turn in social problems theorizing, centers my concern. As the authors make abundantly clear, to think of social problems as accomplishments implies that the problems are not objective conditions but are bound to the rhetorical claims-making activities of those who clarify, redefine, or counter the status of putatively objectionable conditions in society. The question is: Is the accent to be on how rhetoric *practically accomplishes* social problems, which Ibarra and Kitsuse repeatedly stress, or on the view that related rhetoric *is* social problems, which the authors seem to presume? In the following comments, I argue by means of a deconstruction of the paper's vocabulary that a perhaps inadvertent accent on the latter eclipses what Ibarra and Kitsuse refer to as *vernacular* constituents of moral discourse. While Ibarra and Kitsuse allege an interactionist focus and write about members and vernacular, their paper is about publicity, conniving rhetoric, and practices that are neither "members'" nor very vernacular.

The Sense of Agency

The question pinpoints the authors' sense of agency. With some telling exceptions, which I will take up later, their vocabulary reveals a world of wily, claims-making rhetoricians.

The Audience

Claims-makers do what they do with a certain aim (for all, or all those within a targeted category, to hear) and with a particular end (to convince everyone of their message). The audience is the public or publics at large, not small worlds such as households or friendship groups, nor delimited domains such as institutions or formal organizations. Whether the goal is to define a putatively objectionable condition or "condition-category" as a social problem or to defend the condition against such a status, messages are conveyed broadly, the more exhaustive the audience the better.

While Ibarra and Kitsuse do not expressly mention Ludwig Wittgenstein, they evidently have him in mind when they refer to a rather different sense of public, one referencing the social or dialogical, not uniquely private, character of discourse. Referring to the process they are studying, the authors state that it is "a language game into which actions are translated as publicly (and variously) readable expressions." To Wittgenstein, language games are not necessarily broadly public in the sense that they are governed by rules oriented to the public at large. Rather, regardless of the particular domain of application, language games are rules of speech and meaning that operate behind participants' backs, which participants' speech tacitly references and whose objects their speech realizes as they actively engage the game. In Wittgenstein's sense, language games are public because they do not uniquely belong to any one participant.

Ibarra and Kitsuse, however, privilege the public at large. As the authors note, "our field is fundamentally concerned with understanding the constitutive ('world-making') and strategic dimensions of claimants' discursive practices in demarcating moral objects of 'relevance' to a 'public.'" This public is the audience that reads newspapers and news magazines, and listens to the broadcast media. It is a decidedly media public, one whose received texts are to be studiously analyzed by the social constructionist for their reality-constituting features and by-products and not the more limited "publics" of smaller worlds. In describing the concept of "protection" as a rhetorical idiom, for example, the authors refer to Operation Rescue as "the name chosen by the now *well-publicized* antiabortion organization" (my emphasis). Later, speaking of the "rhetoric of unreason," they exemplify what they refer to as a "wide range of claims-making activity" in the following way: "teenagers adopt the destructive habit of cigarette smoking because of the way advertisers 'glamorize' it in *targeted promotional campaigns*" (my emphasis). Soon thereafter, in discussing the rhetoric of calamity, the "public press" itself comes to the fore, as in "a claim expressed in this rhetorical idiom may lend itself to garnering high degrees of *serious and prolonged attention in the public press*" (my emphasis). Even while a promotional campaign may be "targeted," the campaign is aimed at that particular, teenage public *at large*.

Targeted or not, the audiences to whom Ibarra and Kitsuse refer, and whom many constructionists study through media analysis, are a socially nebulous lot. While they may be teenagers, we are not invited to get a glimpse of the everyday worlds within which such an audience receives the rhetoric of claims-makers. Because the audience is a public at large, we are hardly apprised of the who, where, when, or how of what this alleged public does with the rhetoric of its forthcoming, shifting, or fictional social problems. The audience seems to be, well, "just there," mostly larger than life, resembling the conceptually fictive public that Herbert Blumer (1969, pp. 195–208) once railed against as an artifact of public opinion research.

I do not mean to suggest that fictive publics are not real in that they do not concretely enter into everyday experience. The conformist culture of teenage life makes what the public or "others" think weigh heavily on comportment, just as the widespread recognition of Alzheimer's disease has made older persons circumspect about forgetfulness in a way they might not have been if the disease had not become such a public issue. Rather, Ibarra and Kitsuse's agent speaks to an audience that is mainly just there to receive, internally undistinguished.

To be fair, Ibarra and Kitsuse do respond to Gusfield's observation about the almost exclusively public affairs focus of constructionists. The authors "broaden the subject matter" of social problems by arguing "for a reconsideration of the kinds of activities worth attending to as claims-making, extending them beyond the 'legal-rational' and state-centered realms." Yet audience still remains nebulous, for what broadening means in the text following this statement is an expansion of the research agenda to include diverse claims-making *styles,* variously appropriate to particular issues or appealing to particular audiences, among them the scientific (or styleless) style of persuasion, the comic, civic, journalistic, legalistic, and subcultural styles. The realms to be considered are stylistic, not the realms of interaction ostensibly promised by the "interactionist-based" program said to comprise Spector and Kitsuse's ([1977] 1987) original statement of the constructionist approach. Accordingly, we are not as much to be apprised of how, say, scientists and their audiences articulate and respond to diverse rhetorical idioms in practice, as Bruno Latour and Steve Woolgar (1979) describe for laboratory life, but rather how scientists, like other claims-makers, communicate with publics at large to specify or discount the problematic character of select social issues. For example, the disinterested, sober scientific style might be analyzed as a usage to convince the public that, indeed, *the* data do *clearly* speak for themselves in order to show that the ozone layer is being depleted and that, moral considerations notwithstanding, on *objective* grounds alone, there is reason to be alarmed.

The Rhetorician

Ibarra and Kitsuse's vocabulary conveys an agent who not only makes claims to publics at large, but does so as a complete rhetorician. The so-called objectivist concern with the object of a social problem and the conditions that bring the problem about gives way to a "different subject matter for the sociology of social problems" (Spector and Kitsuse [1977] 1987, p. 39). Analytically center stage are those who are engaged in *"proposing or contesting* the designation of a category of putative behaviors, expressions, or processes as 'offensive,' about which something of a remedial nature should be done, i.e., 'claims-making and responding activities'" (Ibarra and Kitsuse, quoting Spector and Kitsuse, [1977] 1987, p. 76).

But we do not encounter the actual claims-makers, only their claims, and counterclaims of course. Ibarra and Kitsuse's analytic categories are not behavioral, interpersonal, or situational; they are rhetorical. The categories serve to catalog very public speech, not conduct. Indeed, the speech is passive in the sense that its data are textual. As the authors note regarding the strict constructionist, who "never leaves language," "Whether s/he is paraphrasing members' arguments or recording their deeds, s/he is always in the realm of the textual." For Ibarra and Kitsuse, textuality refers to concrete texts—primarily the related contents of the print and broadcast media. The rhetorician is not an active persuader, who stands next to, over and above, or beneath his or her audience.

To the extent public texts become publicity, they affirm the presence of the agent. When there is a great deal of publicity for or against a putatively objectionable condition, Ibarra and Kitsuse's social constructionist subject is being loudly, and it is hoped clearly, heard. When there is little publicity, the social problem under contention hardly exists. When there is no publicity, the agent is analytically nonexistent, even while there may be actual proponents or opponents of the objectionable quietly, but "silently," festering somewhere, perhaps in laboratories, in households, in community interest groups, in political organizations, among other not so public forums.

This raises an important methodological issue. If the existence of the agent is bound to publicity, then the social constructionist who cannot find related data in public texts must conclude that there is no social problem under construction. The concrete social relations that produce public texts are irrelevant, since the relations only gain their significance in respect to putatively objectionable conditions when publicity textualizes and broadcasts the reality of the conditions. Thus a social problem is constructively born, and only then. Events leading up to the decision to "go public" are given short shrift. Strictly speaking, the events are analytically silent, not gatherable as constructionist facts because they are not publicized. We cannot know how a public social problem affects the everyday lives of those who suffer its objectionable conditions until their lives are broadcast.

When publicity is the criterion for the birth of agency, the hard work of nonpublicly formulating putatively objectionable conditions into problems is lost. Fleeting as it might be, publicity must be about something and requires some form of evidence of the objectionable to be available to go public about, even while the "evidence" may be socially constructed and suffused with rhetoric in its own right. Except for public hoaxes, whose facts are otherwise real enough before they are revealed and accepted as hoaxes, a reality that can be convincingly conveyed as "observable" in circumstances of everyday life is required for there to be a social problem. Discerning reality by publicity, however, suggests problems are purely rhetorical on the large scale. Even Baudrillard's (1988) simulacra represent something and thus require the practical work of generating facsimiles (without reference to an actual source).

My own constructionist experience studying and analyzing the Alzheimer's disease movement has shown that the movement's publicity is linked to related, nonpublic neurophysiological, cognitive, and behavioral facts in a complex way (Gubrium 1986). Accompanying the movement's publicity, which began in 1979, was a new reading of neurophysiological and psychological facts in "senile" materials and data. There was, and now to a lesser degree continues to be, nonpublic controversy, mainly in academic journals, about whether the facts of senility are those of extended normal aging or disease. At this level, it is unclear whether or not there is a social problem in the related, putatively objectionable conditions. [But see Hernandez (1991) and Russo, Vitaliano, and Young (1991) for controversy even at the level of what is to be considered objectionable.]

Knowingly or unknowingly, the movement has chosen to categorically separate normal aging and disease and their related facts so that it is forcefully claimed that "Alzheimer's disease is *not* normal aging!" Interestingly, the movement's success in turning public, political, and financial attention to the objectionable "disease" (not normal) facts has been accompanied by a lessening of the debate in academic texts. The point is that the hard, nonpublic side of the movement worked up what was needed for purposes of publicity, making it possible for certain scientific facts to be selectively and publicly referenced as the concrete neurophysiological and behavioral grounds of a disease. In turn, the academic controversies surrounding the facts are hardly, if ever, publicized. (My study itself remains academic and even rather esoteric at that.) This relatively unpublic activity is an important part of what Gale Miller and James Holstein (1989) generally call "social problems work."

While I have no reason to believe that the suppression of factual neurophysiological and psychological material has occurred in the Alzheimer's disease movement in order to sustain the public purity of the disease as a category separate from normal aging, limiting constructive agency to publicity does keep sociologically hidden what is publicly hidden. A good deal of what Ibarra and Kitsuse's social constructionist takes to be real as far as social problems are concerned might be the result of the less public work of concertedly or inadvertently insulating ontologically controversial material. It could very well be in the interest of the rhetorician of the putatively objectionable not to go public about such matters, that is, the difficult epistemological issues surrounding the nature of the reality that ostensibly is objectionable and that the rhetorician aims to call or not call a social problem, as the case might be. Evidence of this might be sociologically available in relatively nonpublic texts if not in the otherwise "hidden" confines of organizations linked in various ways to the putatively objectionable.

Ibarra and Kitsuse's rhetorician also is calculating. The language here is quite telling. The rhetorician not only is in the business of persuading or influencing, as a dictionary definition informs us is his or her stock in trade, but does so with guile. A social problem resembles a public chess game, with moves, gambits, and countermoves. As the authors write,

> When viewed in general terms, the social problems process resembles a kind of game whose "moves" are perennially subject to interpretation and reinterpretation, whose aims are subject to dispute, whose players are ever shifting, whose settings are diverse, and whose nominal topics

stretch as far as the society's classification system can provide members with typifications of activities and processes.

Later, in describing "naturalizing" as a counterrhetorical move, they write that "the user of this *gambit* runs the risk of being labeled a 'cynic' or 'pessimist' (my emphasis).

Yet, it is a very strange chess game because the players constantly change and so do the aims. The imagery of the game regularly gives way to a sense of cabal with plots, intrigue, and schemes as the undergirding of publicity. Curiously, the very public text or publicity that is the admittedly limited area of the strict constructionist has a hidden agent, one that is not at all public in the sense of being evident in the media, whose texts are read by both the public at large and the constructionist. This wily hidden agent is read for us in the publicity by the strict constructionist, presenting the social movement to us as a "put on" or public drama of the objectionable. There is something not so textual that, by implication, animates the word, as if to inform us that the text really has no life of its own.

The Contrasting Tone of the Vernacular

This sense of the agent and the audience contrasts with the ontological tone of other terms—vernacular, mundane, member, and practical—telling exceptions to the foregoing vocabulary. It is not that these terms cannot refer to publicity and the rhetorician engaged in ordinary and practical activities, as agents might appear if conduct were analyzed as the everyday work of constructing social problems. However, the very public texts and wily rhetoricians inhabiting Ibarra and Kitsuse's social problems world do not appear to be featured in the vernacular, even while the term is assigned special significance because it appears in the title of their paper. It is said that moral discourse has "vernacular constituents," which I take to mean native and natural. As the authors point out, "Analysis consists of reconstructing the vernacular, not downgrading it or leaving it unexplicated."

The Mundane

In the context of this vocabulary, the mundanity of social problems activity is highlighted. Following Pollner's (1978, 1987) usage, Ibarra and Kitsuse urge us to feature the construction of social problems, not the conditions presumed to generate them, not acting as if the problems were categorically distinct from their production. We are to look upon those engaged in the construction of social problems as *orienting* to the world, specifically, orienting to its more or less objectionable aspects as real and separate from themselves. As Ibarra and Kitsuse explain, this is

> predicated upon what Pollner (1978) has called "mundane ontology," which entails a strict demarcation between the objects in the world, including the moral objects studied by sociologists, and persons' "perceptions," "beliefs," and "ideas" regarding those objects.

The orientational, not objective, quality of the demarcation is underscored as Ibarra and Kitsuse add, "What authorizes, idiomatically, the social problems process is the mundane *claim* that objects and their qualities have an existence independent of their apprehension" (my emphasis).

But in what sense can the mundane appear on the surface of the public texts and in the purview of the public at large, which are taken to constitute the ordinary actors and interactions of social problems formation? Are they not mere words in media? Are they not bereft of the practical activities—interpretation, definition, perception, ad hocing, categorizing, concrete denotation—that constitute texts and publicity? Where is the hard reality work that generates the publicity, belying the "moves" and "gambits" that media audiences hear or read about?

Like the public that is a thing at large, not a feature of language, and like the agent whose ordinary psychology is inferred from beneath cabalistic texts, the mundane in Ibarra and Kitsuse's framework is something vividly extraordinary. The strange chess game that is the construction of social problems is the work of actors without a concrete world, who, while the authors take the actors to be oriented to reality, are presented to us as oriented purely to publicity, to what can be put over on anyone suggestible enough to believe public claims.

But there is a vernacular world of the real even among the actors of this strange chess game, which Ibarra and Kitsuse's concentration on publicity does not open to view. The real is made up of potential-realities-for-their-more-or-less-wily-agents, among these the "angles," "stories," "images," "presentations," "reports," and other scenarios that are worked up to encapsulate what is intended for publics at large (see, for example, Altheide 1976, Tuchman 1978). The hyphenation is meant to underscore the intentionality of the real, where practice is part and parcel of the objects of production. Practice of the mundane is totally lost to inspection in exclusive attention to by-products such as publicity. As Marx noted in his reference to commodity fetishism in the economic analysis of products, we are not apprised of the social relations of production and how relations enter into the products of labor. We cannot escape the real (and its conditions), even while the real may be claimed to be images.

Members

Is the public, in general or in particular, simply a nebulous mass of receptive agents? This brings us to another term—member—which Ibarra and Kitsuse use extensively. For example, they write with regard to their perspective, "If then we change our perspective and assume the gaze of *members*, 'social problems' appears in a different light" (my emphasis). The world of social problems formation is peopled by members, which one would understand to include the public. Shortly thereafter, the authors further specify membership as practical in their view, stating that the constructionist's methodological stance "transforms members' practically based resources into researchable topics."

The term *member* is borrowed from ethnomethodology (Garfinkel 1967; Heritage 1984) and it is important to stress that, like the term *vernacular*, member implies member-of-something. In ethnomethodological usage, it highlights the contextuality of the actor's orientation to everyday life. As members, actors orient to objects, events, and information in terms of the concrete business at hand they have in the world, which is a way of calling attention to its mundane quality. It is sometimes said that these objects, events, and information are "indexical," their reality-for-the-actor indicative of his or her membership in a particular context of the real, with no irony intended. Contexts might otherwise be called the "language games" in which the actor participates.

Ibarra and Kitsuse's borrowing has special implications for the connotation of the public. If those who receive and respond to claims are members, which we would presume all actors to be in the authors' framework, there can be no practical public at large, select or otherwise. In practice, there are only mundane members of this or that circumstance to whom claims are made. In the vernacular, members are to be taken as native to their worlds, which, in turn, present natural objects and borders of life, as mundanely extraordinary as those natural objects and borders might sometimes be.

My studies of the Alzheimer's disease movement can shed concrete light on how membership mediates the public reception of disease claims (Gubrium 1986, 1991). The Alzheimer's Disease and Related Disorders Association (ADRDA) has mounted an extensive media campaign to tout and inform the public about the so-called disease of the century. Diverse images and detailed depictions of both the victim's and the caregiver's (the "second victim") experiences are publicized through a variety of mediums, from television programming to educational videotapes and chapter newsletters. I have been interested in how a particular public, namely, family members and significant others, responds to the publicity, especially how organizations and circumstances mediate the interpretation of public claims about the disease and its typical care experiences.

Support groups for caregivers and local chapters of the ADRDA were observed over a three-year period in two North American cities. Some groups were closely affiliated with the ADRDA through a local chapter; others were not. Although all groups to some extent made use of ADRDA-educational materials and usually were aware of ADRDA publicity, member responses to ADRDA claims and information depended on a group's culture of disease experiences. A few groups were decidedly self-help entities and could be stridently antiprofessional, at such times claiming that only laypersons with hands-on caregiving experience could know "what it's like," not the professionals. On these occasions, members tended to look upon professionally sponsored ADRDA claims with skepticism, preferring to see what was or was not disease, or disease related, in their own terms. Other support groups memberships readily accepted information provided in educational material and encountered in the media, identifying and organizing the interpretation of their personal experiences according to the patterns and schemes presented.

It was often claimed that the caregiver goes through distinct stages in responding to the mental demise of a loved one, usually a spouse or parent. While this was very public information, the claim took on its meaning in the context of its reception. In support groups whose members were positively disposed to the educational materials and ADRDA publicity, members tended to interpret their own and others' disease experiences according to received experiential chronologies. Their individual problems and caregiving histories accorded with the personal side of the social problem the disease was claimed to be. In groups emphasizing self-help, members were more likely to scoff at any received pattern for the disease experience, especially on occasions of decidedly antiprofessional sentiment (Gubrium 1987b). Individual experiences, it was locally claimed, were too complicated to be captured by formulas. Group differences suggested that membership was more than a matter of the mundane, constructing reality on membership's own terms, including what is or is not a problem of everyday life.

For a Cautious Naturalism

If we are to attend to the process of social construction, as rhetorical as it might be, and if we are at the same time to treat the process as mundane and undertaken by members, we must attend to interactional practice. Practice provides an analytic context that tolerates simultaneously both Ibarra and Kitsuse's vocabulary of agency and their contrasting overture to the vernacular (see Bourdieu 1977, ch. 2). On the one hand, the language of rhetoric, publicity, and publics at large tends to decontextualize and deconcretize the social construction process in order to highlight its idiomatic quality, emphasizing its concertedly public discourse. On the other hand, the language of mundanity and membership concretizes and contextualizes, stressing what might be called the ordinary life worlds of publicity—the production, management, and consumption of images, slogans, and scripts. The view to practice centers on an agent whose enduring project is to resolve the seeming contradiction, displacing the contradiction from being theoretical to being a problem of everyday life.

We can think of the agent as a practitioner of everyday life (Gubrium 1988). As agent, the practitioner is located somewhere and therein is engaged in a project of meaning attuned both to the local conditions of his or her activity and the overall products of the enterprise. The conditions can be thought of as the *embeddedness* of the social construction process (Gubrium 1988; Gubrium and Holstein 1990), stressing the formal and informal organizational parameters of meaning that impinge on the agent or, putting it in reverse order, that provide the agent with interpretive resources. The agent's constructive activity is embedded in a context of interpretation. For example, whether or not the putatively objectionable condition of Alzheimer's disease home care is construed as a problem depends on the caregiver's interpretive resources. A support group whose local culture provides a well-articulated reading of disease and caregiving embeds the caregiver in a different understanding of what is going on at home than a support group that defends participants from the dubious interpretive claims of professionals. There are, of course, other layers of embeddedness, from the mediating conditions of gender (Smith 1987) to the categorical diversities of history and society (Foucault 1973), that figure in the social construction process. Yet location and embeddedness do not determine the social construction process. The practitioner of everyday life is a "bricoleur" in Levi-Strauss's (1962) sense of the term, making use of the bits and pieces of available interpretive material and rules of understanding to attach meaning to experience, as Weber (1947, p. 88) puts it. It is in the presentation, not the process of attachment that Ibarra and Kitsuse's rhetorical framework comes to the fore, providing a rich and intriguing set of categories for analysis.

The ordinary, practical quality of constructive agency requires one to methodologically tolerate the tension between culture and nature, attending to the mundane resolutions of practitioners. While on the one hand Ibarra and Kitsuse seem to catapult squarely into persuasive culture to argue their brand of social constructionism, their accompanying attraction to the language of the ordinary, on the other hand, suggests that a cautious naturalism is indicated. To put it simply, features of everyday life are treatable as natural and native, even if they are constructed. Members' projects take the things for granted as real and immutable. Thus what is understood as nature fixes culture, until it seems natural to undo or reinvent what was, as Garfinkel (1967) might put it, unnatural "all along." To conflate the vocabularies of rhetoric and the mundane as Ibarra and Kitsuse do, without a clear appropriation to interpretive practice, commits the kind of error that Norman Denzin (1970) made years ago in tying wholesale symbolic interaction to ethnomethodology (Zimmerman and Wieder 1970).

References

Altheide, David L. 1976. *Creating Reality: How TV News Distorts Events*. Beverly Hills, CA: Sage.

Baudrillard, Jean. 1988. *Selected Writings*. Edited by Mark Poster. Stanford, CA: Stanford University Press.

Blumer, Herbert. 1969. "Public Opinion and Public Opinion Polling." Pp. 195–208 in *Symbolic Interactionism*, by Herbert Blumer. Englewood Cliffs, NJ: Prentice-Hall.

Bourdieu, Pierre. 1977. *Outline of a Theory of Practice*. Cambridge: Cambridge University Press.

Denzin, Norman K. 1970. "Symbolic Interactionism and Ethnomethodology." Pp. 261–84 in *Understanding Everyday Life*, edited by Jack D. Douglas. Chicago: Aldine.

Foucault, Michel. 1973. *The Order of Things: An Archaeology of the Human Sciences*. New York: Vintage.

Garfinkel, Harold. 1967. *Studies in Ethnomethodology*. Englewood Cliffs, NJ: Prentice-Hall.

Gubrium, Jaber F. 1986. *Oldtimers and Alzheimer's: The Descriptive and Organization of Senility*. Greenwich, CT: JAI Press.

———. 1987a. "Organizational Embeddedness and Family Life." Pp. 23–41 in *Aging, Health and Family*, edited by Timothy Brubaker. Newbury Park, CA: Sage.

———. 1987b. "Structuring and Destructuring the Course of Illness: The Alzheimer's Disease Experience." *Sociology of Health and Illness* 3:1–24.

———. 1988. *Analyzing Field Reality*. Newbury Park, CA: Sage.

———. 1989. "Local Cultures and Service Policy." Pp. 94–112 in *The Politics of Field Research*, edited by Jaber F. Gubrium and David Silverman. London: Sage.

———. 1991. "Recognizing and Analyzing Local Culture." Pp. 131–41 in *Experiencing Fieldwork*, edited by William B. Shaffir and Robert A. Stebbins. Newbury Park, CA: Sage.

Gubrium, Jaber F. and James A. Holstein. 1990. *What Is Family?* Mountain View, CA: Mayfield.

Heritage, John. 1984. *Garfinkel and Ethnomethodology.* Cambridge: Polity Press.

Hernandez, Gema G. 1991. "Not So Benign Neglect: Researchers Ignore Ethnicity in Defining Family Caregiver Burden and Recommending Services." *Gerontologist* 31: 271–72.

Latour, Bruno and Steve Woolgar. 1979. *Laboratory Life: The Social Construction of Scientific Facts.* Beverly Hills, CA: Sage.

Levi-Strauss, Claude. 1962. *The Savage Mind.* London: Weidenfeld and Nicholson.

Miller, Gale and James A. Holstein. 1989. "On the Sociology of Social Problems." Pp. 1–16 in *Perspectives on Social Problems*, vol. 1, edited by James A. Holstein and Gale Miller. Greenwich, CT: JAI Press.

Pollner, Melvin. 1978. "Constitutive and Mundane Versions of Labeling Theory." *Human Studies* 1:269–88.

———. 1987. *Mundane Reason.* New York: Cambridge University Press.

Russo, Joan, Peter Vitaliano, and Heather Young. 1991. "Russo and Colleagues Reply." *Gerontologist* 31:272.

Smith, Dorothy. 1987. *The Everyday World as Problematic: A Feminist Sociology.* Boston: Northeastern University Press.

Spector, Malcolm and John I. Kitsuse. [1977] 1987. *Constructing Social Problems.* Hawthorne, NY: Aldine De Gruyter.

Tuchman, Gaye. 1978. *Making News: A Study in the Construction of Reality.* New York: Free Press.

Weber, Max. 1947. *Theory of Social and Economic Organization.* New York: Free Press.

Zimmerman, Don H. and D. Lawrence Wieder. 1970. "Ethnomethodology and the Problem of Order: Comment on Denzin." Pp. 285–98 in *Understanding Everyday Life*, edited by Jack D. Douglas. Chicago: Aldine.

4

The Reflectivity of Constructionism and the Construction of Reflexivity

Melvin Pollner

Constructing Social Problems (*CSP*; Spector and Kitsuse [1977] 1987) advanced one of the more radical and reflexive programs of its time. In lieu of the traditional focus on the "objective conditions" comprising social problems (as defined by the sociologist), *CSP* recommended focusing entirely on the definitional or claims-making processes through which "social problems" were constituted as such. *CSP*'s reflexive sensibility was evident in its critique of sociologists' failure to apply the "practiced skepticism" they apply to the claims of other groups to their "own causal analyses or explanations of social phenomena" (p. 64). The privilege given social science accounts in the analyses of social problems, argued Spector and Kitsuse, "ignores the fact that such statements are the *social constructions of social scientists*" (p. 65, italics in original). As these and other statements suggest, *CSP*'s constructionism was a reflexively attuned radical departure from the "objectivist" position.

Evolving reflexive concerns in sociology and other disciplines, however, seemed to outflank constructionism. Specifically, Woolgar and Pawluch (1985) argued that *CSP* and constructionism generally were guilty of "ontological gerrymandering." Despite programmatic ambitions to abandon a focus on objective conditions in favor of a claims-making approach, constructionism, it was alleged, imported objectivist assumptions into the definition of the phenomenon. Moreover, though prepared to view the claims of others in constructionist terms, constructionists exempted their own formulations from consideration as "social" or constructionist achievements. Thus, constructionism became vulnerable to both objectivist and reflexive critiques: The former bemoaned the intrusion of relativism, while the latter decried the vestiges of objectivism.

The reflexive critique is especially insidious in that regardless of how constructionism responds it is unlikely to produce a satisfying resolution. From a reflexive point of view, constructionist claims about the

discursive or rhetorical construction of, say, social problems are themselves discursive constructions as, indeed, are determinations of their
truth or falsity as, indeed, are the very concepts that initiate and suffuse
constructionist inquiry—such as truth, falsity, and constructionism itself. In applying the principles of constructionism to those very principles and their products, constructionism leads itself to analytic paralysis
or infinite regress. Alternatively, if constructionism circumvents the
paradoxes of reflexivity by exempting itself from reflexive review, it
exposes itself to the criticism that it fails to provide a complete account of
social life: Constructionist explanations have not been accounted for.
Thus, constructionism is in a double- or even triple-bind: Whether it
opts for or against the reflexive turn, the program is liable to charges of
inconsistency, incompleteness, or both.[1]

How then does constructivism respond? In this paper, I explore the
emendation of constructionism by Ibarra and Kitsuse (in this volume) in
response to the critique by Woolgar and Pawluch. The emended constructivist position completely purges objectivism from the formulation
of the *topic* of constructivist inquiry but retains objectivism at the level of
analysis. Although emended constructionism remains reflexively outflanked at the analytic level, Ibarra and Kitsuse suggest that reflexive
approaches might be outflanked sociologically. Specifically, they suggest
studying the conditions that promote or inhibit the emergence of reflexivity. The dialectic between a reflexive sociology and the sociology
of reflexivity comprises, I argue, a growth plate of the sociological imagination.

Objectivist, Topical, and Analytic Constructionism

The term *constructionism* encompasses divergent understandings of
the constructive process and the nature and consequences of reflexivity
(Woolgar 1983; Woolgar and Ashmore 1988). Mundane (Pollner 1978) or
objectivist forms of constructionism presuppose a determinate and analytically specifiable objective order, which actors are conceived to differ-
entially perceive, make claims about, or define. In its objectivist expression, constructionism is concerned with the "subjective," "cognitive," or
"interpretive" cognates of the objective realm. These processes are
themselves incorporated into the objectivist order comprising the focus
of objectivist studies. Thus, objectivist constructionism recognizes that
social problems are variously "defined" by different groups and that the
construction of such definitions falls within the purview of a comprehensive sociology of social problems. Merton (1968) himself acknowl-

edges this form of constructionism in his specification of the scope of the sociology of social problems:

> [F]ull or substantial consensus in a complex, differentiated society exists for only a limited number of values, interests, and derived standards for conduct. We must therefore be prepared to find that the same social conditions and behaviors will be defined by some as a social problem and by others as an agreeable and fitting state of affairs. (p. 786)

For objectivist constructionism, radical reflexivity rarely arises as an issue and appears as anathema, absurd, or pointless when it does. Thus, if it must choose among the varieties of incompleteness and inconsistency, objectivism's preference is to be "incomplete" by exempting its own suppositions and practices from reflexive inquiry.[2]

Constitutive forms of constructionism (Pollner 1978; Woolgar 1988) suspend the distinction between definitional, interpretive, or representational practices on the one hand and the referent of those practices on the other. Constitutive forms, however, vary in their scope. *Topical* constructionism suspends objectivist assumptions in the formulation of the phenomenon or *topic* of inquiry. In crafting the object of its investigations, topical constructionism suspends objectivist assumptions by attending to social reality as inextricably entwined with and constituted through discourse and practice.[3] Objectivist distinctions—between the "objectively determined" and merely labeled, defined, or perceived—are themselves included in the topical field. These distinctions are of interest not as analytic resources for framing and shaping the topic but insofar and in the ways they are presupposed, oriented to, and enacted by the community.

Although advancing a comprehensive constructionist conception of the phenomenon, topical constructionism is objectivist at the level of analysis. At the level of analysis, members' constructionist practices—presuppositions, rhetoric, discourse—are conceived as determinate realities that can be represented veridically by the analyst. Thus, although members are construed as *constituting* reality, analysts are conceived as *discovering* reality. For topical constructionism, reflexive considerations are important in specifying the nature of the phenomenon, especially in identifying importation of objectivist conceptions in the specification of the phenomenon. At the analytical level, however, topical constructionism allies itself with the objectivist project and thus convulses at the prospect of radical reflexivity.

Analytical constructionism brings analysts' as well as members' practices under the purview of the constructionist mandate. Constructionism is no longer confined to the specification of the topic of constructionist studies: It is understood to characterize the studies and their methods as well. Thus, the objects, arguments, accounts, findings, presuppositions, texts, and so forth of the analytic community—including the conceptual infrastructure (Gasché 1986) of the community developing analytical constructionism—are understood as constituting and constituted processes and products.

In its consummate forms, analytical constructionism merges with poststructural critiques (cf. Rosenau 1992). Precisely because the radicalization of constructionism moves beyond the infrastructure of the classical or objectivist tradition, reflexivity or deconstruction is cultivated and encouraged by poststructural perspectives. In contrast to objectivist incomprehension and intolerance of the ambiguities induced by radical questioning, the poststructural preference is for constructionism to pursue the reflexive initiative and thus to reveal (and revel in) the indeterminacies, undecidables, and equivocalities in the constructions of both members and analysts.[4] The preference undermines the possibility of the project of coherent and comprehensive knowledge of a determinate social reality. For radical poststructuralism, however, it is precisely that project that needs be deconstructed. Thus, what seems epistemological suicide from the objectivist perspective is the promise of a kind of insight and enlightenment for analytical constructivism: In turn what seems to be naivete and entrapment from the latter point of view is the guarantee of the possibility of knowledge from the former.

CSP as Topical Constructionism

Woolgar and Pawluch (1985) hold that *CSP* among other constructionist programs retains and indeed requires objectivist assumptions regarding the independence of the conditions described or labeled as social problems from the labeling work itself. *CSP* contains statements that can be read as situated within an ontological space that presupposes an analytically specifiable determinate order, which members may label, perceive, define, or claim to be a "social problem." Spector and Kitsuse, for example, distinguish between the traditional concern with the "objective conditions" and *CSP*'s intention to study "the definitions of them as social problems" (p. 5). "This distinction," the authors argue, "is central to our reformulation of the sociology of social problems" (p. 5). Framed in this fashion, constructionism is situated within objectivist conceptual space and its quintessential distinction between the objective and the subjective.

CSP's objectivism might also be found in the very formulation of the phenomenon as "claims-making." The logical grammar of "claim" presupposes an objective realm about which claims are made. Correlatively, despite their care in invoking the term, Spector and Kitsuse's "putative condition" may be read as oblique reference to an independent and objective reality. Even the encouragement to "set aside the issue of the objective basis of alleged conditions, even to the extent of remaining indifferent to their existence" (p. 78) could be adduced in support of an objectivist interpretation. The objectivist reading would note that *CSP* established the significance of claims by allowing for, but setting aside the relevance of, an objective condition about which claims were being made. Finally, the illustration cited by Woolgar and Pawluch (1985) in which Spector and Kitsuse distinguish between the constancy of marijuana use and varying definitions of marijuana as an addictive substance again suggests the typical objectivist distinction between objective conditions on the one hand and subjective interpretations on the other.

Although selected aspects of *CSP* allow for an objectivist reading, the context and trajectory of the argument indicate that *CSP* is striving to be a coherent topical constructionism (cf. Schneider 1985). Ibarra and Kitsuse's emendations crystallize *CSP* as topical (rather than objectivist) constructionism. For emended *CSP*, objectivist distinctions and discourse are themselves understood as features of the language games through which social problems are constructed as such. In replacing the concept of "putative condition" with "condition-category" they underscore that the term is *not* an oblique reference to objective reality advanced by an omniscient analyst, but a recognition that such references are deployed in the forums of social problems discourse:

> Condition-categories are typifications of socially circumscribed activities and processes—the "society's" classifications of its own contents—used in practical contexts to generate meaningful descriptions and evaluations of social reality. They vary in their level of abstraction and specificity . . . . but they are the terms used by members to propose what the social problem is "about."

Consequently, the analyst of *CSP* persuasion is no longer tempted—if s/he was previously—to divide social problems into objective conditions on the one side and claims about those conditions on the other. Indeed, such a division is part of the phenomenon: The existence (or absence) of a real condition, the specification of its nature and occurrence, and whether it is a social problem are all aspects of the claims-making process studied by the constructionist. The formulating, accounting, and claiming—including the portrayals of the conditions that such discursive practices will be said and heard to be "about"—comprise the phenomena of the construction of social problems.

These emendations remove earlier ambiguities, such as they were, and consolidate *CSP* as topical constructivism. The analyst of claims-making does not invoke a definition of objective reality against which the accuracy of members' definitions are gauged or by reference to which members' responses are conceptualized as definitions or interpretations. Thus, members' constructions are neither right or wrong nor true or false save in the sense that such determinations arise in the claims-making process. The practices and discourse (especially the latter) that occur wherever and whenever social problems are direct or indirect topics are the focus of a constructionist sociology of social problems. Of course, neither the original statement nor the emendation satisfies either objectivists or analytic constructionists.

Anticipating Objectivist and Reflexive Responses

From an objectivist point of view, the crystallization of the *CSP* program into consistent topical constructionism represents an intolerable break with objectivist ontological space. Before the emendation, the ambiguity of the term allowed *putative conditions* to be read as an acknowledgment of the real or objective processes referenced by social problem talk. After Ibarra and Kitsuse, however, there isn't even a "putative" condition. From an objectivist position, emended *CSP* lapses into idealism, as though psychology suddenly claimed that the laws of nature were the experience of the laws of nature and hence physics was no longer necessary. Thus, precisely to the extent that Ibarra and Kitsuse disambiguate the earlier statement by obviating analytic reference to an objective order, they preempt reconciliation with objectivist constructionism. Merton's remarks on the "acid of extreme relativism" (1968, p. 787) might well be the harbinger of critiques yet to come:

> Sociologists need not and do not limit the scope of social problems to those expressly defined by the people they are studying and trying to understand. Fortunately they have an alternative to the doctrine that nothing is either a social problem or a social asset but thinking makes it so. They need not become separated from good sense by imprisoning themselves in the set of logically impregnable premises that only those situations constitute social problems which are so defined by the people involved in them. For social problems are not only subjective states of mind; they are also, and equally, objective states of affairs. (p. 788)

Although analytic constructivism might take issue with Ibarra and Kitsuse's effort to purge objectivism from the topicalizing of constructivist processes, the major objection to emended *CSP* would echo the objection to the original statement: Social constructionism exempts its own practices and determinations from consideration in constructionist terms. As Woolgar and Pawluch argued, selective relativism occurs in the development of constructionism's phenomenon *and* in the development of constructionist analysis:

> Frequently, it is said of certain aspects of social life that things "could have been different." However, the ensuing explanation is not itself subject to this dictate; the analyst's construction of the "explanation" of this state of affairs is emphatically *not* to be regarded as socially contingent, as a result of current conventions, and as lacking logical necessity. In short, explanatory work has to seem distinctively "asocial." The selective application of relativism is thus crucial both in construing phenomena as "social" (for the purposes of establishing a topic for sociological investigation) and in denying the social character of sociologists' own practices. (1985, p.224)

To be sure, both the original and emended statements enunciate a broad and sweeping reflexivity: The sites of social problems discourse encompass the classrooms, conferences, and professional journals—which include, of course, papers such as Woolgar and Pawluch's and this one. Although the program encompasses virtually every aspect of social problems discourse, one aspect is exempted: the practices constituting claims-making, rhetorical moves, and the forums of vernacular discourse as analytically accessible phenomena. The entities, processes, and practices of topical constructionism are conceived as objects independent of the discursive, rhetorical, and enactive work through which their features are represented. In claiming for its objects and inquiries an exemption from the tenets of the constructionist program, topical constructionism remains reflexively incomplete at the analytic level.

Thus, at the end of the day, the double-bind has intensified. For objectivists, the emended *CSP* program is now even more relativistic and subjective—having severed itself from any relation to the objective order. For analytic constructionists, the revised *CSP* remains excessively objectivist in its presumption of an objective field of claims-making processes and practices and, correlatively, the refusal to reckon the work and assumptions of topical constructionism as a focus of study. Thus, Woolgar and Pawluch would not be deterred from their quest:

> [W]e search for forms of argument which go beyond the current impasse between proponents of objectivism and of relativism. Is it possible to establish a form of discourse which is free from the tension engendered by espousals of relativism within the conventions of an objectivist form of presentation? What would an argument free from ontological gerrymandering look like? (1985, p. 224)

These are significant questions. Although there may be forms of argument and analysis free of the tension between objectivism and relativism
and that avoid the conventions of objectivism, I would suggest that it is
unlikely that they will have significant influence within the social sciences.
Objectivism is so insinuated in the infrastructure of disciplinary discourse
and its institutional context that the successful emergence of new forms of
analysis would require new forms of life. In the absence of such a transformation, constructionist analyses—or sociology generally—may chronically find itself in a quandary.

Reflexive Constructionism and the Construction of Reflexivity

Ibarra and Kitsuse refrain from throwing the constructionist into the
reflexive vortex, but they are not cowed by the charge of limited reflexivity. Indeed, in a provocative footnote, they suggest that reflexivity
might be examined empirically:

> The difference between member's and analyst's reflexivity is that the for
> mer's is practical while the latter's is theoretical. Indeed, there are interest
> ing papers to be written about just this topic: how such reflexivity tends to
> emerge, the courses it tends to take, the limitations it must respect because
> of practical considerations, and the ways in which the practice of mundane
> reflexivity may eventuate in the departure from the member's perspective
> altogether in favor of a strictly theoretical reflexivity (in which the "natural
> attitude" is suspended).[5]

Although the sociology of reflexivity intimated by Ibarra and Kitsuse
cannot resolve the binds we have discussed, it suggests that while reflexivity may illuminate sociological argument and inquiry, the latter
may illuminate reflexivity. Specifically, inquiry into the social construction of reflexivity and the contexts that permit or inhibit its emergence
may speak to the prospects of the alternative forms of argument sought
by Woolgar and Pawluch. The sociology of reflexivity, if I am not mistaken, will attest to the difficulty of developing alternatives to "the conventions of an objectivist form of presentation." At the very least, it
marshals a variety of materials suggesting that the conventions of objectivism are deeply rooted in the embodiment of sociological inquirers and
their discursive and institutional contexts.

Elias's ([1939] 1982) study of the "civilizing process" suggests, for example, that the Western sense of self is entwined with objectivism. As
Elias has argued, the notion and experience of the self as an encapsulated entity distinct from an objective external reality develops over a
long-term process of increasing normative restraints on spontaneous

affective behavior. These constraints are internalized and experienced viscerally as separating "self" from "reality." The normative constraints, argues Elias, are products of macrohistorical processes pertaining to the pacification of territory and are incorporated into our musculature as much as they are internalized in our minds. The objectivist metaparadigm is resistant to a radical critique because it is the infrastructure of our embodiment and common sense and, indeed, of our very conceptual resources for formulating and probing the parameters of objectivism.

If inquirers qua members are already constrained from radical questioning by virtue of their embodiment, they are also constrained qua participants in disciplinary discourse. Sociology is premised upon objectivism and assumes a determinate and independent domain of social facts. Insofar as these suppositions are suspended or made problematic, idiomatic concerns such as truth and falsity and eventually the infrastructure of disciplined discourse erode. The intelligibility of concepts such as *reality, truth,* and *representation* are cognate with objectivism and the unsettling of any term reverberates throughout the idiom.[6] From the point of view of objectivism, reflexive efforts to move beyond the objectivist idiom are absurd or unintelligible and given objectivist criteria for determining such matters, the charge is not without substance.

Although discursive challenges and experiments may be tolerated at the margins of the human sciences, it is not likely that objectivism will be abandoned at the core. Peters (1990) argues that the postmodern quest for new discursive styles that recognize the essentially rhetorical nature of all discourse underestimates the connection between "positivist" discursive style, the academy, and the image of self that undergirds the civic life of liberal democracy:

[T]he ways in which academics write is [*sic*] not detached from the ways in which politicians decide or accountants figure; academic institutions, despite the misleading image of the ivory tower, are constituted together with other institutions. The transformation of one awaits the transformation of all. If a rhetorical consciousness is to prevail in academia, we need for a start, theories and practices of meaningful public discourse and public life. After all, it is mainly academics who think that the king is naked and his empire in tatters: in state and society, in the military and industry, in journalism and public talk, positivism—its characteristic attitudes, ambitions, tropes—remains one of the biggest things going. Positivism (again taken loosely as a name for a complex of attitudes about science, truth, talk, and professionalism) remains embarrassingly impervious to our critiques and continues to sustain the institutions that give us our status as professionals. It will not go away just because we stop talking in its style. "Facts" will continue to have paramount persuasive power and objectivity will continue to back up our professional claims to authority when we speak in public. As long as public culture remains as it is, academics will be filmed in front of their book cases (a classic trope of expertise) and queried for their expert opinions, however, severely they criticize the positivism/expertise/social science complex in their writings. (pp. 225–26)

There is nothing intrinsically problematic about incessant reflexivity or the regresses and abysses by which it is supposedly accompanied. They are constituted as unacceptable, intolerable, or unintelligible within forms of life that place a premium on positivist discourse as the basis for subsequent action and inference. These demands are more intense for inquirers who are responsible to objectivist ontology as the grounds for deciding the significance and intelligibility of a claim (cf. Spector and Kitsuse [1977] 1987). Because they are closer to public policy issues, sociologists of social problems are more intensely subject to questions derived from objectivist ontology and therefore required to say something about "out there"—be it the objective conditions comprising social problems or the social construction of social problems. In fateful dialogues presupposing the conventions of objectivism, reflexive discourse is unlikely to be sought or understood.

The embodied, disciplinary, and institutional constraints on new forms of discourse ought not be overstated. It would be presumptuous to suggest that the forms of argument sought by Woolgar and Pawluch are unattainable. The consummate expression of reflexive inquiry, however, seems to require a transformation of deep, diffuse, and entwined forms of embodiment, discourse, and institutions. Short of that transformation, radically reflexive efforts *within* the social sciences are likely to have limited success and those that do succeed are likely to be limited in their radicalism (cf. Hilbert 1990).

The bleak prospects for a fully realized reflexive sociology do not entail abandoning efforts to move beyond the conventions of objectivism. On the contrary, it is through such efforts that a view is gained, however dim, of the profile of the forms of embodiment, discourse, and institutions suffusing contemporary projects and practices. While sociology teaches reflexive inquiry that it is a socially constituted (or denied) possibility, reflexivity teaches sociology (and constructionism) about the equivocality and contingency of its own discourse, practices, and accounts.

Conclusion

Three points emerge from a consideration of Ibarra and Kitsuse's emendation of *CSP*. First, emended *CSP* crystallizes the topic of constructionist investigations in consistent constructionist terms. Thus, *CSP* is not vulnerable to Woolgar and Pawluch's charge of ontological gerry-mandering in terms of the definition of the phenomenon. In exempting constructionist initiatives and practices from reflexive consideration, however, emended *CSP* is vulnerable to a reflexive critique (as is virtually any form of inquiry that purports to be about the world; Pollner 1987). Second, a sociology of reflexivity or an ethnography of argument—that is, the study of how forms of argumentation, representation, explanation, and demonstration are variously open or closed to radical questioning—is a powerful and productive response to the reflexive critique. Reflexive concerns need not always outflank sociological inquiry: Sociology can hold reflexivity responsible to understanding how reflexive questioning is a socially constructed achievement. Although there is an unresolvable tension between reflexivity and sociology, the dialogue between these contrary movements harnesses the deconstructive energy of reflexivity to the sociological imagination. Third, conjectures regarding the sociology of reflexivity indicate limitations to a fully realized reflexive sociology. Insofar as the conventions of objectivism are the infrastructure of the bodies, discourse, disciplines, and institutions within which reflexivity is pursued, it is unlikely that radical reflexivity can be conceptualized let alone implemented within the academy.[7] The Sisyphean efforts to overcome these conventions, however, are the very resources for revealing their presence and potency.

Notes

1. The concept of the double-bind emerged from the Palo Alto school's (Bateson, Jackson, Haley, and Weakland 1956) efforts to explain the ostensibly unintelligible communications of diagnosed schizophrenics. The double-bind referred to situations structured such that regardless of what the individual said or did, s/he would anticipate or experience some form of loss or punishment. The apparent unintelligibility of schizophrenic communication, it was hypothesized, is an adroit effort to respond to these insidious circumstances by making communication highly ambiguous. Thus, for example, the individual might comment about the immediate circumstances and then in the next (or same) utterance negate it or use abstract metaphors without any indication that they are metaphors. In these and other ways (cf. Haley 1959), individuals who took themselves to be in double-binds might make a move and simultaneously retract it, cancel it, or make it unintelligible. The parallels between double-binds and the plight of deconstructionists, radical constructionists, and reflexive sociologists warrants attention.

2. Modernism attends to itself within the framework of its own suppositions. Thus, objectivist thought tames or "disciplines" reflexivity by permitting a reflection whose loyalty to (enlightened or postpositivist) objectivist thought is

assured. Thus, within modernism, reflexivity is transformed into a self-reflection regarding the adequacy of its own practices to provide an accurate rendering of reality.

3.   For topical constructionists, members' activities are not subjective or interpretive in the sense these terms are used in modernist constructionism, where they imply a response to an already given order of objects, facts, stimuli, etc. Rather, these terms connote a constitutive process in which the domain is "realized."

4.   The double-bind predicament may characterize any discipline or perspective pretending to a general or total explanation. Thus, a physics that does not explain its own findings and foundations in physical terms is incomplete: A physics that does explain its findings and foundations is inconsistent. Recognition of these issues may require marginality in relation to what passes for normal science within the discipline. Constructionism strives for a marginality and thus encounters ontological and epistemological issues to which more settled or central perspectives are indifferent and oblivious but whose resolution reverberates to the core.

5.   The proposal resonates with *CSP*'s discussion of the circumstances inhibiting appreciation of a labeling or definitionalist stance with regard to social problems. Spector and Kitsuse ([1977] 1987, pp. 63–72) described how sociologists are diverted from a definitionalist approach by virtue of their perspective as ordinary members and as members of a profession, department, and discipline competing with others to provide an account of social problems. The extension of the sociology of knowledge perspective also complements Woolgar and Pawluch's (1985) "ethnography of argument," which adopts a "distanced" or "anthropologically strange" view of activities such as reasoning, explaining, persuading and understanding" (p. 214). A significant difference, however, is that the ethnography of argument (Woolgar 1988) seems to focus on the internal structure of textual arguments and analyses: A *sociology* of argument, by contrast provisionally use that term, examines the text in context, i.e., the social context that sustains particular forms of argumentation and analysis. The difference is akin to focusing on language games in contrast to language games as shaped by the forms of life from which they emerge and within which they function.

From this broader perspective, features apparently endemic to certain forms of argumentation and explanation (e.g., "ontological gerrymandering") may prove to reflect processes within the form of life. Thus, to use a crude example, the evasions and deferrals of reflexivity (Watson 1987) may not derive from inherent limitations in argumentation per se but the relations between explainers and those who are responding to, using or paying for those explanations. They might be unwilling or uninterested in being permanently unsettled by ceaseless reflexivity. Yet Woolgar, whose studies, regardless of rubric, are central to the reflexive examination of sociology and the sociological examination of reflexivity, increasingly recognizes something outside the text. Woolgar writes that "the ethnography of the text must develop an understanding of the text as just one element in a reader-text community" (1988, p. 32).

6.   Innumerable practices presuppose and promote objectivist discourse. Lynch's (1991) discussion of the "prejudice of the page," for example, suggests how the page constrains and conditions efforts that would try to go beyond the conventions of "sensible pictures" of reality (p. 18).

7.   Mulkay (1988, pp. 213–23) offers a provocative conjecture on what the

world might be like if "serious" or objectivist discourse was displaced from its privileged position.

References

Bateson, Gregory, Don D. Jackson, Jay Haley, and John Weakland. 1956. "Toward a Theory of Schizophrenia." *Behavioral Science* 1:251–64.
Elias, Norbert. (1939) 1982. *The Civilizing Process*. Translated by Edmund Jephcott. Oxford: Blackwell.
Gasché, Rodolphe. 1986. *The Tain of the Mirror: Derrida and the Philosophy of Reflection*. Cambridge, MA: Harvard University Press.
Haley, Jay. 1959. "An Interactional Description of Schizophrenia." *Psychiatry* 321–32.
Hilbert, Richard A. 1990. "The Efficacy of Performance Science: Comment on McCall and Becker." *Social Problems* 37:117–32.
Lynch, Michael. 1991. "Pictures of Nothing? Visual Construals in Social Theory." *Sociological Theory* 9:1–21.
Merton, Robert K. 1968. "Epilogue: Social Problems and Sociological Theory." Pp. 775–823 in *Contemporary Social Problems*, edited by Robert K. Merton and Robert Nisbet. New York: Harcourt Brace Jovanovich.
Mulkay, Michael. 1988. *On Humour*. Cambridge: Polity Press.
Peters, John Durham. 1990. "Rhetoric's Revival, Positivism's Persistence: Social Science, Clear Communication, and Public Space." *Sociological Theory* 8:224–31.
Pollner, Melvin. 1974. "Sociological and Common Sense Models of the Labeling Process." Pp. 27–40 in *Ethnomethodology*, edited by Roy Turner. Middlesex, England: Penguin.
———. 1978. "Constitutive and Mundane Versions of Labeling Theory." *Human Studies* 1:285–304.
———. 1987. *Mundane Reason: Reality in Everyday and Sociological Discourse*. Cambridge: Cambridge University Press.
Rosenau, Pauline Marie. 1992. *Post-Modernism and the Social Sciences*. Princeton, NJ: Princeton University Press.
Schneider, Joseph W. 1985. "Defining the Definitional Perspective on Social Problems." *Social Problems* 32:232–34.
Spector, Malcolm and John I. Kitsuse. [1977] 1987. *Constructing Social Problems*. Hawthorne, NY: Aldine de Gruyter.
Watson, G. 1987. "Make Me Reflexive, But Not Yet: Strategies for Managing Essential Reflexivity in Ethnographic Discourse." *Journal of Anthropological Research* 43:29–41.
Woolgar, Steve. 1983. "Irony in the Study of Science." Pp. 239–66 in *Science Observed: Perspectives on the Social Study of Science*, edited by Karin D. Knorr-Cetina and Michael Mulkay. London: Sage.
———. 1988. "Reflexivity Is the Ethnographer of the Text." Pp. 14–34 in *Knowledge and Reflexivity: New Frontiers and the Sociology of Knowledge*, edited by Steve Woolgar. Cambridge: Cambridge University Press.

Woolgar, Steve and Malcolm Ashmore. 1988. "The Next Step: an Introduction to the Reflexive Project." Pp. 1–13 in *Knowledge and Reflexivity: New Frontiers and the Sociology of Knowledge*, edited by Steve Woolgar. Cambridge: Cambridge University Press.
Woolgar, Steve and Dorothy Pawluch. 1985. "Ontological Gerrymandering: The Anatomy of Social Problems Explanations." *Social Problems* 32:214–27.

5

Do We Need a General Theory of Social Problems?

David Bogen and Michael Lynch

> We are unable to clearly circumscribe the concepts we use; not because
> we don't know their real definition, but because there is no real "defini-
> tion" to them. To suppose that there must be would be like supposing that
> whenever children play with a ball they play a game according to strict
> rules.
>
> —Ludwig Wittgenstein *The Blue and Brown Books*

Constructionism (or as it is sometimes called *constructivism*) has become
a highly visible and influential perspective for studying social problems.
This development is hardly unique to social problems research. Versions
of constructionism have also become prominent in the philosophy of
science, the sociology of knowledge, legal studies, literary criticism,
history, and archaeology. We are told that there is even a small but
robust group of constructionist accountants.[1] Although it has been
around for some time, constructionism is commonly promoted as a
"new" and "radical" perspective, which contrasts to the "conventional"
epistemology supposedly held by researchers who presume the reality
of the objects or events they study and who seek methodically to establish the referential adequacy of the texts, material residues, and symbolic manipulations through which they try to secure factual claims. The
outlines of a distinctive sociological variant of constructionism were established in Berger and Luckmann's (1966) influential treatment of *The
Social Construction of Reality,* which combined Weberian and Schutzian initiatives in a theory of how social institutions are constituted through an
historical process of ritualization and objectification. In the field of social
problems research, constructionists also draw upon the "labeling theory"
of deviance that was popular in the late 1960s and early 1970s. Ethnomethodology (Garfinkel 1967) gained a foothold in sociology at about
the same time, and as far as many sociologists were concerned Garfinkel
and his colleagues delivered what amounted to an abstruse version of
constructivism. There are definite parallels between the two approaches:

Both emphasize the role of constitutive practices in the formation and maintenance of social order; both develop upon phenomenological initiatives; and both stress the necessity to investigate how the "objects" and "facts" proper to the field of sociology are practical and discursive accomplishments. Many avowed constructionists draw upon ethnomethodological research, and many ethnomethodologists embrace constructionist themes and arguments. Despite such thematic continuities and literary mergers, however, we shall aim in this paper to emphasize the deep differences between constructionism and ethnomethodology.

Discussing differences within a common set of commitments is always dangerous, because it can give rise to the sorts of internecine squabbles that divide communities of scholars and empower their common opponents. While recognizing this, we nevertheless see a point to writing an "internal" critique of some entrenched constructionist tendencies. The point is to clarify differences and resolve equivocalities that are too easily glossed over by citing the literature or repeating familiar slogans. The very term *construction* takes on an equivocal sense in constructionist usage. Ordinarily, *construction* refers to a deliberate process of manufacturing or manipulating an object in accordance with a plan of action, but when used as a theoretical term in philosophy, literary theory, or sociology it describes actions that are performed "unwittingly" or "tacitly," without any overt recognition (and in some cases a denial) that construction is actually taking place.[2] A favored way to set up the general relevance of construction in descriptions of social actions is by treating the actor's vernacular understanding as a naive version of philosophical realism, which differs fundamentally from the constructionist researcher's own analytic vantage point. This distinction enables the researcher to gain leverage for a coherent theoretical position that apparently stands outside the naive "natural theories" held by the ordinary members whose actions are investigated. In this paper, we shall draw upon ethnomethodology and Wittgenstein's later philosophy to question whether it makes sense to consider the member's constitutive relation to social problems as though it was based in a coherent philosophy or theory, and by the same token we shall question the need for a general constructionist theory to guide social problems research.

Our task would be easier if we could simply play ethnomethodology off against constructionism, but since the tendencies we are ascribing to constructionism are no less prevalent in some well-regarded versions of ethnomethodology (Heritage 1984; Hilbert 1990; Pollner 1991), we are faced with having to build the scaffolding for our arguments as we go along. The version of ethnomethodology we advocate resonates with Garfinkel's (1991) and Garfinkel and Sacks's (1970) arguments, but in some respects it is an endangered form of the art, whose survival requires a systematic dismantling of some of the analytic tendencies that have become established in the literature. In this paper, rather than launching into such a project we shall lay out our arguments in a particularized way by focusing on a specific exemplar. Ibarra and Kitsuse's paper in this volume offers a convenient target for our purposes, as it happens to be an excellent example of a constructionist study that draws extensively upon a programmatic distinction between everyday discourse and professional analysis. Our critique begins by questioning whether or not Ibarra and Kitsuse's general theory of the construction of social problems provides a necessary or relevant basis for studies of particular "social problems language games," and in the course of arguing that such games are intelligible and investigable in their own right, and without need for such a theory, we shall have occasion to critically reexamine the fundamental distinction between vernacular and analytic understandings

The Social Problems Language Game

Ibarra and Kitsuse begin their paper by reviewing the major theoretical points of Spector and Kitsuse's *Constructing Social Problems* (*CSP*; [1977] 1987). In that work, they argue, "A fundamental point was made with regard to the ambiguous and often logically inconsistent use of *social problems* as an analytical category in sociology." According to them, one of the central findings of *CSP* was that mainstream approaches to social problems research "typically group[ed] various social conditions (e.g., prostitution, crime) under the rubric *social problems* in an ad hoc manner. In the process, the concept of social problems was rendered without theoretical precision or scope."

On this account, the principal task for a theory of social problems is to improve upon the imprecise and theoretically impoverished conceptual apparatus that has (until now) served social problems research in a merely tacit and ad hoc way. The objection Ibarra and Kitsuse raise to the standing traditions in social problems research is therefore *not* that researchers have *wrongly* theorized the concept of social problems, but rather that they have *under*theorized it; that they have merely *used* a concept of social problems without having given it a clear and unambiguous definition. This is a crucial matter, they argue, because by taking the definition of "social problems" for granted, conventional social problems researchers have adopted commonsense definitions of the phenomena they investigate.

The central aim of the theoretical introduction to Ibarra and Kitsuse's paper seems to be to articulate a blind spot generic to the conduct of social problems research; a meta-analytic puzzle that requires for its solution precisely those theoretical remedies the authors recommend. Hence, the purpose served by identifying defects in conventional studies of social problems is to disclose a space within which theory in general, and their theory in particular, can be seen to be doing some legitimate work.

Creating a space for theory's work is, we shall argue, a canonical move in the language game Ibarra and Kitsuse are playing. We shall call this game "the social problems language game." By that we mean the collection of practices, textual or otherwise, involved in constituting the literary object "social problems per se" as an intelligible, interesting, relevant topic for sociological research. We offer this definition of the social problems language game as a viable, radical alternative to the use Ibarra and Kitsuse make of that terminology. In this way, we mean to distinguish what they are doing from lines of social problems inquiry that remain fundamentally indifferent to the perspective they recommend.

At one point in their argument, Ibarra and Kitsuse note that *CSP*'s central distinction between putative condition and social condition may have amplified the confusion between the different layers of theoretical and mundane discourse, and seduced constructionists into making statements reflecting members' idioms instead of discerning them, thus inhibiting the development of an interpretive theory of the social problems process. While it seems correct to say that the differences between "the different layers of theoretical and mundane discourse" are at times difficult to decipher, and that this tends to inhibit the development of general theory, the confusion Ibarra and Kitsuse mention only arises on the assumption that separate layers must be distinguished in the first place. This confusion arises because one of the principal requirements of a general interpretive theory is the identification of a discrete, isolable, stable—i.e., *researchable*—subject matter. Thus, one of the first things a general theory of social problems needs to do is to provide grounds for drawing a *principled* distinction between sociological and commonsense knowledge of social problems.[3] Only in this way can "members' commonsense knowledge of social problems" emerge as a phenomenon free and clear of the work of sociological analysis.

For Ibarra and Kitsuse, the social problems language game is a coherent organization of the claims-making activities comprising the vernacular or idiomatic resources through which members of the society at large initiate, define, promote, and regulate "the social problems process." As such, they conceive the social problems language game as a "members' phenomenon," where what is meant by this is that members of the society at large engage in the game, independent of professional social scientists' interests in and orientations to social problems.[4] One advantage of this conception of "the social problems language game" is that it neatly distinguishes between professional analyses of social problems and the subject matter of those analyses, namely, "the configuration of premises, conventions, categories, and sensibilities constitutive of 'social problems' as idiomatic productions."

As noted above, we are treating "the social problems language game" as a set of constructive-analytic practices for making a literary-theoretical object of "social problems per se."[5] There is a sense in which our re-characterization of that game may seem unduly restrictive, and even precious. Where Ibarra and Kitsuse recommend the social problems language game as a substantive phenomenon of interest for a large corpus of constructivist investigations, readers may conclude that we identify it as a (mere) construct of Ibarra and Kitsuse's text. Where Ibarra and Kitsuse introduce the social problems language game as a broad way of speaking about members' definitional work in varieties of real-worldly settings, we attribute its nominal coherence to the definitional work accomplished in Ibarra and Kitsuse's text. Where Ibarra and Kitsuse want to investigate the rhetorical practices through which members accomplish the social problems language game, we refuse to separate the existence of that game from Ibarra and Kitsuse's rhetorical practices. Consequently, many readers may be inclined to accuse us of making an ironic substitution of a dry and scholastic subject matter for a lively and significant real-worldly phenomenon. Moreover, they may be inclined to pursue the regress one step further by problematizing our definitional work and our rhetorical construction of Ibarra and Kitsuse's text. Such a regress, however, is precisely what we intend to warn against.

Far from accusing Ibarra and Kitsuse of having made an epistemic blunder, we commend their paper as an outstanding exemplar of the constructivist approach. If their conception of the social problems language game is nothing more than a theoretical invention, it is also nothing *less*. That is to say, it is a seriously intended, seriously used conception that animates a large and lively body of contemporary scholarship, and it figures deeply in the terms of reference, modes of argument, and citational preferences of that literature. Ibarra and Kitsuse formulate their theory of social problems with exemplary clarity and courage, and by so doing they bring a common discursive tendency to a head.[6] When we criticize that tendency, we do not mean to imply that constructivist research generally is worthless, nor do we mean to detract from the instructive quality of Ibarra and Kitsuse's discussion of narrative frames in public controversies over health risks, environmental hazards, abortion, and other issues. Indeed, one of the most striking things about Ibarra and Kitsuse's paper is that the analysis is extremely convincing even though the theory upon which it (presumably) is based is not.

Hence, the point of interrogating their text is not only to question their particular conception of the social problems language game, but more importantly to raise the question of whether social problems research needs a general theory at all. We want to ask, What *use* is a general theory for studies of the various social problems? In trying to provide an answer to this question we need first to consider what the relationship is between theoretical statements and the subject matter they presume to be about, and second, what place (if any) theorizing has within persons' displayed mastery of social practices.

Membership Has Its Privileges

In his essay, "Dennis Martinez and the Uses of Theory," Stanley Fish (1989, p. 372) describes an interview between Dennis Martinez, who at the time was a pitcher for the Baltimore Orioles, and Ira Berkow, a local sports writer.[7] Berkow had apparently wandered into the Orioles' locker room just prior to the start of a game with the Yankees and noticed Martinez talking to his manager, Earl Weaver. Thinking that there might be a story in it, Berkow approaches Martinez and asks him what he and Weaver had been talking about. Martinez turns to Berkow and says, "He said, 'throw strikes and keep them off the bases,' and I said, 'O.K.'" As Fish continues:

> This is already brilliant enough, both as an account of what transpires between fully situated members of a community and as a wonderfully deadpan rebuke to the outsider who assumes the posture of an analyst. But Martinez is not content to leave the rebuke implicit, and in the second stage he drives the lesson home with a precision that Wittgenstein might envy: "What else could I say? What else could he say?" (p. 372)

The point Fish makes with this story concerns a fundamental difference he sees between the *doing* of some activity or practice, on the one hand, and what he terms "the practice of discoursing on practice" (p. 377) on the other. Having established a use of this distinction in baseball, Fish goes on to discuss its relevance to legal disputation and scientific research. In the latter case he applies the distinction to a discrepancy between the way a team of industrial researchers collaboratively come up with a novel solution to an engineering problem versus the way they "theoretically" account for their innovation after the fact.[8] This discrepancy is well established in constructivist studies of natural science, where it is often pointed out that what scientists actually do in their laboratories differs in many respects from how they report upon their methods and findings in published articles (Latour and Woolgar 1979; Knorr-Cetina 1981), but Fish encourages a nonstandard conclusion about the discrepancy. Rather than suggesting that "fully situated members" (whether they be industrial engineers or baseball players) produce *deficient* accounts of their methods, he questions the whole point of assuming an analytic stance toward members' practical actions.[9] Although sports writers and sociologists certainly have rights to describe and analyze the practices of ball players, natural scientists, police officers, and social workers, just as members of those professions have rights to develop formal accounts of their practices, Fish refuses to accord a *special epistemic status* to formal analytic accounts, over and against members' ad hoc uses of expressions and actions. In his view, formal accounts do not necessarily consolidate a dispersed array of partial and deficient, lower-level accounts within a more comprehensive framework of understanding. Instead, formal accounts are produced and justified *as further versions* that have their own rhetorical and practical uses. This cuts to the quick of a fundamental distinction that Ibarra and Kitsuse repeatedly stress, namely "the distinction between the sociologist's perspective and the member's." Like Fish, Ibarra and Kitsuse distinguish the practical circumstances of everyday discourse and action from the adoption of an analytic or theoretical posture. But, unlike Fish, they propose that something *in general* is missing from "mundane" accounts, something that theoretical analysis can supply. In this, they align with the very sort of analytic enterprise that gets squelched for soliciting an account of the "what else" Martinez and Weaver might have said in their reportedly banal conversation.

So how could Fish, with a touch of irony, speak of Martinez's riposte to Berkow as displaying "a precision that Wittgenstein might envy?" Weaver's recommendation to "throw strikes and keep them off the bases," hardly counts as an interesting, original, or exacting formulation of a pitcher's actual practices, so the "precision" of Martinez's utterance must lie elsewhere. And indeed, the point of the story is that the sense and adequacy of Martinez's utterance has nothing to do with describing, explaining, or analyzing the game, but has instead to do with the fact that persons who have no need to describe the general practice of playing baseball nevertheless have things to say to others of their kind.[10] The *intelligibility* of "throw strikes and keep them off the bases" consists in its use as a maxim or reminder—a kind of litany—to be rehearsed *for* the game and recalled *in* the course of game-specific situations. The precision of Martinez's rebuke consists in his use of Weaver's words to exploit a kind of natural equivocality intrinsic to the baseball cliché: namely, that although overhearers may take it to be nothing more than a trite restatement of the obvious, for players engrossed in the game it is not only about all they can say, it is also enough.

To imagine a need to describe the skills and situations of the game comprehensively—i.e., in other than an occasional or ad hoc way—is to demand something extraordinary. This demand is far from extraordinary to those of us who work in the academy, and in the present context it has a dignified history that can be traced back to a legacy from transcendental philosophy that has become entrenched in constructivist sociology.

Distinguishing Topics from Resources

Like many before them, Ibarra and Kitsuse utilize a series of visual metaphors to distinguish the member's "perspective" on social problems from that of the analyst. When acting as agents in the social problems language game, members "perceive" through a "viewpoint" that projects a particular objective definition on one or another social problem. In the familiar language of art criticism, members see the trompe l'oeil composition *as* a realistic portrait or pastoral scene, while ignoring the artful arrangement of brush strokes and the conventions of linear perspective that establish, rely upon, and systematically hide the relational context of the realistic illusion (Gombrich 1960). The analyst steps outside the frame of the naturalistic illusion in order to disclose the artful practices and conventions that "the gaze of members" ecstatically ignores.[11]

This perspectivist picture has a certain classical pertinence, though it becomes far less apt when applied to nonrepresentational modes of art or speech, and it stretches the imagination rather painfully to treat "the members' orientation to social problems" as though it could be like gazing at a visual field from a fixed standpoint. Ibarra and Kitsuse articulate a kind of moral translation of this perspectival picture: Lines of sight become moral commitments, and a focal theme becomes an *idée fixe*. In order to get a glimpse of the invisible grid that locks the member's gaze in place, the analyst must withdraw from the conventional commitments that articulate the relation between field and standpoint. Ibarra and Kitsuse acknowledge that the analyst's task is by no means easy, and that it requires a severe methodological discipline in order to resist the "seductive" tendency of "going native": "In other words, it has proved difficult for constructionists to avoid 'making moves' in the social problems language game." The key, as they elaborate it, is to place vernacular or "folk" versions of social problems into a state of suspended animation in order to maintain a "basic distinction between vernacular resources and analytic constructs."

The distinction between vernacular resources and analytic topics is a long-standing theme in ethnomethodology and phenomenological sociology. In an early statement, Sacks proposed that in order to emerge as a science, sociology "must free itself not from philosophy but from the common-sense perspective."[12] This, he added, distinguishes its historical task from that of the natural sciences:

> Its predecessors are not such as Galileo had to deal with, but persons concerned with practical problems, like maintaining peace or reducing crime. The "discovery" of the common-sense world is important as the discovery of the problem only, and not as the discovery of a sociological resource. (Sacks 1963, pp. 10–11)

For Ibarra and Kitsuse, however, there is little difference between the commonsense perspective and a particular philosophy that stands in the way of a constructivist theory. According to their distinction between member and analyst, the vernacular or commonsense perspective is placed on one side of a dialectic, while constructivist analysis is placed on the other. Common sense is characterized as a coherent epistemological orientation; a dim version of positivism or naive realism. This treatment of common sense as a coherent, although naive, variant of a philosophical position is a well-established maneuver in constructivist and ethnomethodological theorizing. Pollner (1987), for instance, speaks of "positivistic common sense," and Holstein and Miller characterize an "everyday life" orientation to "a reality that is objectively 'out there,' existing apart from the acts of observation and description through which it is known" (1990, p. 104). This imputation of a coherent philosophical view to the ordinary member is similar to the tendency in sociology of scientific knowledge to attribute a positivistic or realist orientation to the practicing scientist as well as the philosopher of science (Pickering 1984, pp. 3ff.).

According to Ibarra and Kitsuse, members are practical rather than analytic or theoretical, and yet the member's perspective consists in a philosophically coherent, "mundane ontology" dominated by a demarcation between words and things. Essential to this ontology is the "mundane claim" that objects and their qualities have an existence independent of their apprehension. Members' conceptions of social problems are "grounded in a folk version of the correspondence theory of meaning." In short, members—a category that now includes most social problems researchers—are made out to be "philosophical dopes," whose commonsense reasoning is captivated by a folk ontology that *to them*, but not to the analyst, is indistinguishable from the world itself.

At this point it might be well worth asking what leads members to be so persuaded by *that* particular ontology, but to paraphrase Garfinkel (1967, p. 68) we are led instead to ask, "What are analysts *doing* when they make members out to be philosophical dopes?" When construed as a philosophical dope, the member becomes an agent who takes for granted a "mundane world" that the analyst recasts as the product of taken for granted "social" practices.[13] This construal not only creates endless work for analysts (a central task for any theory), it also sets up a familiar move in the ubiquitous realist/constructivist debate. Once the member is made out in the image of a realist philosopher, constructivist researchers can accuse their professional colleagues who express realist or objectivist tendencies of taking for granted an unanalyzed member's sense of the objective facticity of social structure. Their very espousal of objectivism thus affiliates such researchers with the commonsense knowledge they despise! The constructivist analyst then shows that this sense of objective facticity is interactively constructed and retained: It is a reality that is "talked into being" (Heritage 1984, p. 290) or constituted through "mundane reason" (Pollner 1987). *Analysis* undermines the claim that members, whether lay actors or sociologists who tacitly adopt members' presuppositions, are reporting about an objective reality. Consequently, within constructionist arguments, social, rhetorical, and interactional agencies—i.e., constructive practices and ethnomethods—occupy the grammatical role of presuppositions in a classic idealist rebuttal to philosophical realism.

The injunction to treat commonsense reasoning, natural language categories, and vernacular intuitions as topics and not analytic resources for sociological investigation has been stated so often in the ethnomethodological canon it has become something of a central dogma (Garfinkel and Sacks 1970; Zimmerman and Pollner 1970; Heritage 1984; Schegloff 1987; Hilbert 1990). When presented to readers who presume that sociology ought not to be contaminated by its subject matter it is an effective rhetorical device, but when taken literally—as Ibarra and Kitsuse seem to take it—it implies that an analyst can somehow stand outside the commonsense world when investigating its constitutive organization. Somehow, it would seem, the analyst must conduct an activity that is not itself practical, vernacular, conventional, mundane, or informed by intuitive categories. Although they do not make a major point of it, Ibarra and Kitsuse apparently call upon a Husserlian solution to this problem of transcending the mundane perspective of members when they propose "bracketing of the 'natural attitude.'"[14] For our purposes, it is worth reconsidering the consequences such a classic phe-nomenological solution for a constructivist theory of social problems.

A Multiplicity of Attitudes

In his essay "The Problem of Rationality in the Social World," Schutz characterized the "attitude of scientific theorizing" as being remote from the world of everyday practical relations:

> This [everyday] world is not the theatre of his [the scientific theorist's] activities, but the object of his contemplation on which he looks with detached equanimity. As a scientist (not as a human being dealing with science) the observer is essentially solitary. He has no companion, and we can say that he has placed himself outside the social world with its mani-fold relations and its system of interests. Everyone, to become a social scientist, must make up his mind to put somebody else instead of himself as the center of the world, namely, the observed person. But with the shift in the central point, the whole system has been transformed, and, if I may use this metaphor, all the equations proved as valid in the former system now have to be expressed in terms of the new one. If the social system in question had reached an ideal perfection, it would be possible to establish a universal transformation formula such as Einstein has succeeded in es-tablishing for translating propositions in terms of the Newtonian System of Mechanics into those of the theory of Relativity.
>
> The first and fundamental consequence of this shift in the point of view is that the scientist replaces the human beings he observes as actors on the social stage by puppets created by himself and manipulated by himself. What I call "puppets" corresponds to the technical term "ideal types" which Weber has introduced into social science. (1964, p. 81)

Accordingly, the scientist performs a kind of transcendental reduction of the everyday natural attitude in order to construct a simulacrum of the actor's practical orientation. In contrast to Garfinkel's (1967, pp. 68ff.) later discussion of the "cultural dope" of classic social theory, Schutz explicitly ascribed legitimacy to the ideal-typical puppet's con-struction. Although the puppet incorporates only and entirely what the social theorist puts into it, Schutz does not repudiate the project of constructing "personal ideal types," but he demands that any such type be checked against the "mind of the individual actor" described by it.[15]

By invoking a version of the Schutzian opposition between "the natu-ral attitude" and the "attitude of scientific theorizing,"[16] Ibarra and Kit-suse put themselves in an awkward position with respect to other constructivist studies. Numerous studies on the social construction of

scientific knowledge have rejected the image of the scientist as a cogitat-
ing ego withdrawn from the myriad embodied skills, social interactions,
and practical interests in the everyday life-world.[17] The scientist now
appears to be more of a *bricoleur*. But this characterization itself poses
problems for constructivist analysis.

The image of the *bricoleur*—a kind of jack-of-all-trades and handy-
man—is owed to Lévi-Strauss (1966), who contrasts the *bricoleur's* im-
provisory use of the array of tools ready to hand with the engineer's
explicitly planned and rationally articulated choice of means to a specific
end. In his essay, "Structure, Sign, and Play in the Human Sciences,"
Derrida expounds upon the internal relation between *bricolage* and the
figure of the engineer in Lévi-Strauss's work.

> If one calls *bricolage* the necessity of borrowing one's concepts from the text
> of a heritage which is more or less coherent or ruined, it must be said that
> every discourse is *bricoleur*. The engineer, whom Lévi-Strauss opposes to
> the *bricoleur*, should be the one to construct the totality of his language,
> syntax, and lexicon. In this sense the engineer is a myth. A subject who
> supposedly would be the absolute origin of his own discourse and sup-
> posedly would construct it "out of nothing," "out of whole cloth," would
> be the creator of the verb, the verb itself. The notion of the engineer who
> supposedly breaks with all forms of *bricolage* is therefore a theological idea;
> and since Lévi-Strauss tells us elsewhere that *bricolage* is mythopoetic, the
> odds are that the engineer is a myth produced by the *bricoleur*. As soon as
> we cease to believe in such an engineer and in a discourse which breaks
> with the received historical discourse, and as soon as we admit that every
> finite discourse is bound by a certain *bricolage* and that the engineer and
> scientist are also species of *bricoleurs*, then the very idea of *bricolage* is
> menaced and the difference in which it took on its meaning breaks down.
> (1972, p. 285)

On Derrida's account, the Lévi-Straussian engineer who dwells in an
idealized world of rational choice is an absurdity, and so would be the
Schutzian scientist who theorizes with an "attitude" divorced from the
everyday world. The use of these figures as ideal-typical constructs—
viz., as methodological heroes, and even straw men—is accompanied
by a principled acceptance of a performative contradiction: "conserving
all these old concepts within the domain of empirical discovery while
here and there denouncing their limits, treating them as tools which can
still be used" (Derrida 1972, p. 284). An entire edifice of contrastive
terms—engineer/*bricoleur*, scientist/practical reasoner, and in the present case, analyst/member—becomes "menaced" by the effervescence of
the initial term in each of these pairs into a "mythopoetic" counterpart of
the other. All we are left with are *bricoleurs*, practical reasoners, and

ordinary members who occasionally, contingently, and opportunistically conjure up various mythic creatures: gods, heroes, rational actors, scientists, engineers, social theorists, and analysts.

As soon as they deny the possibility of transcending the natural attitude, along with its vernacular accounts and ordinary linguistic categories, aspiring analysts might seem doomed to succumb to the "seductions" of membership. To paraphrase Dennis Martinez, "What else could they do?" In line with Derrida's suggestion, however, the very coherence of the natural attitude is itself "menaced" by the absence of a contrastive category (the attitude of scientific theorizing), and hence there is no longer any reason to impute a coherent philosophical standpoint to something so inclusive. It makes just as much sense to suppose that the natural attitude includes every imaginable scientific, philosophical, and mundane "attitude." This, in turn, would mean that the natural attitude comprises a multiplicity of attitudes, none of which constitutes a standpoint from which to view the entire array.

A Plurality of Language Games

We began this essay by proposing a conception of the social problems language game that would open up a radical alternative to the program of constructive analysis proposed by Ibarra and Kitsuse. We argued that the phenomenon they theorize—viz., "social problems per se"—appears in and only in the conduct of "the social problems language game." We argued further that even (and perhaps especially) the claim that the "social problems process," the "social problems language game," or "social problems per se" exist independently of the work of constructive analysis is itself a move in the social problems language game.

Lest we be read as having reached a purely negative conclusion regarding the prospects of Ibarra and Kitsuse's program of research we wish to reiterate that we are quite untroubled by the kind of analysis they pursue, that we find it informative and rewarding, and that it is only for this reason that we have been caused to wonder what the connection between their study and their theory might be.

Clearly there are differences between the program that Ibarra and Kitsuse are recommending and the methods of research toward which we incline, and it has been our argument that many of those differences can be brought to light by examining their use of "the social problems language game." Such differences arise whenever parties to a discourse are operating with understandings of a concept that are so different that the difference itself needs to be thematized. For our part, the issue that

spells the difference is not that we disagree about how properly to conceive "the social problems language game," rather, it is that we disagree
about the relevance of such disputes to the conduct of social problems
research. This point can perhaps be made clearer by considering how
the concept of language games arises as a topic of concern for the social
sciences in the first place.

Wittgenstein's concept of language games (if indeed it is a concept) is
subject to innumerable interpretations, but one thing that is especially
clear is the *plurality* of different examples he gives of them. At one point
in the *Philosophical Investigations* he writes that "the term 'language-
game' is meant to bring into prominence the fact that the *speaking* of
language is part of an activity, or of a form of life." He then lists the
following examples of language games:

> Giving orders, and obeying them—
> Describing the appearance of an object, or giving its mea-
> surements—
> Constructing an object from a description (a drawing)—
> Reporting an event—
> Speculating about an event—
> Forming and testing a hypothesis—
> Presenting the results of an experiment in tables and diagrams—
> Making up a story; and reading it—
> Play-acting—
> Singing catches—
> Guessing riddles—
> Making a joke; telling it—
> Solving a problem in practical arithmetic—
> Translating from one language into another—
> Asking, thanking, cursing, greeting, praying. (Wittgenstein
> 1958b, §23)

These various language games do not seem to form a unitary cognitive
system. Although Wittgenstein never wrote of "social problems" language games, we can imagine that were he to do so he would not write
of *the* social problems language game at all, nor would he describe "it" as
a coherent metaphysical picture. More likely, he would list an array of
social problems language games or, more precisely, a plurality of language games affiliated with specific orders of activity that are in turn
associated with the various substantive topics included in lay and professional discussions of social problems. Since "crime and the criminal
justice process" has an unquestioned place in contemporary discussions

of social problems, consider the following list of language games associated with that topic:

> Arresting a suspect and reading him his rights—
> Cross-examining a witness in a trial—
> Plea bargaining—
> Selecting a jury—
> Jury deliberations—
> Doing "count" in a maximum security prison—
> Generating a picture of an assailant from a victim's description—
> Cooling out the mark in a con game—
> Interviewing victims of a burglary—
> Examining a corpse for evidences of "foul play"—
> Passing contraband at a prison visitation facility—
> Tap codes among inmates—
> Receiving emergency calls and dispatching police—

Many of these language games have been investigated in detail by ethnomethodologists and constructivist sociologists (Garfinkel 1967; Sudnow 1965; Bittner 1967; Cicourel 1968; Wieder 1974; Maynard 1984; Brannigan and Lynch 1987; Goffman 1952; Atkinson and Drew 1979; Pomerantz 1987; Whalen and Zimmerman 1987; Meehan 1989).[18] Note, however, that these language games are constituents of various substantive actions and institutions associated with a *presumptive* condition-category of social problem. The status of crime as a social problem for the most part is not thematic to the various language games in criminal justice institutions, nor is it thematized in studies of those particular language games. It would be unusual to find, for instance, adversaries in a criminal trial debating about whether or not "common assault" is a "social problem." They would more likely argue about whether or not a particular defendant committed the assault in question, whether his "joining a fight" in fact constituted "an assault," or whether, having been convicted, the assailant remains a "menace to society."

When in the later part of their article Ibarra and Kitsuse outline the properties of the social problems language game, it is not clear that they bring into relief a *general* set of properties that covers the range of language games that social problems researchers typically investigate. Instead, they seem to be thinking of some language games and not others. The various rhetorical claims and counterclaims Ibarra and Kitsuse describe *do* have a recognizable place in the way many public controversies are prosecuted. Some of the things that come to mind are the language used in junk mail sent to potential contributors to single-issue causes; the arguments and counterarguments used in dialogues between callers and radio talk show hosts; slogans shouted at protest marches and pasted on bumper stickers; journalistic summaries of arguments on both sides of a public controversy; or the arguments used in a class action suit in which the plaintiff charges a company with having created a public hazard by releasing industrial wastes into a local river.[19] Ibarra and Kitsuse's paper sketches a set of rubrics that may assist researchers to develop and deepen their understandings of an array of such controversies. But even in these cases, the slogans and terms of debate are circumscribed by sets of considerations that are conceptually distinct from a definition of *the* social problems language game in general. By analogy, one can say that players in a game of chess are "playing a board game," and it may even be possible to develop an abstract conception of what it is that all board games typically have in common, but it would be odd to say that a particular move in chess was a move in *the* board game.[20]

The important feature of the social problems language game for Ibarra and Kitsuse is that the condition-categories featured in an interchange of slogans and arguments are *relativized* by reference to a chronic standoff between the disputants' positions. Where antiabortionists define the condition category of "abortion" as "murder," advocates of legalized abortion argue that it should remain a matter of "right" and "free choice"; where opponents of smoking emphasize the harmful effects and social costs of "secondhand smoke," advocates argue that smoking should remain a matter of "right" and a "free choice." In classic sociology of knowledge fashion, Ibarra and Kitsuse treat the interplay of positions in these public disputes as an opportunity to distance their analysis from the substantive claims identified with the contending positions. Such contentious situations are as though tailor-made for a program of analysis that distinguishes the formal properties of the partisan "claims" from assumptions about their truth and moral virtuousness.

Although many such controversies and disputes can be analyzed in the way Ibarra and Kitsuse recommend, not all social problems language games necessarily take the form of opposing arguments by different sides. From the short list of crime and criminal justice language games listed above, we can see that all sorts of routines, arguments, and modes of symmetrical and asymmetrical exchange have a constitutive role in their production. If the language games associated with crime and criminal justice are diverse and difficult to group under a covering definition or a coherent set of narrative frames, the difficulties get much worse when we consider the full range of topics commonly represented in social problems literatures.

Concluding Discussion

Ibarra and Kitsuse are bothered by the "heterotopias" (Foucault 1970, p. xviii) of vernacular categories that researchers adopt when they study diverse social problems. As a solution, they propose a general interactionist theory as a remedy for the "ambiguous and often logically inconsistent use of 'social problems.'" The problem as they see it is that researchers too often presume the relevance of particular social problems to their studies, without *defining* how the discursive organization of, for example, "plea bargaining" or "passing contraband" is related to social problems, generally speaking. We have argued that to stipulate such a relation as a criterion for social problems research buys little in the way of either theoretical clarity or analytical advance. Although it is sometimes helpful to have in hand a definition of social problems, to us it would seem unduly restrictive to limit the agenda for social problems research to the study of those language games where the status of a given condition-category as a social problem is called into question, and we do not figure that Ibarra and Kitsuse would want to impose such definitional limits on what counts as a bona fide topic for social problems research.

Ibarra and Kitsuse say that constructivists should bracket particular condition-categories, because analysts should not trade upon vernacular conceptions of "abortion," "child abuse," or "hazardous pollutants'. Note, however, that when they give examples they do not carry this bracketing to absurd extremes. They do not bracket everything having to do with the ontological status of the social problems they examine. Following their policies we would be careful to say that some groups *claim* or *define* abortion as [murder] while others define it as a morally legitimate [choice], and we would not say that abortion *really is* "an act of murder" or that it *really is* "a legitimate choice." To follow Ibarra and Kitsuse's policies in this case would neither be impossible nor senseless, since the intelligibility of the bracketing is *internal* to the substantive dispute being investigated (the vernacular terms of the dispute themselves establish *just* what is problematic about "abortion"), but it would be absurd to generalize the analytic procedure in an attempt to transcend an entire "members' ontology." Notice, for instance, that Ibarra and Kitsuse do not suggest that we should refer to abortion clinics as [abortion] clinics (or as abortion [clinics]), as though to suggest that what *abortion* or *clinic* denotes in such a context should be bracketed for the sake of analysis. Disputes about abortion clinics do not problematize the matter of whether or not abortions actually occur, or whether or not there actually exist facilities called abortion clinics . Even the most radical antiabortionist saboteurs give little thought to such ontological concerns when they stage their protests or plant their bombs.[21] Consequently, in order to have anything specific to say about the abortion controversy, social problems researchers must trade upon vernacular concepts of clinic and abortion. The lesson from Dennis Martinez and Wittgenstein is that *this is not a problem* (and therefore it is not a problem to be re-medied by a theory), since it is their vernacular concepts that enable members and analysts alike to problematize what they see fit to debate about, explicate, or relativize in accordance with some language game.

This returns us to the question we asked earlier: What use is a general theory for studies of the various social problems? From what we can see it is of very little use, either for investigators who study particular lan-guage games associated with conventionally recognized types of social problem, *or* for Ibarra and Kitsuse when they begin to explicate some of the narrative tropes that come into play in various public disputes. Al-though we applaud their having begun a study of an array of language games specific to a variety of social movements and public controver-sies, we see no reason to believe that their study, however promising and insightful, will yield a *comprehensive framework* for investigating the myriad language games that in one way or another constitute the famil-iar themes and settings associated with the various vernacular categories of social problem.

From what we have said thus far, readers may be inclined to ask, "So what are you trying to do? What would you suggest as an alternative?"[22] One thing we are *not* aiming to do is to offer an alternative theory to supplant the one proposed by Ibarra and Kitsuse. Despite the fact that we have focused our critique on their theory, we would not want readers to conclude that their theory is inadequate compared to another actual or possible theory of the social problems process. Instead, we have questioned their initial conception of the field of social problems—and of social action more generally—that sets up a need for a general theory. We have suggested some reasons for doubting whether a general social problems process subsumes the various language games associated with the public manifestation and practical management of members' social problems. Although we recognize that what counts as a social problem is a "members' phenomenon," which therefore can change with different social and historical conditions of membership, we see little reason to believe that a general theory of how members rhetori-cally constitute social problems would fare any better than an objective definition of the social problems themselves.

It might seem at this point that we are advocating a hyperrelativistic perspective that disavows any possibility of investigating substantive social problems. Such a position would be far from what we are in fact advocating. It would be a fundamental mistake to suppose that because social problems are vernacular, rhetorical, or indexical phenomena researchers should first devise a stricter and more demanding conception of the field before they can hope to investigate those phenomena. To suppose this would be to forget that students of social problems are masters of the vernacular (that is, they are members) before they begin their studies, and that the many ordinary and more specialized discursive practices pertinent to the transgressions, institutionalized routines, disputes, and negotiations that make social problems accountable are *finely ordered.* Although a vernacular concept is far from an epistemological guarantee, and there may be no invariant definition of social problems or of the discursive practices associated with their production and recognition, this should not deter researchers from taking up the task of explicating the way those practices are ordered (Sharrock and Anderson 1991, p. 52). The fact that social problems may always be bound to temporal and practical circumstances does not make them unreal, nor does it justify an invariant attitude of skepticism toward them. So far from arguing in favor of a remote epistemological attitude toward the field of social problems research, we would rather encourage further research about the discursive practices through which social problems manifest in specific social and historical circumstances. As mentioned earlier in this paper, numerous studies of this sort are in hand, and while they may not provide readers with a coherent and noncontentious perspective on a general social problems process, they do provide occasional glimpses into the unfathomably complex fields of practical action in which social problems arise.

Notes

1. This information comes in a personal communication from Richard Harper, of Rank Xerox, Ltd., Cambridge EuroPARK. According to Harper, these accountants adopt a version of deconstructionism, which for present purposes can be treated hand in glove with constructionism.

2. See Fish (1989, p. 226) for a discussion of this "equivocation."

3. By principled, here we mean a distinction that must be seen to identify nonarbitrary qualities of the members' phenomenon under study, as distinct from the contingent products of a methodological interest that ignores or overrides the system of relevancies interior to the production of the phenomenon. This is a particular way of attending to the "postulate of adequacy" that Schutz develops from Weber:

> Each term used in a scientific system referring to human action must be so constructed that a human act performed within the life-world by an individual actor in the way indicated by the typical construction would be reasonable and understandable for the actor himself, as well as for his fellow men. (1964, p. 85)

Note, however, that this postulate retains a strong element of methodological individualism (the reference to the "individual actor") that does not operate when "actor" is transformed into "member" (see note 4).

4.   In ethnomethodology, the term *member* refers not to a person but to "mastery of natural language" (Garfinkel and Sacks 1970, p. 342). Ibarra and Kitsuse apparently use the term in the more familiar sense of *member of a society or group,* although they do associate members with particular rhetorical practices.

5.   Garfinkel and Sacks (1970, pp. 339–40) use the term *constructive analysis* to cover a "remedial program of practical sociological reasoning" that aims to accomplish "a thoroughgoing distinction between objective and indexical expressions." Among the specific research objectives and tasks listed under this "remedial program" are

> the elaboration and defense of unified sociological theory, model building, cost-benefit analysis, the use of natural metaphors to collect wider settings under the experience of a locally known setting, the use of laboratory arrangements as experimental schemes of inference, schematic reporting and statistical evaluations of frequency, reproducibility, or effectiveness of natural language practices and of various social arrangements that entail their use, and so on. (p. 340)

Although Ibarra and Kitsuse align with ethnomethodology's program and obviously oppose "objectivistic" modes of research, their effort to build a general theory of "the social problems language game" that remedies the "ambiguous" and "ad hoc" uses of the concept in the research literature is a prime example of the constructive analytic enterprise.

6.   Ibarra and Kitsuse's paper also displays a kind of groundless optimism with regard to the future prospects of the theory and its consequences for the actual conduct of research that is a characteristic (perhaps essential) feature of "programmatic" theorizing. This faith in theory's power to redefine our ordinary concepts is a variant of what Fish (1989, p. 322) has dubbed "theory hope," or "the hope that our claims to knowledge can be 'justified on the basis of some objective method of assessing such claims' rather than on the basis of the individual beliefs that have been derived from the accidents of education and experience."

7.   The interview took place in 1985. Dennis Martinez is now a veteran pitcher for the Montreal Expos, had outstanding 1991 and 1992 seasons, and pitched a perfect game on July 28, 1991. As Jim Holstein (personal communication) put it: "Something must be working for Martinez—Weaver's litany, a rejuvenated fastball, his newfound sobriety—that surely wasn't doing the trick in 1985."

8.   Fish (1989, pp. 374ff.) draws this example from Schön (1979).

9.   Compare, for instance, Aronson (1984, pp. 7ff.), who argues that the disjuncture between science methods and scientists' descriptions of their methods should make us skeptical of the facticity of science findings. Notice, however, that this skepticism arises only once we suppose that *descriptions* of science methods ought to map directly onto those methods in situ—i.e., that there ought to be some direct correspondence between the two—rather than that science methods and scientists' descriptions of those methods are, practically speaking, designed simply to do different kinds of work. It is perhaps for this reason, and not because they are interested in veiling their actual practices (although they sometimes are), that scientists' reports cannot possibly meet the criteria of correspondence implicit in Aronson's treatment of their factual claims.

10. This is related to the argument about formulations made by Garfinkel and Sacks (1970). By "formulating" they mean giving a verbal account that says "in-so-many-words-what-we-are-doing" (p. 351). Like the more familiar varieties of scribes and pundits, social scientists have an occupational interest in formulating what various other members of the society are doing when they engage in their activities. For instance, when conducting interviews they demand explicit verbal accounts that stand as indicators of attitudes, practical skills, and bodies of knowledge. Often such inquirers get disappointing results when they ask for explicit accounts from practitioners, but they are able to fall back on some well-established techniques for clarifying, coding, elaborating, and enriching partial, cryptic, and even hostile answers. Consequently, it can often seem that ordinary usage is inherently partial, schematic, unreflective, ambiguous, or otherwise faulty until an accompanying formulation can draw out its meaning and clarify its sense. This, according to Garfinkel and Sacks, places an undue burden upon formulating. For them, the intelligibility of ordinary usage does not depend upon an accompanying formulation to clarify it:

> [I]nsofar as formulations are recommended to be definitive of "meaningful talk," something is amiss because "meaningful talk" cannot have that sense. This is to say either that talk is not meaningful unless we construct a language which is subject to such procedures, or that *that* could not be what "meaningful talk" is, or "meaningful actions" either. (p. 359)

In the case at hand, an expression like "throw strikes and keep them off the bases," is a disappointing cliché when what is wanted is an elaborate formulation of how a wise old manager instructs a nervous pitcher prior to a big game. But, in line with Garfinkel and Sacks's argument, to hear it *only* as a description answerable to an outsider's inquiry would be to miss its role in the game.

11. For an instructive essay on the limitations of visual metaphors in sociological and psychological theory, see Coulter and Parsons (1991).

12. Although it is not of concern to us here, Sacks expresses a puzzling view of the relationship between natural science and "the common-sense perspective." Bacon's protoexperimental program was set off against the "idyls" of common sense, and while it is well documented that Galileo and other seventeenth-century heroes struggled against theological orthodoxy, they did not at the time propose to free their inquiries from philosophy. For a discussion of related considerations see Lynch and Bogen (forthcoming).

13. Pollner's (1987) account of the epistemic limitations of "mundane reason" has made this move virtually paradigmatic for constructivist social science. See Bogen (1990) for a critical discussion of Pollner's notion of the "mundane world."

14. Although Ibarra and Kitsuse cite Pollner (1975, 1978) as proximate authority, it should be evident from the expression "bracketing the 'natural attitude'" that they are indebted to Husserl and Schutz. Husserl (1970) proposed the "transcendental reduction" as a method through which the solitary theorist reflectively withdraws from active engagement in the life-world in order to thematize the pre-predicative "acts" through which a cognizing subject apprehends real-worldly objects and their categorical relations. Schutz elaborated upon Husserl's analysis of the life-world, and he revised transcendental phenomenology in order to make it more suitable for social scientific investigations. Like many others, Schutz (1966) found Husserl's concept of the "transcendental ego" to be an inadequate starting point for investigating the intersubjective structures of the life-world, and he attempted critically to integrate Husserlian phenomenol-

ogy with established theoretical traditions in sociology. For Schutz, "the attitude of scientific theorizing" offered a perspective—analogous to that of Husserl's transcendental ego—for viewing "the natural attitude" of daily life as though from outside its sphere of operations.

15.   Schutz raises the question, "But why form personal ideal types at all?" (1964, p. 84), but then goes on to formulate a postulate of subjective interpretation that regulates the analytic construction by reference to "what happens in the mind of an individual actor whose act has led to the phenomenon in question" (p. 85).The only alternative Schutz considers is to simply collect empirical facts, and he argues that one cannot do this without taking account of subjective categories.

16.   Ibarra and Kitsuse make only brief mention of Schutz. Nevertheless, we read their article to be indebted to the conceptual distinction between the attitude of sociological theorizing and the "natural attitude" of everyday life (or, as they sometimes put it, the contrasting "perspectives" of the member and the sociological theorist), which is a familiar tenet of much constructivist and ethnomethodological writing, and which was given extensive and original development in Schutz's seminal writings.

17.   See Lynch (1988) for a critical discussion of Schutz's cognitivist views on natural science. A more charitable clarification of Schutz's distinction between the theoretical and everyday attitudes is given by Sharrock and Anderson (1991).

18.   This is but a small sample of a much larger group of studies relevant to various "language games" associated with discursive activities and institutions that presuppose the "problematic" character of condition-categories like mental illness, poverty, and contagious disease. See the extensive bibliography of ethnomethodological studies by Fehr, Stetson, and Mizukawa (1990), for other examples. Many of these studies employ variants of the programmatic distinction between analysis and vernacular orientation that is so central to Ibarra and Kitsuse's theory, and they are therefore not exempt from the critique of the member/analyst distinction we are giving in this paper. The point of mentioning these studies here is to argue that the diverse "language games" they investigate do not readily fall under the rubric of a general "social problems process."

19.   In note 3, Ibarra and Kitsuse mention a "paradigm case" where members "self-reflexively comprehend the social problems process." This is where political consultants advise presidential election campaigns on strategies for topicalizing "social problems" for different audiences. In our terms, such strategy sessions are no more or less "reflexive" than are any other natural language activity, nor do they provide a "window" on a general social problems process that remains obscure within less "self-reflexive" uses of language. See Czyzewski (forthcoming) for a criticism of the conflation of ethnomethodological "reflexivity" with a cognitive concept of "self-reflection."

20.   Wittgenstein (1958b, §2) makes a related point: "It is as if someone were to say: *A game consists in moving objects about on a surface according to certain rules* . . . . —and we replied: You seem to be thinking of board games, but there are others. You can make your definition correct by expressly restricting it to those games."

21.   'Ontological gerrymandering" (Woolgar and Pawluch 1985) is not the issue here. *Gerrymandering* suggests a kind of arbitrary or unwarranted definitional project, while the controversy in this case establishes what it is about abortion that is problematic; and not *everything* about abortion is arbitrary as far as participants or analysts are concerned. Woolgar and Pawluch's argument has

"devastating" effects only for readers who continue to suppose that social problems researchers should not trade upon *any* vernacular characterizations of the phenomena they study. We are suggesting that there is a world of difference between locally and accountably "problematic" vernacular characterizations versus those that are used and accepted as a matter of course for the sake of some argument.

22. We are indebted to Jim Holstein for raising these questions about an earlier draft.

References

Aronson, Naomi. 1984. "Science as a Claims-Making Activity: Implications for Social Problems Research." Pp. 1–30 in *Studies in the Sociology of Social Problems,* edited by J. W. Schneider and J. I. Kitsuse. Norwood, NJ: Ablex.

Atkinson, J. Maxwell and Paul Drew. 1979. *Order in Court: The Organisation of Verbal Interaction in Judicial Settings.* London: Macmillan.

Berger, Peter and Thomas Luckmann. 1966. *The Social Construction of Reality.* New York: Anchor Books.

Bittner, Egon. 1967. "Police Discretion in Emergency Apprehension of Mentally Ill Persons." *Social Problems* 14:278–92.

Bogen, David. 1990. "Beyond the Limits of Mundane Reason." *Human Studies* 13:405–16.

Brannigan, Augustine and Michael Lynch. 1987. "On Bearing False Witness: Perjury and Credibility as Interactional Accomplishments." *Journal of Contemporary Ethnography* 16:115–46.

Cicourel, Aaron V. 1968. *The Social Organization of Juvenile Justice.* New York: Wiley.

Coulter, Jeff and E. D. Parsons. 1991. "The Praxiology of Perception: Visual Orientations and Practical Action." *Inquiry* 33:251–72.

Czyzewski, Marek. Forthcoming. "Reflexivity of Actors vs. Reflexivity of Accounts." *Theory, Culture, and Society.*

Derrida, Jacques. 1972. "Structure, Sign and Play in the Discourse of the Human Sciences." Pp. 242–72 in *The Structuralist Controversy: The Languages of Criticism and the Sciences of Man,* edited by R. Macksey and E. Donato. Baltimore, MD: Johns Hopkins University Press.

Fehr, B. J., Jeff Stetson, and Yoshifumi Mizukawa. 1990. "A Bibliography for Ethnomethodology." Pp. 473–559 in *Ethnomethodological Sociology,* edited by J. Coulter. London: Edward Elgar.

Fish, Stanley. 1989. *Doing What Comes Naturally: Change, Rhetoric, and the Practice of Theory in Literary and Legal Studies.* Durham, NC: Duke University Press.

Foucault, Michel. 1970. *The Order of Things.* Translated by Alan Sheridan. New York: Pantheon.

Garfinkel, Harold. 1967. *Studies in Ethnomethodology.* Englewood Cliffs, NJ: Prentice Hall.

_____. 1991. "Respecification: Evidence for Locally Produced, Naturally Accountable Phenomena of Order*, Logic, Reason, Meaning, Method, etc. in and as of the Essential Haecceity of Immortal Ordinary Society, (1)—An

Announcement of Studies." Pp. 10–19 in *Ethnomethodology and the Human Sciences*, edited by G. Button. Cambridge: Cambridge University Press.

Garfinkel, Harold and Harvey Sacks. 1970. "On Formal Structures of Practical Actions." Pp. 337–66 in *Theoretical Sociology: Perspectives and Development*, edited by J. C. McKinney and E. A. Tiryakian. New York: Appleton-Century Crofts.

Goffman, Erving. 1952. "On Cooling the Mark Out: Some Aspects of Adaptation to Failure." *Psychiatry* 15:451–63.

Gombrich E. H. 1960. *Art and Illusion: A Study in the Psychology of Pictorial Representation*. Princeton, NJ: Princeton University Press.

Heritage, John. 1984. *Garfinkel and Ethnomethodology.* Oxford: Polity Press.

Hilbert, Richard. 1990. "Ethnomethodology and the Micro-Macro Order." *American Sociological Review* 55:798–808.

Holstein, James and Gale Miller. 1990. "Rethinking Victimization: An Interactional Approach to Victimology." *Symbolic Interaction* 13:103–22.

Husserl, Edmund. 1970. *The Crisis of European Sciences and Transcendental Philosophy.* Translated by David Carr. Evanston, IL: Northwestern University Press.

Knorr-Cetina, Karin. 1981. *The Manufacture of Knowledge: An Essay in the Constructivist and Contextual Nature of Science.* Oxford: Pergamon.

Latour, Bruno and Steve Woolgar. 1979. *Laboratory Life: The Social Construction of Scientific Facts.* London: Sage.

Lévi-Strauss, Claude. 1966. *The Savage Mind.* Chicago: University of Chicago Press.

Lynch, Michael. 1988. "Alfred Schutz and the Sociology of Science." Pp. 71–100 in *Worldly Phenomenology: The Influence of Alfred Schutz on Human Science*, edited by L. Embree. Washington, DC: Center for Advanced Research in Phenomenology and University Press of America.

Lynch, Michael and David Bogen. Forthcoming. "Harvey Sacks's Primitive Natural Science." *Theory, Culture, and Society.*

Maynard, Douglas W. 1984. *Inside Plea Bargaining: The Language of Negotiation.* New York: Plenum Press.

Meehan, Albert J. 1989. "Assessing the 'Police Worthiness' of Citizen's Complaints to the Police: Accountability and the Negotiation of 'Facts'." Pp. 116–40 in *The Interactional Order: New Directions in the Study of Social Order*, edited by D. T. Helm, W. T. Anderson, A. J. Meehan, and A. W. Rawls. New York: Irvington.

Pickering, Andrew. 1984. *Constructing Quarks: A Sociological History of Particle Physics.* Chicago: University of Chicago Press.

Pollner, Melvin. 1975. "'The Very Coinage of Your Brain': The Anatomy of Reality Disjunctures." *Philosophy of the Social Sciences* 5:411–30.

———. 1978. "Constitutive and Mundane Versions of Labelling Theory." *Human Studies* 1:269–88.

———. 1987. *Mundane Reason: Reality in Everyday and Sociological Discourse.* Cambridge: Cambridge University Press.

———. 1991. "Left of Ethnomethodology." *American Sociological Review* 56:370–380.

Pomerantz, Anita M. 1987. "Descriptions in Legal Settings." Pp. 226–43 in *Talk and Social Organization*, edited by G. Button and J. R. E. Lee. Clevedon, UK: Multilingual Matters.

Sacks, Harvey. 1963. "Sociological Description." *Berkeley Journal of Sociology* 8:1–16.

Schegloff, Emanuel A. 1987. "Between Micro and Macro: Contexts and Other Connections." Pp. 207–34 in *The Micro-Macro Link*, edited by J. Alexander, B. Giesen, R. Münch, and N. Smelser. Berkeley: University of California Press.

Schön, Donald. 1979. "Generative Metaphor: A Perspective on Problem-Setting in Social Policy." Pp. 254–283 in *Metaphor and Thought*, edited by A. Ortony. New York: Cambridge University Press.

Schutz, Alfred. 1964. "The Problem of Rationality in the Social World." Pp. 64–90 in *Collected Papers II*, by A. Schutz. The Hague: Martinus Nijhoff.

———. 1966. "The Problem of Transcendental Intersubjectivity in Husserl." Pp. 51–83 in *Collected Papers III*, by Alfred Schutz. The Hague: Martinus Nijhoff.

Sharrock, Wes and Bob Anderson. 1991. "Epistemology: Professional Scepticism." Pp. 51–76 in *Ethnomethodology and the Human Sciences*, edited by G. Button. Cambridge: Cambridge University Press.

Spector, Malcolm and John Kitsuse. [1977] 1987. *Constructing Social Problems*. Hawthorne, NY: Aldine de Gruyter.

Sudnow, David. 1965. "Normal Crimes: Sociological Features of the Penal Code in a Public Defender's Office." *Social Problems* 12:255–76.

Whalen, Marilyn R. and Don H. Zimmerman. 1987. "Sequential and Institutional Contexts in Calls for Help." *Social Psychology Quarterly* 50:172–85.

Wieder, D. Lawrence. 1974. *Language and Social Reality: The Case of Telling the Convict Code*. The Hague: Mouton.

Wittgenstein, Ludwig. 1958a. *The Blue and Brown Books*. Oxford: Basil Blackwell.

———. 1958b. *Philosophical Investigations*, translated by G. E. M. Anscombe. Oxford: Basil Blackwell.

Woolgar, Steve, and Dorothy Pawluch. 1985. "Ontological Gerrymandering: The Anatomy of Social Problems Explanations." *Social Problem* 32:214–27.

Zimmerman, Don H. and Melvin Pollner. 1970. "The Everyday World As a Phenomenon." Pp. 80–103 in *Understanding Everyday Life: Toward the Reconstruction of Sociological Knowledge*, edited by J. D. Douglas. Chicago: Aldine.

6

But Seriously Folks: The Limitations of the Strict Constructionist Interpretation of Social Problems

Joel Best

Ibarra and Kitsuse's chapter in this volume, "Vernacular Constituents of Moral Discourse," is the most recent contribution in the distinguished career of John I. Kitsuse. For thirty years, Kitsuse's writings have influenced developments, first in the sociology of deviance, and later in studies of the social construction of social problems. In particular, three of his works became touchstones for labeling theorists and constructionists: "Societal Reaction to Deviant Behavior" (Kitsuse 1962), "A Note on the Use of Official Statistics" (Kitsuse and Cicourel 1963), and *Constructing Social Problems* (Spector and Kitsuse [1977] 1987). Citing these pieces has been almost obligatory, a convention that obscures the different ways Kitsuse's writings can be read.

Much of Kitsuse's work is subject to both strong and weak interpretations. A strong reading is radically phenomenological; it calls into question all commonsensical assumptions about deviant labels, official statistics, social problems, and the like. Kitsuse favors a strong reading; he has consistently criticized both labeling theorists and constructionists for presuming to know the objective reality of deviance or social problems (Kitsuse and Spector 1975; Spector and Kitsuse 1987; Kitsuse and Schneider 1989).

The irony is that many of those being criticized have been influenced by Kitsuse's writings. This is because weak readings of Kitsuse's work far outnumber strong readings; his considerable influence is due to interpretations of his work that Kitsuse himself rejects. Take "A Note on the Use of Official Statistics." There can be little doubt that most readers leave this essay with a sense that official statistics should be understood as products of organizational practices, and should be interpreted with caution. In this interpretation, Kitsuse and Cicourel (1963) merely criticize sociologists for treating official statistics as a straightforward reflection of objective reality. This is a weak reading, in that many analysts who cite Kitsuse and Cicourel proceed to use official statistics, albeit self-consciously, handling them with some care, so that the statistics are now seen as reflecting some combination of organizational practices and the social world. For instance, an analyst may acknowledge that procedures for census-taking cause poor blacks to be undercounted, yet presume that the census results are otherwise more or less accurate. A strong reading of Kitsuse and Cicourel leads in a very different direction: Given official statistics' inherent ambiguity, the analyst should avoid using them. Obviously, the weak reading is more popular; many sociologists want to continue (carefully) using census figures and other official statistics as (imperfect) indicators. They may be willing to toss the bathwater, but they want to hang on to the baby.[1]

I believe that Ibarra and Kitsuse's "Vernacular Constituents of Moral Discourse" should be read with these issues in mind. It offers a new reclarification of the authors' thoughts on the constructionist perspective. Like its predecessors, this paper is susceptible to both strong and weak readings, and once more, the weak reading is likely to be more popular and, in Ibarra and Kitsuse's view, less correct. My critique of Ibarra and Kitsuse requires first reviewing the emergence of what I've called strict constructionism (Best 1989) and discussing the limitations of that stance, before turning to their paper to identify what I see as the attractions of a weak reading and the limitations of a strong interpretation. On occasion, I will use the current concern over satanism to illustrate my points.

The Satanic Panic

The contemporary campaign against satanism began gaining force roughly ten years ago. By the late 1980s, warnings about the satanic menace could be found on television talks shows and the networks' prime-time offerings, and in dozens of books and countless articles in magazines and newspapers. Police officers and social workers could learn about occult or ritual crimes at professional seminars, presentations that described a huge, powerful, secret conspiracy, a blood cult centered around rituals of sexual abuse and human sacrifice. U.S. satanists were estimated at more than one million, their sacrificial victims at sixty thousand per year. Warnings about satanism linked such diverse phenomena as serial murder, missing children, multiple personality disorder, child sexual abuse, illicit drugs, heavy-metal music, and fantasy role-playing games in one great web of evil.

If accusations of a great satanic conspiracy seem unfamiliar, it may be because this volume's readers tend to get their news from Mac-Neil/Lehrer rather than Geraldo, from the prestige press rather than more popular or local media. But the general public is familiar with the blood cult story, and they are concerned: In a recent Texas poll, 63 percent of the respondents rated satanism a "very serious" problem, while another 23 percent said it was "somewhat serious." Moreover, academics have begun warning about satanism. One recent trade book about the satanic threat is written by a religious studies professor at the University of Denver (Raschke 1990); references to satanism and its victims can be found in the literature of criminology, child welfare, psychiatry, and other helping professions (e.g., Holmes 1989).

At this point, I could begin examining the "construction of the satanism problem," the nature of the "claims-makers" and their "claims," and so on. After all, the constructionist approach has become a—perhaps the—leading school of social problems theory, a perspective often used to study the emergence of newly recognized social problems such as satanism.[2] However, my purpose is not to interpret the rise of satanism, but to use satanism as a convenient example of the limitations of strict constructionism. I intend to show that strict constructionism places unreasonable constraints on sociologists who hope to understand social problems.

Consider the sorts of questions one might have after hearing about the blood cult menace. Most obviously, one might ask whether the warnings are correct. Is there a satanic conspiracy with a million—or perhaps only one hundred thousand or even ten thousand—members? Does the cult claim tens of thousands—or maybe just dozens—of victims each year? Further, one might wonder about the people issuing the warnings. Who are they, and what motives or interests lie behind their claims? And is the evidence they offer persuasive? How should we respond to statements linking hundreds of teen suicides to playing *Dungeons and Dragons*, to testimony by adult multiple-personality-disorder patients that they suffered ritual abuse during childhood, to discoveries of satanic graffiti and sites that seem to have been used for strange rituals, to reports by therapists that they've interviewed children who were victims of systematic sexual abuse at their preschools, or to typologies of occult crime offered by police officers? These are sensible questions, and they might seem particularly amenable to constructionist analysis. They are also the sorts of questions that John Kitsuse and other leading figures in constructionist theory—the strict constructionists—argue analysts ought not address. To understand why constructionist sociologists increasingly turn away from such interesting questions, we must consider the perspective's development.

The Emergence of Strict Constructionism

Statements by Herbert Blumer (1971) and John I. Kitsuse and Malcolm Spector (1973, 1975; Spector and Kitsuse 1973, [1977] 1987) laid the foundation for contemporary constructionism.[3] They sought to turn social problems—a concept that rarely figured in sociological analysis, other than as a topic for beginning undergraduate courses and textbooks—into a subject for serious study. They began by criticizing the standard definitions, which equated social problems with objective conditions:

> It is a gross mistake to assume that any kind of malignant or harmful social condition or arrangement in a society becomes automatically a social problem for that society. The pages of history are replete with instances of dire social conditions unnoticed and unattended in the societies in which they occurred. (Blumer 1971, p. 302)

The key to any condition becoming a social problem was subjective: "The existence of social problems depends on the continued existence of groups or agencies that define some condition as a problem and attempt to do something about it" (Kitsuse and Spector 1973, p. 415). Moreover, these collective definitions were what conditions labeled social problems had in common; there were no objective qualities shared by all the chapter topics in a standard social problems text.

This argument led to new, subjectivist definitions of social problems: "social problems lie in and are products of a process of collective definition" (Blumer 1971, p. 301); or "[W]e define social problems as *the activities of groups making assertions of grievances and claims with respect to some putative conditions*" (Kitsuse and Spector 1973, p. 415, emphasis in original). These definitions radically shifted the focus of the sociology of social problems away from social conditions and onto the process of collective definition or claims-making. Both Blumer and Kitsuse and Spector outlined agendas for further constructionist research, including natural history models of social problems construction (Blumer 1971; Spector and Kitsuse 1973).

In directing attention toward claims-making, the constructionist theorists often suggested that claims could be located within their social context. Their early articles featured many references to the empirical reality of social conditions. Thus, Blumer clearly assumed that sociologists could evaluate the truth of claims:

> [R]ecognition by a society of its social problems is a highly selective process, with many harmful social conditions and arrangements not even making a bid for attention and with others falling by the wayside in what is frequently a fierce competitive struggle, (Blumer 1971, p. 302)

and "knowledge of the objective makeup of social problems . . . . should be sought as a corrective for ignorance or misinformation concerning this objective makeup" (p. 305). Kitsuse and Spector made a similar point:

> [T]he relationship between "objective conditions" and the development of social problems is variable and problematic. It is an empirical question whether certain types of conditions are correlated with or associated with certain types of claims (Spector and Kitsuse 1973, p. 148; see also Kitsuse and Spector 1973, p. 414)

They also suggested that the sociological analyst can assess claims-makers' motives ["groups defining conditions as social problems then, may be kept going by interests or values, or any mixture of combination of them" (Kitsuse and Spector 1973, p. 415)]; experiences ["the experience of dissatisfaction will influence the kind of claims that a group will make" (Spector and Kitsuse 1973, p. 150)], and power [("a genuinely powerful group may not be willing to expend its resources on a certain issue" (p. 149)]. Such statements do not imply a strong reading; they suggest that constructionist analysis might locate claims within their broader social context.

In their later papers, Kitsuse and Spector began adopting a more cautious epistemological stance. They noted that "sociologists are participants in the definitional process," and warned that analysts must "achieve the distance needed to focus on the definitional process, rather than unknowingly participate in it" (Kitsuse and Spector 1975, p. 585). Attempts to incorporate both subjective definitions and objective conditions in the same analysis—"the balanced view"—inevitably sacrifice "the integrity of the definitional process" (p. 589). Therefore, analysts should forgo all statements about objective conditions:

> [W]e assert that even the existence of the condition itself is irrelevant to and outside of our analysis. . . . . If the alleged condition were a complete hoax—a fabrication—we would maintain a noncommittal stance toward it unless those to whom the claim were addressed initiated their own analysis and uncovered it as a hoax. (Spector and Kitsuse [1977] 1987, p. 76)

This led to recommendations that "certain kinds of questions . . . . be set aside," e.g., that analysts not attribute claims-making to the participants' motives or values (Spector and Kitsuse [1977] 1987, p. 96). In sum, Kitsuse and Spector increasingly advocated a strong reading, urging analysts to avoid discussing social conditions.

Objectivist Responses

Most critiques of the constructionist position ignored these epistemological concerns. These critics worried about constructionism's relativism; if social problems are equated with claims-making, then those who are too poor—or weak or alienated—to make claims may never attract the analyst's attention (Collins 1989; Eitzen 1984; Young 1989). One could, they insisted, define social problems objectively, and they suggested different bases for such definitions, including "moral imperatives and human needs that are trans-societal and trans-historical" (Eitzen 1984, p. 11), "the knowledge related values of science" (Manis 1985, p. 5), and "an overarching ethical framework" (Collins 1989, p. 90).

Most of those defending the objectivist conception of social problems did not reject constructionism. Rather, they proposed integrating the two perspectives, borrowing insights from each to develop a more complete interpretive framework. For instance, Jones, McFalls, and Gallagher (1989) present a model in which objective conditions cause subjective reactions, with visibility, expectations, and values acting as intervening variables. For constructionists, such models were founded on the very objectivist assumptions about social life and sociology that they had begun by rejecting, and the proposals had little appeal (Spector and Kitsuse 1987).

Ontological Gerrymandering

A far more influential critique came from within the subjectivist ranks.[4] Woolgar and Pawluch charged that constructionists inevitably adopt an epistemologically inconsistent position through what they call ontological gerrymandering:

> The successful social problems explanation depends on making problematic the truth status of certain states of affairs selected for analysis and explanation, while backgrounding or minimizing the possibility that the same problems apply to assumptions upon which the analysis depends. (1985a, p. 216)

Their first example was from a passage in *Constructing Social Problems* about changing definitions of marijuana in which Spector and Kitsuse remark: "The nature of marijuana remained constant" ([1977] 1987, p. 43). Woolgar and Pawluch noted: "[T]he key assertion is that the actual character of a substance (marijuana), condition, or behavior remained constant" (1985a, p. 217).[5] Even Spector and Kitsuse, authors of repeated warnings about the need to avoid assumptions about objective conditions, made such assumptions:

[P]roponents fail to live up to the programmatic relativism which they espouse in calling for a purportedly different, definitional perspective. In the course of specific, empirical case studies, the programmatic claims give way to clearly discernible lapses into realism. (Woolgar and Pawluch 1985a, p. 224)

Of course, Woolgar and Pawluch were right. I have already shown that Blumer's and Kitsuse and Spector's theoretical writings often implied—even stated—that analysts could and might want to assess objective conditions. The notion that sociologists must not presume any knowledge of those conditions did not appear until Kitsuse and Spector's later work. Moreover, as Woolgar and Pawluch charged, case studies routinely failed to attain this analytic ideal.

Strict Constructionism

"Ontological Gerrymandering" attracted a good deal of attention among constructionists. Joseph Gusfield's (1985) response (discussed below) was critical, but other prominent constructionists tried to defend the perspective while simultaneously accepting Woolgar and Pawluch's standards for evaluating research. Thus, Schneider's review article on constructionist research stated: "The criticism is justified for many [constructionist] studies" (1985b, p. 224). But, in his reply to Woolgar and Pawluch, Schneider dismissed their examples as "mistakes in applying the definitional perspective, ... instances of careless talk" and spoke of "researcher carelessness and confusion" (1985a, p. 233). Similarly, Spector and Kitsuse acknowledged the tendency for analysts to lapse:

[W]hen confronted with a "disjunction," analysts infer that the member/participants' definitions of social realities reflect "misinterpretations" of the "facts," incomplete knowledge or other inadequacies. [This] . . . . may reflect a "social scientistic" arrogance that seduces the analyst away from a study of definitions and leads to assuming a warrant to identify and to correct the definitional "errors" of member/participants. (1987, p. 14)

Still, they insisted that an internally consistent analysis—one that avoided ontological gerrymandering—was possible.

The debate over Woolgar and Pawluch's critique served to redefine and harden the strict constructionist position. Epistemological concerns, which had not figured prominently either in the perspective's initial theoretical statements or in the case studies that had appeared, now became central to both discussions about constructionist theory and evaluations of new research. Analysts were urged to avoid any contamination by objectivism, to shun all assumptions about the empirical world.

The Possibility and Price of Strict Constructionism

Calls for sociologists to stay within the analytic boundaries of strict
constructionism, coupled with admissions that most—if not all—constructionist case studies fail to meet those standards, raise the question
whether a strict constructionist analysis is possible, or even desirable.
Here, it may help to return to the example of satanism and consider
what a strict constructionist treatment of the topic might involve.

Claims about a secret, conspiratorial blood cult are untestable, since a
successful conspiracy is one that cannot be proven to exist. Critics of the
antisatanism movement are reduced to arguing that a conspiracy on the
scale described in antisatanist claims would inevitably leave some trace.
Thus, the FBI's Kenneth Lanning notes the failure to find even one
victim's body:

> Not only are no bodies found, but also, more important, there is no physi-
> cal evidence that a murder took place. Many of those not in law-
> enforcement do not understand that, while it is possible to get rid of a
> body, it is much more difficult to get rid of the physical evidence that a
> murder took place, especially a human sacrifice involving sex, blood, and
> mutilation. . . . . Those who accept these stories of mass human sacrifice
> would have us believe that the satanists and other occult practitioners are
> murdering more than twice as many people every year in this country as
> all other murderers combined. (1989, p. 20)

Strict constructionism allows us to note these claims (e.g., satanists sacrifice sixty thousand victims per year) and counterclaims (e.g., antisatanist claims are implausible), but enjoins us from assessing their relative
merits. Not only must analysts not presume to know the truth about the
blood cult—something that can never be known, since an absence of
evidence may only show that the conspiracy works—but they must not
let their analysis be affected by judgments that one set of claims presents
a stronger case.

This suggests that strict constructionists will recognize no difference
between claims about satanism and, say, claims about AIDS. Both, after
all, emerged as subjects of claims-making during the 1980s, both are said
to kill thousands of people each year (admittedly, the claimed death toll
for AIDS is considerably lower). In both cases, the claims-makers have
attracted critics, and the strict constructionist will find no differences
between Special Agent Lanning and someone arguing that the purported AIDS crisis is a hoax.

Constructionist analysts rarely declare that they know the truth about
objective conditions.[6] For example, even antisatanism's critics must con-
cede that there *might* be a blood cult out there. But analysts are likely to

make less explicit assumptions about objective conditions, assumptions that frame the research agenda. Thus, a sociologist who doubts the reality of the satanic menace is more likely to try to account for antisatanism's spread ("Who believes this stuff, and why?"), than to ask how major institutions manage to ignore the blood cult ("Why haven't the authorities done more about this?"). It may be possible to avoid overt "lapses"—outright declarations about objective reality—but implicit assumptions about objective conditions will almost inevitably guide researchers.

Contrast the sorts of questions analysts are likely to ask about satanism and AIDS. By strict constructionist standards, the journalists and sociologists who have written about the construction of AIDS have addressed a series of inappropriate topics (cf. Albert 1989; Fumento 1990; Gamson 1989; Shilts 1987). When they ask why the federal government was slow to respond to the epidemic, or why the press began focusing on the risk of transmission via heterosexual intercourse, or why activists chose to adopt unconventional forms of protest, we can detect a hidden, forbidden assumption that frames their research: People are sick with AIDS. A strict constructionist can no more assume that AIDS exists than presume that there's probably no large, satanic blood cult at work. This suggests that strict constructionist researchers must ask the same questions about each claims-making campaign, rather than focusing on the interesting aspects of a particular case. After all, how can an analyst who refuses to presume anything about a case identify its interesting features?

What can a strict constructionist say about satanism? What sorts of analysis are acceptable? Spector and Kitsuse (1973, [1977] 1987; Kitsuse and Spector 1973) suggest that it may be fruitful to explore claims-makers' interests. Thus, we might discover that Christian Evangelists are among the most prominent antisatanist claims-makers, that many of the police officers, psychiatrists, and therapists who warn about occult crimes acquire money, status, and influence through anticult activities (and make references to their own religious beliefs in their presentations), and that many adult cult survivors have lengthy histories of psychiatric problems. A standard constructionist interpretation might note that these claims-makers stand to gain converts, money, etc. through their claims-making. But don't such interpretations also violate the tenets of strict constructionism, don't they "background" assumptions about objective reality, e.g., by presuming that Evangelists want to convert others and that such conversions are in the Evangelists' interest? How can we know what is in a claims-maker's interest—or even have a concept of interest—without making assumptions about objective conditions?[7]

It becomes impossible to say where we might draw the line. Is there anything an analyst might say about the construction of a particular social problem, such as satanism or AIDS, that does not require the analyst to make assumptions about objective reality? Must the study of social problems wait until someone writes *Principia Sociologica*, identifying the minimum assumptions needed for sociological analysis? No wonder strict constructionists have begun suggesting that analysts avoid case studies. Case studies inevitably violate the guidelines for strict constructionist analysis. These theorists have painted themselves into an armchair.[8]

It is difficult to miss the irony in the strict constructionist position. Constructionist theorists have always insisted that their theory is empirically based, but strict constructionism demands that analysts avoid references to the empirical world in order to maintain the theory's epistemological integrity.

Contextual Constructionism

Even if it is not impossible to do empirical research within the constraints imposed by strict constructionism, there remains the question whether these limits are desirable. Analytic purity comes at a high price. Urging that analysts "move beyond constructivism" to explore the nature of sociological inquiry, Woolgar and Pawluch raise a set of new questions, acknowledging: "They will not contribute . . . . to our understanding of the world as we have traditionally conceived that pursuit" (1985b, p. 162). Similarly, Kitsuse and Schneider contrast strict constructionist concerns with "research on social problems where the researcher participates, with members, in the practical projects of documenting and explaining a state of affairs that they find objectionable or important and that they may want to change" (1989, p. xiii). In short, strict constructionists must forgo most sorts of sociological analysis.

Among the major figures in the constructionist camp, only Joseph Gusfield challenged the value of Woolgar and Pawluch's discussion of ontological gerrymandering:

> I am left uninstructed about the importance of the critique. If it doesn't change the value of the empirical work, is it significant? . . . . Woolgar and Pawluch illustrate too well a kind of sociology that seems to me to be a dead end. It is a preoccupation with the logic of theory as something apart from and independent of the substantive questions to which directed. (1985, p. 17)

For Gusfield, the value of the constructionist position rests in its ability to increase our knowledge of social life:

It provides us with new questions about the emergence, or decline, of phenomena and/or definitions of the phenomena. . . . . It raises questions about the nature of "facticity" that heretofore sociologists have not routinely raised. This is most useful, especially in a society heavily committed to information and comment through mass media, governmental organizations and professional agencies. (p. 17)

Gusfield's position can be characterized as contextual constructionism (Best 1989). Contextual constructionists study claims-making within its context of culture and social structure. In practice, this means that an analyst may doubt claims that satanists sacrifice sixty thousand victims annually (on the grounds that the antisatanist claims-makers are unable to offer much evidence to support their charges), while generally accepting the Centers for Disease Control's figures for the numbers of AIDS victims (on the grounds that there is some limit to the degree organizational practices are likely to distort the collection of these official statistics). Note, however, that the analyst's focus remains the construction of social problems. For constructionists, the issue is unlikely to be the precise number of satanist or AIDS victims. The analyst is more likely to be interested in the ways statistics are collected, the role they play in claims-making rhetoric, the responses they elicit from the media, officials, and the public, and so on. But contextual constructionists assume that claims-making occurs within some context: Thus, a sociologist studying satanism may marvel that estimates of human sacrifice victims are supported by so little evidence, and ask why these claims are relatively successful; while a sociologist studying AIDS may wonder why, in the face of accumulating evidence of a serious problem, it took officials and the press so long to attend to AIDS.[9]

Contextualist assumptions are—as the strict constructionists charge—detectable throughout the constructionist literature: in the theoretical writings of Blumer—and Kitsuse and Spector—and Gusfield; and in (no doubt all of the) dozens of case studies. These works assume that we will understand the empirical world better if we pay attention to the manner in which social problems emerge and, at a more basic level, they also assume that understanding the empirical world is desirable. That is, contextual constructionism is inspired by a sociological imagination.

This Way to the Egress? Ibarra and Kitsuse

Debate, then, has broken out within the constructionist camp, with a growing body of critiques, responses, and rejoinders concerning the appropriate stance for analysts. Although Spector and Kitsuse noted: "We hope to avoid the interminable conceptual analysis and re-analysis that has deflected the so-called labeling theory of deviance from the more important task of building an empirical literature" (1987, p. 13), Ibarra and Kitsuse's paper must be seen within the context of such an ongoing debate. They present a corrective, strong reading of *Constructing Social Problems*: That book was meant as a programmatic statement, and Ibarra and Kitsuse urge sociologists to get with the program.

In particular, they offer a new concept—"condition-category"—as the means for refocusing constructionist analysis. Just as *Constructing Social Problems* shifted the attention of sociologists of social problems away from social conditions and onto claims-making, Ibarra and Kitsuse propose another, albeit more subtle shift, away from claims-making activities and onto the language of claims.[10] The record shows that studying claims-making offers too many temptations for analysts to lapse into ontological gerrymandering. But concentrating on condition-categories—"the strict constructionist never leaves language"—seems to promise to circumvent this problem.

The Attractions of a Weak Reading

Ibarra and Kitsuse, then, explore claims-making as rhetoric. While this is not a new topic for constructionists (cf. Spector and Kitsuse [1977] 1987; Gusfield 1981; Best 1990)—let alone for scholars in speech and communications (e.g., Condit 1990)—their paper offers a fresh approach to the topic, with a useful catalog of rhetorical strategies, motifs, and styles. Constructionist sociologists will find these new concepts helpful.

Unfortunately, many of those who choose to apply these concepts are likely to give the paper a weak reading, to stray from the tight focus on language prescribed by Ibarra and Kitsuse.[11] To understand the attractions of a weak reading, let's imagine a sociologist studying claims about satanism. Once our analyst has collected examples of antisatanist rhetoric, new questions are likely to emerge. Like many social causes, the antisatanist movement is a loose coalition, involving a diverse set of claims-makers, including Evangelists, police officers, psychiatrists, and journalists (with an equally diverse coalition arrayed in opposition). Which claims-makers make which claims (or counterclaims)? And why did they choose those strategies? Do their rhetorical choices reflect their particular values or interests? Do those choices derive from available resources, such as claims-makers' prior experiences with successful or unsuccessful claims-making campaigns? To what degree does their rhetoric reflect contingencies of knowledge (as in the lawyers' aphorism—when the law favors your side, pound the law; when the facts favor your side, pound the facts; and when neither favors your side, pound the table)? In making their rhetorical choices, are claims-makers cynical or sincere—do they believe their own arguments? Another set of questions concerns the audiences for the claims: Who responds to which claims, and how? Why are particular audiences responsive to some claims and not others? Is there a form of feedback involved, in which claims-makers tailor their rhetoric to the anticipated responses of their audience(s)?

Obviously, this list of questions barely scratches the surface. We can imagine all sorts of seductive questions, each tempting our analyst to "leave language" and link rhetoric to social arrangements. And, of course, those who give in to temptation will then number among the fallen, the heretics who engage in ontological gerrymandering and contextual constructionism. Their numbers will grow. The next step, presumably, will be an acknowledgment that "condition-category" has failed to do the job, coupled with yet another reclarification of the strict constructionist position, built around yet another new concept.

In sum, constructionist sociologists are likely to borrow heavily from Ibarra and Kitsuse, but to use their concepts in ways other than those authors intended. The new conceptual apparatus may be popular, but it is unlikely to be proof against a weak reading.

The Limitations of a Strong Reading

Not only are analysts unlikely to restrict themselves to a strong reading of Ibarra and Kitsuse, but it isn't clear that a consistently strong reading is possible. As Woolgar and Pawluch (1985a) noted, strict constructionists are quick to spot the objectivist assumptions in others' work, but slower to acknowledge their own lapses. Consider Ibarra and Kitsuse's list of rhetorical strategies—rhetorics of loss, entitlement, endangerment, unreason, and calamity. They make no claim that theirs is an exhaustive list, as it obviously is not. Rhetorical strategies undoubtedly reflect particular cultures, social structures, and historical circumstances.[12] The language of claims does not exist independently of the social world; it is a product of—and influence on—that world. A strong reading that "never leaves language" is an illusion because language never leaves society. An analyst who ignores the social embeddedness of claims-makers' rhetoric takes that embeddedness for granted; this is another form of ontological gerrymandering.

Ibarra and Kitsuse describe their goal as "an empirically based theory of social problems," and references to the "empirical" foundation of constructionism appear throughout Kitsuse's writings. At the same time, the demands of strict constructionism push analysts away from empirical research. Ibarra and Kitsuse suggest that case studies have proven analytically troublesome:

> [O]ur position is that the project of developing a theory of *social problems discourse* is a much more coherent way of proceeding with constructionism than, for example, the development of a series of discrete theories on the social construction of X, Y, and Z. To develop a theory about condition X when the ontological status of X is suspended results in "ontological gerry-mandering' . . . . which is to say flawed theory. (emphasis in original)

Therefore, instead of studying the rhetoric of antisatanism and other campaigns to construct social problems—research that might provide an empirical foundation for a theory of social problems rhetoric—they present their own list of rhetorical strategies without explaining how it was derived. Where case studies of claims-makers' rhetoric inevitably incorporate assumptions about social conditions, an abstract typology of strategies seems to finesse the problem.

Ibarra and Kitsuse want to reclarify the nature of constructionist analysis; they seek to identify the errors in others' analyses and, through their focus on discourse, show that strict constructionist analysis is possible. Presumably they took great care in writing their paper. Yet assumptions about the social world creep into their analysis. Consider three statements from their discussion of their first rhetorical strategy—the rhetoric of loss:

> This rhetoric works most idiomatically with objects (i.e., condition-categories) that can be construed to qualify as forms of perfection. . . . .
>
> Rhetorical idioms can cut across ideological divisions like liberal and socialist and conservative, inter alia. . . . .
>
> (The rhetoric is wholly unidiomatic when the concern at issue is revealed to be for the loss of "white male privilege.")

These brief passages suggest the sorts of problems that plague Ibarra and Kitsuse's analysis. First, there are the evaluations of rhetoric as being idiomatic or unidiomatic—an undefined standard, but one that certainly seems to "privilege" the analyst. Second, consider the notion that some "objects . . . . can be construed to qualify as forms of perfection." This would seem to assume that culture/social structure somehow shapes the language of claims: if some objects can be construed as perfect, presumably others cannot be so construed—but how can analysts judge which are which? Third, there is the overt assumption that there are ideological divisions among claims-makers. And we could go on. Even in a statement denouncing unwarranted assumptions about the social world, a statement presumably crafted so as to avoid all such assumptions, we find evidence of such assumptions having been made. Even when analysts retreat from any discussion of empirical cases, epistemologically consistent strict constructionist analysis seems to be an unachievable goal. Like their strict constructionist predecessors, Ibarra and Kitsuse set a standard that they themselves cannot meet.

But Seriously Folks

During the 1980s, it became fashionable for sociologists to warn that they intended to "take [this or that] theory seriously." This phrase, like the stand-up comic's transitional "But seriously folks," often signaled that the analyst was about to make statements that ran a risk of seeming silly. Strict constructionism's problems reveal that theory can be taken too seriously.

Just as quantitative researchers continually risk sacrificing sociological substance for more elaborate research designs and more sophisticated statistics, qualitative researchers must balance substance against the demands of theoretical consistency. Analytic purity can come at a terrible cost. Constructionist theory warns against being distracted by the conditions about which claims are made, but the implications of strict constructionism push the analyst well beyond that boundary, into a contextless region where claims-making may only be examined in the abstract. The sociology of social problems began with the assumption that sociological knowledge might help people understand and improve the world; strict constructionism sells that birthright for a mess of epistemology.

Ibarra and Kitsuse characterize social problems claims-making as "a language game." This term seems well-suited for describing the claims and counterclaims in the debate over constructionist theory. For instance, Ibarra and Kitsuse attack contextual constructionism as "a narrow construal of the constructionist project." This criticism deserves inspection. The weak readings of contextual constructionists cause them to ask all manner of research questions that lead the analyst across borders closed to the strict constructionist who "never leaves language." In what sense is contextual constructionism "narrow'? Similarly, strict constructionist discourse conveys a sense of "ownership" (Gusfield 1981) of the right to define such key terms as *social problems* and *constructionism*.[13]

Perhaps the most damaging rhetorical device in Ibarra and Kitsuse's paper is the one quoted above: "the project of developing a theory of *social problems discourse* is a much more coherent way of proceeding with constructionism than, for example, the development of a series of discrete theories on the social construction of X, Y, and Z" (emphasis in original). This is simply a false dichotomy. There is another choice: following the albeit traditional model for qualitative researchers, staying close to the data, and developing grounded theories through analytic induction (cf. Glaser and Strauss 1967). Constructionist research seems well suited for this sort of analysis; the literature has grown dramatically since Schneider's (1985b) review essay identified more than fifty studies. And, of course, there is much relevant information to be found in sociological studies of social movements and deviance, and in the work of historians, political scientists, anthropologists, and so on.

The grounded theory approach—familiar to all qualitative sociologists—can, in fact, produce "an empirically based theory of social problems." It will not, to be sure, meet the strict constructionists' tests for epistemological consistency, but it just might help us understand how social problems emerge and develop. Isn't it time for constructionists to worry a little less about how we know what we know, and worry a little more about what, if anything, we do know about the construction of social problems?

Notes

1.   The tendency to give Kitsuse's other key works a weak reading has been discussed elsewhere. On Kitsuse (1962), see Rains (1975). On Spector and Kitsuse ([1977] 1987), see Woolgar and Pawluch (1985a) and Best (1989).

2.   Sociological analyses of the current antisatanist campaign include Forsyth and Oliver (1990); Richardson, Best, and Bromley (1991) and Victor (1989, 1990).

3.   The argument that objectivist definitions of social problems had inherent flaws was not new. Spector and Kitsuse ([1977] 1987) review the early history of the objectivist-subjectivist debate.

4.   Mauss's (1989) argument that constructionist research on social problems should be subsumed within the sociology of social movements is another subjectivist critique. For a response, see Troyer (1989).

5.   This example seems to flirt with a classic logical fallacy—the argument from ignorance. Critics can always ask how one knows that the nature of marijuana—or oxygen, or Jupiter's orbit—has not changed. But, by traditional standards of inquiry, unless there is some reason to suspect change, a presumption of stability is reasonable.

6.   To be sure, there are analysts who present a sort of "vulgar constructionism" which equates constructionist analysis with debunking claims. For instance, Forsyth and Oliver say: "Basically the constructionist argument is that there has been no significant change in the activity in question, but that activities which were not previously defined as problematic, or rates of activity which were not previously defind [sic] as problematic, have been defined as a problem" (1990, p. 285).

7.   The less specific claims that constructionist analysis can help reveal the workings of racial, sexual, class, and other hierarchies seem vulnerable to the same criticism. Doesn't the analyst first need to accept the objective reality of those hierarchies? This may explain the recent attraction of postmodernism for

some strict constructionists; the conventions of postmodernist prose make it difficult to pin down what, if anything, the analyst believes to be true.

8. Fortunately, most researchers who adopt the constructionist perspective find themselves able to ignore this debate. In particular, the constructionist work that has appeared in sociology's flagship journals pays little or no attention to epistemological issues (Block and Burns 1986; Gamson and Modigliani 1989; Hilgartner and Bosk 1988).

9. Strict constructionists sometimes endorse similar topics: "A putative condition may be defined in terms that are not amenable to 'credible' or persuasive documentation; member/participants may be unable to sustain social problems activity organized on such definitions" (Spector and Kitsuse 1987, p. 14; cf. Kitsuse and Schneider 1989). They do not, unfortunately, explain how the analyst can identify what is credible or persuasive or sustainable without making assumptions about the context of claims-making.

10. Woolgar and Pawluch (1985b) argue for a more radical shift in focus. In their vision, analysts should explore the nature of sociological analysis. At this point, of course, social problems—however defined—cease being the object of study.

11. For instance, when Coltrane and Hickman (1992) compare fathers' and mothers' rhetoric in the debate over child custody and child support laws, they invoke Ibarra and Kitsuse. Yet their analysis links claims-makers' success to "economic, institutional, and ideological contexts."

12. Because a very large share of constructionist research concerns the contemporary United States, it has been easy for U.S. constructionists to take the arrangements in their society for granted. We need more comparative research, examining the construction of social problems in other societies and in other times.

13. Obviously, the same sort of rhetorical analysis can be applied to contextual constructionist statements, including this paper. A contextual constructionist might even venture beyond language to ask sociology-of-science questions about who says what, why, and so on.

References

Albert, Edward. 1989. "AIDS and the Press." Pp. 39–54 in *Images of Issues*, edited by Joel Best. Hawthorne, NY: Aldine de Gruyter.

Best, Joel. 1989. "Afterword." Pp. 243–53 in *Images of Issues*, edited by Joel Best. Hawthorne, NY: Aldine de Gruyter.

———. 1990. *Threatened Children*. Chicago: University of Chicago Press.

Block, Fred and Gene A. Burns. 1986. "Productivity as a Social Problem." *American Sociological Review* 51:767–80.

Blumer, Herbert. 1971. "Social Problems as Collective Behavior." *Social Problems* 18:298–306.

Collins, Patricia Hill. 1989. "The Social Construction of Invisibility." *Perspectives on Social Problems* 1:77–93.

Coltrane, Scott and Neal Hickman. 1992. "The Rhetoric of Rights and Needs." *Social Problems* 39:400–20.

Condit, Celeste. 1990. *Decoding Abortion Rhetoric*. Urbana: University of Illinois Press.

Eitzen, D. Stanley. 1984. "Teaching Social Problems: Implications of the Objectivist Subjectivist Debate." *SSSP Newsletter* (Fall):10–12.

Forsyth, Craig J. and Marion D. Oliver. 1990. "The Theoretical Framing of a Social Problem." *Deviant Behavior* 11:281–92.

Fumento, Michael. 1990. *The Myth of Heterosexual AIDS*. New York: Basic Books.

Gamson, Josh. 1989. "Silence, Death, and the Invisible Enemy." *Social Problems* 36:351–67.

Gamson, William and Andre Modigliani. 1989. "Media Discourse and Public Opinion on Nuclear Power." *American Journal of Sociology* 95:1–37.

Glaser, Barney G., and Anselm L. Strauss. 1967. *The Discovery of Grounded Theory*. Chicago: Aldine.

Gusfield, Joseph R. 1981. *The Culture of Public Problems*. Chicago: University of Chicago Press.

———. 1985. "Theories and Hobgoblins." *SSSP Newsletter* 17 (Fall):16–18.

Hilgartner, Stephen and Charles L. Bosk. 1988. "The Rise and Fall of Social Problems." *American Journal of Sociology* 94:53–78.

Holmes, Ronald M. 1989. *Profiling Violent Crimes*. Newbury Park, CA: Sage.

Jones, Brian J., Joseph A. McFalls, Jr., and Bernard J. Gallagher III. 1989. "Toward a Unified Model for Social Problems Theory." *Journal for the Theory of Social Behavior* 19:337–56.

Kitsuse, John I. 1962. "Societal Reaction to Deviant Behavior." *Social Problems* 9:247–56.

Kitsuse, John I., and Aaron Cicourel. 1963. "A Note on the Use of Official Statistics." *Social Problems* 11:131–39.

Kitsuse, John I. and Joseph W. Schneider. 1989. "Preface." Pp. xi–xiii in *Images of Issues*, edited by Joel Best. Hawthorne, NY: Aldine de Gruyter.

Kitsuse, John I., and Malcolm Spector. 1973. "Toward a Sociology of Social Problems." *Social Problems* 20:407–19.

———. 1975. "Social Problems and Deviance." *Social Problems* 22:584–94.

Lanning, Kenneth V. 1989. *Child Sex Rings*. Washington: National Center for Missing and Exploited Children.

Manis, Jerome G. 1985. "Defining Social Problems: Objectivism-Subjectivism Revisited." *SSSP Newsletter* 16 (Winter):5.

Mauss, Armand L. 1989. "Beyond the Illusion of Social Problems Theory." *Perspectives on Social Problems* 1:19–39.

Rains, Prudence. 1975. "Imputations of Deviance." *Social Problems* 23:1–11.

Raschke, Carl A. 1990. *Painted Black*. San Francisco: Harper & Row.

Richardson, James T., Joel Best, and David G. Bromley (eds.). 1991. *The Satanism Scare*. Hawthorne, NY: Aldine de Gruyter.

Schneider, Joseph W. 1985a. "Defining the Definitional Perspective on Social Problems." *Social Problems* 32:232–34.

———. 1985b. "Social Problems Theory." *Annual Review of Sociology* 11:209–29.

Shilts, Randy. 1987. *And the Band Played On*. New York: St. Martin's.

Spector, Malcolm and John I. Kitsuse. 1973. "Social Problems: a Re-formulation." *Social Problems* 21:145–59.

_____. [1977] 1987. *Constructing Social Problems*. Hawthorne, NY: Aldine de Gruyter.

_____. 1987. "Preface to the Japanese Edition: Constructing Social Problems." *SSSP Newsletter* 18 (Fall):13–15.

Troyer, Ronald J. 1989. "Are Social Problems and Social Movements the Same Thing?" *Perspectives on Social Problems* 1:41–58.

Victor, Jeffrey S. 1989. "A Rumor-Panic about a Dangerous Satanic Cult in Western New York." *New York Folklore* 15:23–49.

_____. 1990. "Satanic Cult Legends as Contemporary Legend." *Western Folklore* 49:51–81.

Woolgar, Steve, and Dorothy Pawluch. 1985a. "Ontological Gerrymandering." *Social Problems* 32:214–27.

_____. 1985b. "How Shall We Move Beyond Constructivism?" *Social Problems* 33:159–62.

Young T. R. 1989. "Deconstructing Constructionism." Paper presented at the annual meeting of the Society for the Study of Social Problems.

PART II

New Directions for Social Constructionism

7

Social Constructionism and Social Problems Work

James A. Holstein and Gale Miller

Since Spector and Kitsuse ([1977] 1987) offered their foundational statement on the construction of social problems, ethnomethodological contributions to the understanding of everyday reality as socially accomplished have been increasingly recognized, accepted, and even appreciated by the sociological community (Pollner 1991). By the late 1980s, ethnomethodologically informed studies regularly appeared in the journal *Social Problems*, some relating to Spector and Kitsuse's constructionist program, others taking alternative approaches and topics. While Spector and Kitsuse avoided drawing explicit connections between their version of constructionism and ethnomethodology, their approach was clearly compatible with the ethnomethodological tradition (Troyer 1989).

In this volume, Kitsuse and his colleague Peter Ibarra cogently respond to many of the issues arising from various challenges to the constructionist perspective, but their arguments seem most pointedly directed to long-standing ethnomethodological concerns. While still hesitant to openly embrace an explicitly ethnomethodological stance, Ibarra and Kitsuse draw upon ethnomethodological resources to reiterate and underscore the radical impulse of their constructionist position. The task of social problems theorists, they write, is to reconstruct members' ways—their vernacular discourse practices—of constituting social problems as moral objects. The argument clarifies some possible ambiguities in earlier statements by unequivocally directing the constructionist program toward the conventional features of the social problems "claims-making" process, focusing on the "condition-categories" that are applied and used in practical circumstances to produce meaningful descriptions and evaluations of social reality.

Ibarra and Kitsuse's focus on interaction and language use certainly highlights the constitutive practices that are ethnomethodology's concern as well. Indeed, in statements like the following, Ibarra and Kitsuse's constructionist project sounds distinctly similar to ethnomethodological proposals (see Garfinkel 1967; Heritage 1984; Pollner 1987):

[O]ur field is fundamentally concerned with understanding the constitutive ("world-making") and strategic dimensions of claimants' discursive
practices. . . . We conceive of social problems as "idiomatic productions"
to accentuate their status as members' accomplishments.

In application, however, Ibarra and Kitsuse's proposal—like Spector
and Kitsuse's—emphasizes the construction of social problems categories through "large-scale" public rhetoric—"publicity," as Gubrium (in
this volume) calls it. Neglected are the myriad everyday interactional
matters that constitute social problems on a smaller scale. Ibarra and
Kitsuse point the study of social problems in the direction of processes
by which collective representations are assembled and promoted. While
this is certainly vital to a sociological understanding of the phenomenon,
a more ethnomethodological concern for the interpretive practices by
which everyday realities are locally accomplished, managed, and sustained urges constructionism to broaden its focus to include those practices that link public interpretive structures to aspects of everyday reality, producing recognizable instances of social problems. We refer to
such practices as *social problems work* (Miller and Holstein 1989, 1991;
Miller 1992).

This essay outlines an approach to the study of social problems work,
linking ethnomethodological concerns for constitutive practice with constructionist interests in social problems categories. It illustrates the articulation of problem categories with concrete cases, the interactional bases
of the attachments, and the open-ended nature of the process. The essay
concludes with some prospects for a sociology of social problems work.

Social Problems Work

Both the original constructionist statements (Kitsuse and Spector
1973, 1975; Spector and Kitsuse 1974, [1977] 1987) and Ibarra and Kitsuse's refinements tend to gloss over the interactional production of
concrete instances of social problems, even as they focus on forms of
vernacular usage as the constitutive source of social problems as social
forms. A sociology of social problems work neither contradicts nor deni-
grates this project. Rather it both expands and transforms the constructionist project to address how social problems categories, once publicly
established, are attached to experience in order to enact identifiable
objects of social problems discourse. The approach combines ethnomethodological impulses with concerns for collective representation
(Durkheim 1961) and discourse structures and gaze (Foucault 1972,
1973).

While ethnomethodologists have traditionally been interested in local practices of enactment, they have generally been reluctant to explicitly engage the challenge posed by the recurrence of patterned interpretations. Interpretation is certainly "artful" (Garfinkel 1967), but it also produces and reproduces categorizations that are recognizable as instances of the same phenomenon. Interpretive practice attaches meaning to occurrence in familiar ways. That sense of familiarity, of course, is not merely a matter of recognition; it, too, is artfully accomplished. Still, the analytic challenge for a more comprehensive constructionist approach lies in explicating the articulation of culturally recognized images with aspects of experience in ways that produce identifiable, indicatable instances of social problems that can be cited, in everyday interaction and through vernacular usage, as evidence of the problem's objective status.

Durkheim's analysis of social forms and collective representations provides a resource for linking everyday articulation practices to public interpretive structures (Gubrium 1988). For Durkheim (1961), social reality is enacted through collective representations—culturally recognized and shared categorization systems. As Douglas (1986, p. 96) notes, Durkheim considered collective representations to be "publicly standardized ideas (that) constitute social order." Durkheim pays scant attention to the constitutive processes through which a sense of order is achieved, but the basic framework is useful for understanding how meaning is accomplished. Indeed, analyzing the processes by which collective representations constitute order provides a link between Durkheimian structural concerns and phenomenological, ethnomethodological, and constructionist considerations.

Collective representations can be analyzed as interpretive structures that are constituted in a manner similar to Schutz's (1970) "schemes of interpretation"—that is, experientially acquired frameworks for organizing and making sense of everyday life. The structures are grounded in individual biography but reflect and perpetuate culturally promoted and shared understandings of and orientations to everyday experience. Social problems work involves procedures for expressing and applying these culturally shared categories to candidate circumstances. Interpretations are shaped by the interpretive structures and resources that are locally available and acceptable. For example, labeling persons "mentally ill" or "homeless" requires the availability of the categories plus the interpretive activity through which a category is articulated with a case.

In elaborating a neo-Durkheimian view, Mary Douglas (1986) suggests that human reason is organized and expressed through social structure by way of processes of "institutional thinking." Using this process as a metaphor, Douglas argues that socially organized circumstances provide models of social order through which experience is assimilated and organized. She states, for example, that "An answer is only seen to be the right one if it sustains the institutional thinking that is already in the minds of individuals as they try to decide (Douglas 1986, p. 4).

According to Douglas, institutions are organized as social conventions involving typical and routine ways of representing social reality. As she formulates them, representational conventions are similar to what Foucault (1972) analyzes as discursive formations. Contextually grounded discourses, vocabularies, and categories are part of local interpretive cultures (Gubrium 1991), resources for defining and classifying aspects of everyday life. Miller (1991), for example, shows how the local interpretive culture of a Work Incentive Program provides distinctive ways of formulating identities, problems, and solutions. Similarly, Gubrium's (1992) study of two family therapy agencies contrasts the ways the two institutions formulate what a family "really" is, citing distinctive local cultures and interpretive resources as the source of the differences.

Collective representations that emanate from social problems claims-making are merely candidate structures for making sense of objects and events. While they have been promoted as viable ways of understanding social conditions, there are myriad possible ways to define experience, so interpretive practices must articulate any particular structure with its object. Social problems designations are assigned, legitimated, and conventionalized as persons interpret and apply problem definitions in terms of the representational resources available to them. Social problems categories thus become a part of persons' and groups' ways of understanding and representing their everyday experience—locally available resources for constructing instances of social problems.

Social problems work articulates interpretive resources with concrete experience to constitute instances of social problems. Whereas the term can be used to characterize the activity of "street-level bureaucrats" whose formal job it is to formulate and apply general social problems policies to the concrete circumstances of everyday life (Lipsky 1980), we suggest that social problems work be more broadly understood to include any and all activity implicated in the recognition, identification, interpretation, and definition of conditions that are called "social problems." It is any practice contributing to the practical construction or definition of an instance of a social problem.

Accordingly, a sociology of social problems work focuses on interaction, conversational practice, and interpretive resources in the diverse settings where instances of social problems might be identified. Such practices and resources orient the way individuals and groups organize their interpretations, including the ways that they attach meaning to behavior. If we construe the outcomes of large-scale social problems claims-making as candidate "reality structures," we can analyze social problems work for the ways that these structures routinely infuse instances of everyday life with their social problems status.

Social problems work is a potential aspect of all social relationships and interactions where dissatisfaction with a putative condition might emerge. When individuals formulate the condition as a type of problem that warrants their attention or remedial concern, they engage in social problems work as an aspect of their ordinary conversation. In making claims and expressing complaints, persons portray aspects of relationships and circumstances as unsatisfactory, assign them to culturally known categories, and justify actions intended to change them. As Emerson and Messinger (1977) suggest, when third parties are consulted or when "troubleshooters" intervene to produce change, the problem becomes more concrete and public. Involvement of new participants provides new sources for additional social problems work, which may precipitate new depictions of the nature and causes of problems as well as remedies for them.

Analysis of social problems work may procede in several interrelated ways as it focuses on a constellation of phenomena and concerns. The following sections discuss three ways in which such analysis may be developed. First, the social problems work perspective can address the diverse interpretive and interactional procedures and occasions through which otherwise mundane aspects of everyday life are cast as social problems. Studies of social problems work analyze the attachment of shared cultural images and categories to aspects of experience to produce concrete instances of problems category members. A second, and related, focus is the interactional basis of the social problems work process. Instances of social problems are constructed through the often seen but unnoticed (Garfinkel 1967) practices of mundane interaction. Consequently, analysis of social problems work centers on the interactional dynamics of practical interpretation. Finally, social problems work is ongoing, situated, and contingent, a process that is never complete. Instances of social problems are constantly in the making—under construction, but provisional, so to speak. Analysis of the everyday construction work may thus consider the locally managed practices and practical circumstances that condition the articulation of social problems imageries with concrete cases.

Producing Concrete Cases

Instances of social problems are routinely produced and reproduced in everyday circumstance, through a variety of interpretive procedures. The activity is so commonplace that it may be all but invisible. Reference to an individual as a gang member, or reports of a particular event as an instance of child abuse, for example, constitute as they describe. The dynamics of social problems work is perhaps most visible when the problem is the overt concern of a particular setting. Human service organizations are exemplary in this regard, as they routinely deal with, and constitute, persons and occurrences as problems (Holstein 1992). Indeed, social problems work may be the primary preoccupation of the human services (Miller 1992), even if it is not recognized as such.

As an illustration, consider how an instance of "mental illness" was publicly established during an involuntary commitment hearing. Mental illness is widely recognized and legitimated as a category for defining incomprehensible cognition, affect, and/or behavior—both professionally and in vernacular usage. It has been available in Western culture as a collective representation and interpretive resource for quite some time. Foucault (1965), for example, has described the historical emergence of the concepts and discourses of madness, insanity, mental illness, and related terms dating back to the Middle Ages, while more recent movements to popularize and institutionalize the mental illness metaphor have also been documented (Sarbin 1969; Sarbin and Mancuso 1970). The issue for the study of social problems work, then, is the local articulation of the collective representation with a concrete aspect of experience.

Involuntary mental hospitalization can be enforced only if the candidate patient is found to be mentally ill and dangerous to self or others in a court of law. Thus, commitment hearings are scenes for the assignment of social problems categories to actual cases. In the following extract from hearing testimony, a psychiatrist testifies regarding the mental condition of Gerald Simms, the candidate patient. The doctor accounts for a diagnosis of "chronic schizophrenia" by displaying evidence of the problem that justifies the label. The diagnostic work and testimony can thus be analyzed as an instance of social problems work—interpretive activity through which a category is formally attached to an individual:

> Mr. Simms suffers from drastic mood swings. His affect is extremely labile. One minute he'll be in tears, the next he's just fine. He fluctuates. His affect may be flattened, then elevated. One moment he'll be telling you about his cleaning business, then he'll flip out of character and cry like a brokenhearted schoolgirl over the most insignificant thing. Something that should never upset a grown man like Mr. Simms. During his periods of flattened affect, he seems to lose all interest. . . . . His passivity—he's almost docile in a very sweet sort of way. He just smiles and lets everything pass. It's completely inappropriate for an adult male. (Holstein 1987, p. 145)

Note that while the psychiatrist is ostensibly describing Mr. Simms's condition and behavior, his description is also rhetorical. He selects aspects of a range of reportable features and advocates them as definitive characterizations. In the process, he constitutes Mr. Simms as a member of the problem category, interpretively attaching the definition in a fashion that is accountable to locally prevailing legal and psychiatric standards.

In addition, the psychiatrist descriptively accomplishes Mr. Simms's mental illness with reference to normal types, pointing out in the process how Mr. Simms's traits and behaviors are anomalous—that is, unmotivated by other circumstances that are described. Social problems work of this type routinely involves rhetorical devices that Dorothy Smith (1978) calls *contrast structures* to display problems or troubles. Contrast structures juxtapose characterizations of traits or behaviors with statements that supply instructions for seeing the traits or behavior as unusual or problematic (Smith 1978). Anomalies—in the case above, documents of mental illness—are accomplished by constructing relationships between rules or definitions of situations and descriptions of an individual's behavior so that the former do not properly provide for the latter.

In the Simms case, for example, the described anomalies make it "evident" that the candidate patient is mentally ill. The psychiatrist explicitly contrasted descriptions of Mr. Simms's behavior with normal expectations for a person of his gender and age. Mr. Simms's emotions, for example, were portrayed as those of "a brokenhearted schoolgirl" crying over matters that should "never upset a grown man." His "passivity" was "inappropriate for an adult male." Mr. Simms's age and gender were made salient and consequential to the diagnosis as standards for invidious comparison. Apparent incongruities between expected and encountered behaviors and traits were then noted as evidence that a problem existed, and the problem was identified as mental illness (Holstein 1993).

This interpretive technique is similar to the use of complementary oppositions, a practice often employed to establish persons or events as problematic (Douglas 1986; Loseke 1992; Miller 1991, 1992). Oppositional forms include distinctions between nature and culture, normal and unusual, good and bad. The oppositions may be explicitly expressed as orientations to matters of practical concern or used as implicit background assumptions justifying persons' orientations. In this way, complementary oppositions are linked to other oppositions and expressed as ideologies that justify and perpetuate the institutional discourses from which they are built. Oppositional forms and other contrastive structures can thus be used to attach social problems categories to concrete cases, specifying what a problem is as opposed to what it is not.

Loseke's (1989, 1992) analysis of the social construction of wife abuse in battered women's shelters further illustrates the practical interpretive work that goes into assigning individuals to a social problems category. The problem of battered women and wife beating was publicly constituted and recognized through a variety of claims-making activities culminating in the 1970s and 1980s (Studer 1984, Tierney 1982). The practical work of shelter workers, according to Loseke, is deciding and justifying which women to assign to the category. As an everyday matter, this amounted to accountably deciding which potential clients wanted and needed what the organization had to offer, and which women would become good members of the shelter community. This involved the practical articulation of client characteristics with organizational goals and resources using commonsense or folk reasoning and typification. Seeing candidate clients in terms of oppositional forms— "appropriate" or "inappropriate" clients, "battered" or "not battered" women—shelter workers produced decisions that were justified by their constructions of the women and their circumstances.

Social problems work is apparent in staff members' entries in the shelter "logbook," which offered accounts for the full range of workers organizational decisions and actions. Log entries noting admission decisions illustrate the application of the "battered woman" image. Consider the following entries:

> 8:30 P.M. Susan called. Needs shelter badly, has four children, husband searching for her. She's been battered and is frightened—requires shelter till she can relocate. Called [another worker] and we think we should pick her up. (Loseke 1992, p. 85)

> She seems like a classic battered case. Had a long session with her, she was crying and very hurt. Absolutely no self-esteem, husband treated her like a little child but she is still in love with him. . . . . She feels very helpless and lonely. (Loseke 1989, p. 184)

According to Loseke, Susan—from the first entry—was constructed as a member of the battered woman type by portraying her as frightened and in danger, a woman wanting to remain independent from an abusive partner and therefore a woman who could not be turned away. The battered woman collective representation reflexively emerged from the descriptions and served as an interpretive scheme for understanding and categorizing Susan's behavior and circumstance. The second woman was assigned to the battered woman type by noting that she was oppressed by her husband and felt helpless and isolated.

In contrast, many women were turned away from the shelter. The battered woman image was typically invoked as part of logbook accounts for their rejections:

[hospital] called. Wanted to dump a woman on us because she had no place to go. She wasn't a battered woman, referred to [another shelter]. (Loseke 1992, p. 83)

Crisis call from J.E., rather elusive, claims to battery. Husband has kicked her out of the house and refuses to let her return. She requested a place to sleep for 2–3 days. I do not see an immediate need here, she has mother, friends here. (Loseke 1989, p. 186)

The first of these entries glosses over the criteria used to deny admission, relying on the claim that the candidate client "wasn't a battered woman" to justify her exclusion. The second entry builds a case against the application of the battered woman label by first casting doubt on the woman's experiences, noting the woman's "claims to battery" rather than, say, simply reporting that she had been battered. Then it lists three characteristics of the candidate client that are not typically linked to the battered woman type: She lacked proper motivation for seeking shelter ("she requested a place to sleep"), she was not trapped in a violent situation ("husband has kicked her out"), and she was not socially isolated ("she has mother, friends here"). The woman was thus accountably constructed as "not battered" within the practical context and local interpretive culture of this particular shelter. As in the instances where women were taken into the shelter, social problems work attached or withheld membership in the battered woman category.

Concrete instances of social problems do not exist apart from the interpretive work that produces them. The "homeless mentally ill" (Campbell and Reeves 1989), the "chronically unemployed" (Miller 1991), "juvenile delinquents" (Emerson 1969), and myriad other everyday instances of abstract social problems are constituted through social problems work. A social constructionist approach should include an explicit focus on this work.

Interactional Bases

As an interpretive project, social problems work is interactive as well as rhetorical. Social problems designations are not unilaterally enforced, simply applied or withheld; instead they emerge from talk, interaction, and negotiation. Consider, for example, how a child is assigned to the social problem category "emotionally disturbed" in a meeting of a multidisciplinary team of mental health professionals and educators (Buckholdt and Gubrium 1985). The team has been assigned the responsibility of certifying children for ongoing care at a juvenile treatment facility. In the meeting concerning student Teddy Green, we encounter commonplace interpretive practices that select information from Teddy's case file and assemble it in a coherent pattern that documents his ostensible disturbance and membership in the problem category.

In the following excerpt, note how Dee Lerner (DL) and Dave Bachman (DB), a clinical educator and school psychologist, respectively, typify the child at several points, attempting to fill in what is lacking in Teddy's file to produce a consistent portrait of Teddy's problem. At one point Lerner and Bachman, together with Floyd Crittenden (FC), the facility's principal, focus on Teddy's home neighborhood and the family's residential origin as the relevant interpretive framework for understanding his problems. They use this to make further inferences about the nature of Teddy's disturbance. Decision-making rests on the unspoken assumptions that emotional disturbance exists in principle as an educational and behavioral deficit—a collective representation. The principal opens the meeting:

FC: We have new psychs [complete psychological reports] on Green and Jones.

DB: Good. Green first then.
[Staffers try to locate Green's home address because it is not clear in the file where his parents reside.]

DL: When I don't know the home address, I put the local foster home down. I guess it doesn't matter as long as *I'm* consistent. Everyone does these [multidisciplinary team reports] differently. [Turning to Bachman] You know that, don't you? I'll put that down anyway. He's ten years old. So he's three years below grade level. Right?

DB: Uh-huh.
[There is a five-minute pause for writing.]

DB: He's from Mayville.

FC: They moved into Morley [the local metropolitan area] on Logan Street. Have you ever seen Logan Street? It's like an alley. It's narrower than an alley.

DB: [Laughing as he reads Teddy's file] When he's in the classroom it says here that the teacher had to put him in his seat at least twice [on the average] in ten minutes of the school day.

FC: [Sarcastically] Active.

DB: That was two years ago.

DL: It says here that he's two years below grade level. But I think he's three years below. So I'll put that down.
[There is another pause for writing, then conversation resumes, first turning to Teddy's physical condition, then his behavior in the program.]

DB: [Laughing as he reads the file] It says you've decreased his running [being away from the center without permission]. He only runs to the A&P now.

FC: Yeah. You should have seen him go before.
     [Teddy's running behavior is discussed and elaborated. There is much amused commentary and sarcasm over the image of Teddy's running being generated. Staffers then return to their report writing.]

DB: Millikin [one of the center's consulting psychologists] questioned the language dysfunction here. [He reads from Teddy's file.] Two or three years below average. Do you thing we should put that in?

FC: He doesn't have a speech problem, really.

DL: I think it's cultural deprivation. They seem like hill people. They live in an alley on the south side.

FC: They're from the South, and you might say that they're hill people. He doesn't have any deficiency in swearing though. You should see his home. What a mess!

DL: It's funny about emotionally disturbed children. They really know how to swear. I became an adult after I started to work with these kids . . . .

FC: The mother used to drive me crazy. She was always telling me when Teddy ran. He'd run from anxiety, frustration, and all that.

DB: Is the mother divorced?

FC: No. But whenever the mother disciplines the kids, it's always, "I'll club you."
     [Crittenden's pager buzzes and he leaves. Bachman and Lerner take a ten-minute break, then resume their report writing.]

DL: [She talks as she read's Teddy's file] This is a classic, isn't it. The typical emotionally disturbed kid: nothing exceptional, just problems of one sort or another. (Buckholdt and Gubrium 1985, pp. 197–99)

As the participants sort through and highlight various aspects of information that might be relevant to the case at hand, they produce documents of what ultimately comes to be seen as a typical example of emotional disturbance. The selective description assembles the working picture of the student, providing the warrant for the categorization. Teddy's status is "worked up" as the staffers interactively consider his case, ultimately placing him in the emotionally disturbed category.

Social problems work need not be so intentional. Nor is it necessarily one-sided, with commonsense interpreters assigning or withholding others' membership in problem categories. Individuals may claim membership for themselves, as when an "unemployed" person applies for welfare assistance or a "battered woman" applies for shelter. Or they might resist, as in involuntary commitment hearings or criminal trials, for example. Documents that are used to justify category membership may even be collaboratively produced—not only in the intentional fashion described in the example directly above, but through practices unremarkable to those involved. This happens frequently in involuntary commitment hearings, for example.

As representatives of the district attorney's (DA) office argue that candidate patients are mentally ill and in need of hospitalization, they attempt to produce evidence of these charges to support their case. Psychiatric testimony, as we have seen, provides one form of documentation. Further evidence often emerges from the hearing interactions, not necessarily in terms of answers to testimony or narrative testimony, but through the conversational exchanges themselves. In the case considered below, the DA had asked fourteen prior questions, one immediately following the other, regarding where Lisa Sellers—the candidate patient—intended to live if she were released. The DA then initiated the following sequence:

1. DA2:   How do you like summer out here, Lisa?
2. LS: It's OK.
3. DA2:   How long have you lived here?
4. LS: Since I moved from Houston
5.   (Silence)
6. LS: About three years ago.
7. DA2:   Tell me about why you came here.
8. LS: I just came.
9.   (Silence)
10. LS: You know, I wanted to see the stars, Hollywood.
11.   (Silence)
12. DA2:   Uh huh.
13. LS: I didn't have no money.
14.   (Silence)
15. LS: I'd like to get a good place to live.
16.   (Silence five seconds)
17. DA2:   Go on.((spoken simultaneously with onset of next utterance))
18. LS: There was some nice things I brought.
19.   (Silence)
20. DA2:   Uh huh.
21. LS: Brought them from the rocketship.
22. DA2:   Oh really?
23. LS: They was just some things I had.
24. DA2:   From the rocketship?
25. LS: Right.
26. DA2:   Were you on it?
27. LS: Yeah.
28. DA2:   Tell me about this rocketship, Lisa. (Holstein 1988, p. 467)

The sequence culminates in the patient's reference to a rocketship. Later, the DA summarized the case, stating that this sort of talk—the "delusions" about the rocketship in particular—clearly indicated that Ms. Sellers was "mentally ill," unable to manage her life, and in need of hospitalization. While the talk about the rocketship was ostensibly produced by Ms. Sellers, close examination of the extract reveals the conversational work done by the DA that contributed to the final outcome.

Note how the DA encouraged extended and unfocused turns at talk by the way he managed his participation in the conversation. First, he altered the structure of the conversation from what may have come to be understood as a "normal" or "expected" sequence of questions and answers. In the fourteen exchanges immediately prior to this extract, and continuing in lines 1 through 4, the DA questioned the patient, then directly followed the patient's answers with questions, allowing no notable gaps between answers and next questions. Silence, however, followed line 4, to be terminated by the patient's elaboration. In line 7, the DA solicited further talk, but not in the form of a question. This was a very general request for the patient to provide more information, but the adequacy of a response to this type of solicit is more indeterminate than for a direct question. The DA's discretion is deeply implicated in what may come to be seen as adequately fulfilling the request, the completeness of a response depending, in part, on how the DA acknowledges it.

The DA did not respond at the first possible speaker transition point after the patient's next utterance (lines 8 and 9), and declined possible speakership or minimally filled turnspaces through line 20. The patient's mention of a rocketship finally elicited an indication of apparent interest ("Oh really?") from the DA at line 22. The DA then asked two additional questions before soliciting further talk about the rocketship. Once again this was done without asking a direct question, instead making a general request for information.

This segment of cross-examination produced an instance of hearably "crazy" or delusional talk that was ultimately cited as evidence of the *candidate patient's* mental illness. But it is clear that this testimony is an interactional achievement. The DA requested testimony from the patient, but repeatedly withheld acknowledgment of the testimony's adequacy, promoting further talk in the process. He further encouraged the patient to speak, using "Uh huh" to indicate an understanding that an extended unit of talk was in progress and was not yet complete (Schegloff 1982), and by declining possible turns at talk altogether. The patient, for her part, sustained the ongoing conversation by terminating silences that had begun to emerge at failed speaker transition points. She repeatedly elaborated responses, and eventually produced the "crazy" talk that was cited as evidence of her interactional incompetence. But, in a sense, it was her cooperation with the DA in extending the conversation—her conversational competence—that allowed for the emergence of that very talk. As an instance of social problems work, we can see both parties to the interaction engaged in the production of verbalizations that were subsequently used to document social problems claims.

Perhaps inadvertently, but nonetheless actively, both parties contributed to the production of documents used to further social problems claims-making. The social problems work leading up to categorization was thoroughly interactional.

Social Problems Work as Open-Ended Process

The processes by which representations of social problems are applied are essentially open-ended. Analysis of the emergent construction of instances of social problems thus requires a natural history framework rather than an "endpoint" or retrospective point of view (see Emerson and Messinger 1977). If analysts simply focus on cases where an instance of a problem has been identified, the events and interpretive work leading up to the present-time definition take on a somewhat "determined" quality. That is, events and interpretations appear to lead logically to the outcome—the problematic status of the case at hand. This ignores the myriad contingencies that affect what happens in any candidate case where a problem category might be applied. Whereas a case might be assigned to the problem category, it is possible that it might also be defined differently—that is, as an instance of something other than a social problem. For example, Steve Howe, pitcher for the New York Yankees, was suspended from major league baseball for repeated drug abuse—labeled a chronic instance of a social problem. In an appeal of his suspension, however, his attorney argued that he should be tested and treated for "adult attention deficit disorder"—a medical condition—thus opening up the definitional possibility for just what Howe was and how he should be treated (*Sporting News*, August 8, 1992).

Processes of social problems work are ongoing, locally managed, and sensitive to practical circumstances. Analysis should therefore recognize that categorization is always uncertain, that more than a single category might be interpretively related to any candidate case, and that the designation of any particular instance is provisional, for the practical purpose at hand, and always subject to change.

Consider the complexities, for example, of the social problems work that might be involved in constructing concrete instances of "juvenile delinquency." Such interpretation first requires the availability of the collective representation or category as a constructive resource. Thus, images of both "juvenile" and "delinquency" must exist for instances of the problem to be constructed. Aries (1965) documents the emergence of the concept of childhood, the seeming prerequisite for juvenile problems, while others have outlined the emergence of the notion of a particular brand of trouble involving children—juvenile delinquency (Empey

1982; Platt 1969; Schlossman 1977). With the category available as an everyday interpretive resource, under what circumstances will it be applied?

Certainly the behavior of the youth in question is relevant. Its importance, however, is not because the youth's actions determine whether he or she is labeled as a problem. Rather, aspects of the youth that are made topical—matters of behavior, character, background, and the like—are themselves available as interpretive resources, factors that can be described, interpreted, and defined in the process of making sense of any particular person or situation. While interpretations of persons or actions may not be infinitely variable, neither are they certain to lead to any particular depiction; meaning is always mediated by interpretive process. Thus, analysis of social problems work must focus on what is interpretively *done* with aspects of experience to assign them to particular categories.

Analysis must also avoid presuppositions about what sort of instances may eventually be made into problems. Informal reactions and interpretations may place occurrences in a problem category, but they are also capable of making candidate problems into more-or-less "normal" aspects of everyday life (Lynch 1983; Pollner and McDonald-Wickler 1985), or locating them in alternative "problem" categories. The interpretive activity that differentiates "childish pranks" from "juvenile delinquency" is commonplace. As mundane as it is, and as overlooked in the study of social problems as it might be, the process by which "nothing" is made of a candidate problem is an important aspect of social problems work.

The same is true of more formally organized social problems work. Citizen complaints to the police, for example, must be organized into organizationally relevant response categories. Meehan's (1989) study of telephone requests for service suggests that the telephone conversations involve complex interpretive work to produce police categorizations of, and responses to, what are designated (and recorded in police records) as instances of juvenile delinquency and youth gang activity. Similarly, police encounters with juveniles are open-ended, deeply implicating the officers' interpretive practices in determining what will be made of the persons and circumstances they encounter (Cicourel 1968; Meehan 1986; Piliavin and Briar 1968; Sanders 1977). Indeed, studies of what has come to be known as the exercise of police "discretion" in the application of the law might be recast as studies of social problems work in the field.

Being an open-ended process, the designation of a case as an instance of a social problem does not finalize its interpretation. A police officer, for example, may categorize an instance of juvenile delinquency, but its classification is always subject to change. Screening procedures "divert" many cases referred by the police before they are adjudicated. Who is treated as a "delinquent" or who is disposed of in some other fashion—as a minor trouble that will go away on its own, or as a psychiatric or medical matter, for example—is determined through organizationally circumscribed interpretive procedures that construct and manipulate the "facts" of the case at hand in light of practical objectives and circumstances (Needleman 1981). Similarly, when cases reach juvenile courts, they are once again interpreted to see whether they coincide with the categories of "normal," "hard core or criminallike delinquent," or "disturbed" (Emerson 1969). Subsequently, court personnel employ "pitches" and "denunciations"—rhetorical maneuvers—to warrant their categorizations, once again "working up" the example of the social problem in the routine course of doing the work of the court.

The upshot of ongoing social problems work is that a case is never fully or finally constituted as juvenile delinquency. New processing venues may interpretively transform the problem from one form to another. As Emerson's (1969) study of juvenile court illustrates, court decision-making may construct either juvenile delinquents or emotionally or psychiatrically disturbed children from the same candidate cases. Probation officers may then have to convince the involved juvenile and his or her family that the categorization is proper—"in the best interest of the child"—often "cooling out" persons who have vested interests in alternative definitions in the process (Darrough 1984, 1989, 1990).

With the creation of medical definitions for troublesome childhood behavior—hyperkinesis, for example (Conrad 1975)—candidate juvenile delinquents may also be categorized as medical rather than social problems. And with the proliferation and popularization of psychiatric and "substance abuse" terminology, diverse resources are increasingly available for constructing instances of problems of various sorts. Categorization is transinstitutionalized (Warren 1981) as organizational settings provide distinctive orientations, vocabularies, and interpretive resources that condition the ways cases are defined.

Ultimately, the results of the varied interpretations and decisions may be tallied to produce statistical documents of the incidence and prevalence of juvenile problems. But these "hard data" that ostensibly indicate that the various problems do, "in fact," exist are themselves products of social problems work (Gubrium and Buckholdt 1979, Kitsuse and Cicourel 1963).

And as final as a statistical tally may make any particular interpretive project seem, social problems work is always open to revision. An instance of a problem is never permanently constituted. A case involving a client and workers of a Work Incentive Program (WIN) illustrates the way today's problem may interpretively evolve into something else (Miller 1985). The client (CL) had developed a reputation among WIN staff as a troublesome character, a man with a "bad attitude." In most respects he was considered an example of the "hard-core" unemployed, an especially salient category for WIN personnel. Considered a nearly hopeless case, the client was sent for some routine diagnostic tests at the Alternate Education Center. Much to everyone's surprise—including the client himself—the scores were much higher than anticipated. In light of the new information, previous formulations of the client's biography, attitude, and problems were revised, as was evident in the following discussion with a WIN staff member (SM):

SM: You've got a brain. You just haven't always used it to make wise choices. I'll bet your problem in school was that you were bored.
CL: Yeah, I was bored. About the ninth grade I lost all interest.
SM: You didn't do the work, you acted out and you got put in the dummy group. You should have been in the gifted class or at least at the top of your group. You got in a group that didn't care and you didn't either. . . . Maybe you should think about college. You could go to [a local college]. What would you like to be, an engineer? (Miller 1985, p. 387)

The reassessment was profound. "He's really changed. He is taking control of his life. It's so easy to work with him," noted a staff member (p. 388). Relying upon the "documentary method of interpretation" (Garfinkel 1967), old "facts" were assimilated to a new pattern. Within a very short time, the client was interpretively transformed from the embodiment of a social problem into "the success story of the year" (Miller 1985, p. 388). As an open-ended process, interpretive practice reconstituted the client's identity and past, but left the possibility open for future interpretive revision.

Prospects and Implications

A sociology of social problems work considers how interpretation proceeds in the myriad everyday settings where instances of social problems might be constructed. There is no *theoretical* reason to assume that any individuals or groups, or any organized settings, are more appropriate than others as sites of social problems work. Instances of social problems may be constructed anywhere social problems rubrics might be invoked, anywhere problems become interpretive possibilities. As a practical matter, settings where problematic or troublesome behavior is routinely and specifically topicalized are the most likely to produce social problems discourse. Human service and social control settings are therefore rich in opportunities to observe the attachment of social problems representations to concrete cases.

But the work in these settings cannot be considered more "authentic" than other constructions; their enacted problems are no more objective or "real" than those assembled in alternative settings. Social problems work by human service or social control professionals might generally be accorded a practical legitimacy that encourages others to take professional interpretations more "seriously" than others' interpretations. But that legitimacy is also an ongoing social accomplishment.

Some forms of social problems work may also have more far-reaching effects than others. The mass media, for instance, not only participate in the promotion of social problems categories, but they provide widely publicized examples of the image as it is attached to experience. We see living representations of the homeless mentally ill, for example, in network television news programming that selects concrete cases and portrays them as the embodiment of the social problems image. Campbell and Reeves (1989) argue that television news publicizes the distinction between mainstream populations and those designated as problems of mental illness and homelessness, artfully manipulating visual images and verbal commentary to attach "public idioms" to selected aspects of experience in contrast to others. The dynamics of how interpretations are promoted, legitimated, and sustained, and the informal, professional, and technical practices used to interpret cases are thus important topics for analysis.

While studies of social problems work focus on interpretive practice, they also incorporate context. Not only are social problems representations organizationally produced and preferred models for interpretation, but their use is conditioned by prevailing local preferences, practices, and resources. Both image and attachment are organizationally embedded (Gubrium 1988); categories and the practices through which they are applied reflect local interpretive circumstances and culture. Contextual influence is apparent, for example, when we observe how juvenile problems are variously formulated in law enforcement, psychiatric, and medical surroundings. Each setting has its available resources, institutionalized procedures, and practical discourses for dealing with matters they routinely encounter. While the contexts neither predict nor determine individual outcomes, they provide orientations and resources that generally distinguish the interpretation process in one circumstance from that in another. Studies of social problems work therefore consider the practical contingencies and discursive and interactional structures that characterize the contexts within which the work takes place. Practice remains central, with recognition of its situated, contextualized character.

As social problems work is increasingly carried out in formal organizations that process and channel everyday life, interpretation may become increasingly "professionalized" and "institutionalized." Public bureau-cracies, human service organizations, and social control agencies routinely formulate problems and their solutions, their work being organized around the rhetorical production of the troubles and problems they ostensibly address (Miller 1990, 1991). This suggests a more general issue regarding the pervasive bureaucratization and rationalization of experience. Weber (1958, 1968) referred to "formal rationality" as the organization of conduct according to calculated principles, formal rules, and institutionalized procedures. He argued that rationalized social relations adhere to generalized principles that promote the sort of predictability that facilitates bureaucratic activity. As life comes progressively under formal and official auspices, meaning is increasingly institutionalized. Interpretation is totalized as the tendencies of organizations assert themselves to overwhelm individual differences in representational practice.

From Weber's standpoint, the representation of experience is progressively "disenchanted" in that there is no room left for personalized, spontaneous thought and action (Bendix 1960). A social problems work perspective, however, reasserts the importance of practice without denying the role of context. Interpretive structure and culture cannot be as totalizing as Weber suggests because they must always be applied—situatedly, yet creatively, articulated with selected aspects of experience (Gubrium 1992). People are not mere captives or extensions of organizational thinking and discursive structures. They exercise interpretive discretion conditioned by a complex layering of interpretive resources and influences. So, whereas personnel in a particular human service agency may orient to social problems in organizationally promoted ways, they bring multiple resources and vocabularies to any interpretive occasion, encouraging diversity in the identification of problem cases. Practical interpretation, then, is almost unavoidably paradoxical: Individual practice yields spontaneity and diversity, while context and interpretive structure promote pattern.

A sociology of social problems work thus addresses both interpretive structure and practice as they jointly produce everyday instances of social problems. This dual focus on social process and representational resources reveals a new dimension to the construction of social problems.

References

Aires, Phillippe. 1965. *Centuries of Childhood. A Social History of Family Life.* New York: Vintage.
Bendix, Reinhard. 1960. *Max Weber: An Intellectual Portrait.* New York: Doubleday.

Buckholdt, David R. and Jaber F. Gubrium. 1985. *Caretakers*. Lanham, MD: University Press of America.
Campbell, Richard and Jimmie. L. Reeves. 1989. "Covering the Homeless: The Joyce Brown Story." *Critical Studies in Mass Communication* 6:21–42.
Cicourel, Aaron. 1968. *The Social Organization of Juvenile Justice*. New York: Wiley.
Conrad, Peter. 1975. "The Discovery of Hyperkinesis." *Social Problems* 23:12–21.
Darrough, William D. 1984. "In the Best Interest of the Child: Negotiating Parental Cooperation for Probation Placement." *Urban Life* 13:123–53.
———. 1989. "In the Best Interest of the Child II: Neutralizing Resistance to Probation Placement." *Journal of Contemporary Ethnography* 18:72–88.
———. 1990. "Neutralizing Resistance: Probation Work as Rhetoric." Pp. 163–87 in *Perspectives on Social Problems*, vol. 2, edited by G. Miller and J. Holstein. Greenwich, CT: JAI Press.
Douglas, Mary. 1986. *How Institutions Think*. Syracuse, NY: Syracuse University Press.
Durkheim, Emile. 1961. *The Elementary Forms of the Religious Life*. New York: Collier-Macmillan.
Emerson, Robert M. 1969. *Judging Delinquents*. Chicago: Aldine.
Emerson, Robert M. and Sheldon L. Messinger. 1977. "The Micro-politics of Trouble." *Social Problems* 25:121–34.
Empey, Lamar. 1982. *American Delinquency*. Homewood, IL: Dorsey.
Foucault, Michel. 1965. *Madness and Civilization*. New York: Random House.
———. 1972. *The Archaeology of Knowledge*. New York: Pantheon.
———. 1973. *The Birth of the Clinic*. New York: Random House.
Garfinkel, Harold. 1967. *Studies in Ethnomethodology*. Englewood Cliffs, NJ: Prentice-Hall.
Gubrium, Jaber F. 1988. *Analyzing Field Reality*. Newbury Park, CA: Sage.
———. 1991. "Recognizing and Analyzing Local Cultures." Pp. 131–41 in *Experiencing Fieldwork*, edited by W. Shaffir and R. Stebbins. Newbury Park, CA: Sage.
———. 1992. *Out of Control*. Newbury Park, CA: Sage.
Gubrium, Jaber F. and David R. Buckholdt. 1979. "Producing Hard Data in Human Service Institutions." *Pacific Sociological Review* 22:115–36.
Heritage, John. 1984. *Garfinkel and Ethnomethodology*. Cambridge: Polity Press.
Holstein, James A. 1987. "Producing Gender Effects on Involuntary Mental Hospitalization." *Social Problems* 34:141–55.
———. 1988. "Court Ordered Incompetence: Conversational Organization in Involuntary Commitment Proceedings." *Social Problems* 35:801–16.
———. 1992. "Producing People: Descriptive Practice in Human Service Work." Pp. 23–40 in *Current Research on Occupations and Professions*, vol. 7, edited by G. Miller. Greenwich, CT: JAI Press.
———. 1993. *Court-Ordered Insanity: Interpretive Practice and Involuntary Commitment*. Hawthorne, NY: Aldine de Gruyter.
Kitsuse, John I. and Aaron Cicourel. 1963. "A Note on the Use of Official Statistics." *Social Problems* 11:131–39.
Kitsuse, John. I and Malcolm Spector. 1973. "Toward a Sociology of Social Problems." *Social Problems* 20:407–19.

———. 1975. "Social Problems and Deviance: Some Parallel Issues." *Social Problems* 22:584–94.

Lipsky, Michael. 1980. *Street-Level Bureaucracy.* New York: Russell Sage Foundation.

Loseke, Donileen R. 1989. "Creating Clients: Social Problems Work in a Shelter for Battered Women." Pp. 173–94 in *Perspectives on Social Problems,* vol. 1, edited by James A. Holstein and Gale Miller. Greenwich, CT: JAI Press.

———. 1992. *The Battered Woman and Shelters.* Albany, NY: SUNY Press.

Lynch, Michael. 1983. "Accommodation Practices: Vernacular Treatments of Madness." *Social Problems* 31:152–63.

Meehan, Albert J. 1986. "Record-keeping Practices in the Policing of Juveniles." *Urban Life* 15:70–102.

———. 1989. "Assessing the 'Police-worthiness' of Citizen Complaints to the Police." Pp. 116–40 in *The Interactional Order* edited, by D. Helm, W. Anderson, A. Meehan, and A. Rawls. New York: Irvington.

Miller, Gale. 1985. "Client Attitude and Organizational Process." *Urban Life* 13:367–94.

———. 1990. "Work as Reality Maintaining Activity: Interactional Aspects of Occupational and Professional Work." Pp. 163–83 in *Current Research on Occupations and Professions,* vol. 5, edited by Helena Lopata. Greenwich, CT: JAI Press.

———. 1991. *Enforcing the Work Ethnic.* Albany, NY: SUNY Press.

———. 1992. "Human Service Practice as Social Problems Work." Pp. 3–22 in *Current Research on Occupations and Professions,* vol. 7. edited by G. Miller. Greenwich, CT: JAI Press.

Miller, Gale and James A. Holstein. 1989. "On The Sociology of Social Problems." Pp. 1–16 in *Perspectives on Social Problems,* vol. 1 edited by James A. Holstein and Gale Miller. Greenwich, CT: JAI Press.

———. 1991. "Social Problems Work in Street-Level Bureaucracies." Pp. 177–202 in *Studies in Organizational Sociology,* edited by G. Miller. Greenwich, CT: JAI Press.

Needleman, Carolyn. 1981. "Discrepant Assumptions in Empirical Research: The Case of Juvenile Court Screening." *Social Problems* 28:247–62.

Piliavin, Irving and Scott Briar. 1968. "Police Encounters with Juveniles." *American Journal of Sociology* 70:206–14.

Platt, Anthony. 1969. *The Child Savers.* Chicago: University of Chicago Press.

Pollner, Melvin. 1987. *Mundane Reason.* Cambridge: Cambridge University Press.

———. 1991. "Left of Ethnomethodology: the Rise and Decline of Radical Reflexivity." *American Sociological Review* 56:370–80.

Pollner, Melvin and Lynn McDonald-Wickler. 1985. "The Social Construction of Unreality: A Case Study of a Family's Attribution of Competence to a Severely Retarded Child." *Family Process* 24:241–54.

Sanders, William B. 1977. *Detective Work.* New York: Free Press.

Sarbin, Theodore R. 1969. "The Scientific Status of the Mental Illness Metaphor." Pp. 9–31 in *Changing Perspectives in Mental Illness,* edited by S. C. Plog and R. B. Edgerton. New York: Free Press.

Sarbin, Theodore R. and James C. Mancuso. 1970. "Failure of a Moral Enterprise:
    Attitudes of the Public Toward Mental Illness." *Journal of Consulting and
    Clinical Psychology* 35:159–73.
Schegloff, Emanuel A. 1982. "Discourse as an Interactional Achievement: Some
    Uses of 'Uh huh' and Other Things That Come Between Sentences." Pp. 71–
    93 in *Georgetown University Roundtable on Language and Linguistics*, edited by
    D. Tannen. Washington, DC: Georgetown University Press.
Schlossman, Steven L. 1977. *Love and the American Delinquent*. Chicago: Univer-
    sity of Chicago Press.
Schutz, Alfred. 1970. *On Phenomenology and Social Relations*. Chicago: University
    of Chicago Press.
Smith, Dorothy E. 1978. "'K is Mentally Ill': The Anatomy of a Factual Account."
    Sociology 12:23–53.
Spector, Malcolm and John I. Kitsuse. 1974. "Social Problems: A Reformulation."
    Social Problems 21:145–58.
———. [1977] 1987. *Constructing Social Problems*. Hawthorne, NY: Aldine de
    Gruyter.
Studer, Marlena. 1984. "Wife Beating as a Social Problem: The Process of Defini-
    tion." *International Journal of Women's Studies* 7:412–22.
Tierney, Kathleen. 1982. "The Battered Women Movement and the Creation of
    the Wife Beating Problem." *Social Problems* 29:207–17.
Troyer, Ronald J. 1989. "Are Social Problems and Social Movements the Same
    Thing?" Pp. 41–58 in *Perspectives on Social Problems*, vol. 1, edited by J.
    Holstein and G. Miller. Greenwich, CT: JAI Press.
Warren, Carol A. B. 1981. "New Forms of Social Control: The Myth of Deinstitu-
    tionalization." *American Behavioral Scientist* 24:724–40.
Weber, Max. 1958. *The Protestant Ethic and the Spirit of Capitalism*. New York:
    Scribners.
———. 1968. *Economy and Society*. New York: Bedminster Press.

8

Claims-Making from the Underside: Marginalization and Social Problems Analysis

Leslie J. Miller

I. Introduction

In the course of their discussion of social problems analysis in this volume, Ibarra and Kitsuse state: "The matter of marginality . . . . is a subject that greatly interests us." They are not alone. The existence of communities whose typical ways of knowing and talking about the world have been discredited, or marginalized, is a matter of increasing interest to scholars within the social problems field as well as outside it. My purpose in what follows is to sift the larger theoretical discussion of marginality for what it has to say to analysts of social problems.

Most sociologists first encountered the issue of marginalization in its epistemological form: What counts as a (legitimate) way of knowing the world? Anchored in the recognition that knowledge was always knowledge from somewhere,[1] this formulation of the question made it plain that *some* ways of knowing (e.g., professional medicine, science) had put to rout *other* ways (e.g., commonsense, the "voice of experience"), which, if they survived at all, had retained little credibility as "prejudice," "ignorance," and "myth."[2] For the analyst of social problems, the question of marginalization takes the form, What counts as a (legitimate) way of talking problems? The question acts as a reminder of the perspectiviality of dominant ways of making claims, and suggests that some ways of raising concerns will be less successful than others. But while the social problems literature reveals little systematic discussion of marginalized social problems talk, it has shown a growing recognition that problems can be talked up in a number of ways.[3]

Several developments in the field have come together to broaden our sense of what counts as social problems talk. The first is a heightened awareness of the highly organized yet heterogeneous character of every-day life, especially the "seen but unnoticed" sphere of women and the family, which has worked to expand the study of claims-making activities beyond its initial focus on what goes on in professional people-processing institutions. Although the centrality of "public problems" to the field is still advocated by some, most sociologists see the merit in extending the study of social problems talk to what Featherstone calls "the life left behind" (Featherstone 1992, p. 160). Sometimes framed as the study of "troubles," this research has demonstrated how people struggle to achieve an account of what's objectionable in their lives long before (or at the same time as) their accounts are reformulated by professional claims-makers and official discourses (e.g., Jefferson and Lee 1981; Emerson and Messenger 1977; Smith 1987).[4]

The second factor is our richer understanding of language and the way it works. Many sociologists now take it as axiomatic that the world is unavailable to us except in language, i.e., in the ways we have to think and speak about it. This means that language is not simply an aspect of social life (a kind of behavior) but the basis of it. Definitional matters have long been seen as important in social problems research (notably in labeling theory) and more recently a different body of scholarship has demonstrated, through a wide array of substantive studies, that "the order of things" is created, sustained, and resisted discursively (e.g., Davies 1989; Gubrium and Holstein 1990; Holstein 1987; G. Miller 1991; L. Miller 1990, 1991; Smith 1987). These studies are a pointed reminder to analysts of social problems that realities are negotiated in talk.[5]

The implication of these developments for social problems theorists is that different communities of speakers will have different ways of making claims, and some of these ways will be less visible than others, as Ibarra and Kitsuse recognize. But the analysis of marginalization as a process in the social problems literature is thin.[6] One reason is that the classic early studies of marginal or deviant subcultures, while documenting insider knowledge and insider jargon, tended to emphasize the legitimate, autonomous social orders these communities displayed, rather than their marginality per se or the impact this had on their characteristic ways of raising problems. In general, these ethnographies showed that subcultural communities were hidden from the perspective of dominant groups, without showing how that invisibility was imposed, sustained, recognized, and resisted. Inspired by the conviction that the social world of the hobo or the hustler was separate but equal, this generation of researchers emphasized cultural difference, rather than domination and resistance. As a result, the features of marginalized worlds (and discourses) were not systematically connected to power—as if these worlds "just happened" to be obscure.

A second reason is the blind spot toward large-scale discourse that has handicapped the ethnomethodological contribution to social problems analysis in the 1970s and 1980s. Ethnomethodologists and conversation analysts have consistently maintained their fealty to the interaction order. While studies have been able to show how social order is achieved in routine interaction, and even how members accomplish domination and subordination in their talk—I am thinking here especially of work on gender and communication—they are unable to account for the fact that different ways of talking (including ways of talking problems) carry different degrees of authority, for these considerations would take them beyond the interactional setting into the historical conditions surrounding the emergence of large-scale hegemonic discourses (such as the institutional discourses of professional medicine, or the commonsense discourses of masculinity and femininity that rose to prominence in the nineteenth century). Ethnomethodological inattention to the insights of scholars like Foucault and Gramsci is based largely on the principled rejection of what they take to be top-down, totalizing discourses, which turn actors into cultural or linguistic dopes. But this view is misguided,[7] and has weakened their ability to offer an adequate treatment of power and marginality. These issues will be taken up elsewhere in the paper.

Finally, social problems theorists have been interested in the question, What counts as a claim? mainly as a way of defining and widening the scope of the field. In effect, the question has been treated as a (theorist's) limit, rather than a (member's) exclusionary practice to be studied. I return to this argument in a later section; for now, the point is that the study of marginalization, as a practice that silences some styles of claims-making, itself remains a marginal issue in the social problems literature.

By contrast, the discussion of marginality *outside* the social problems field is well developed, and it is a discussion that places power at the forefront. A broad scan of the contemporary theoretical scene reveals a growing interest in what we might call, in social problems parlance, "claims-making from the underside." Some sociological perspectives, notably poststructuralism and postmodernism, take their point of departure from Foucault's (1979) recommendation that we amplify the "voice of the other" by "entertain[ing] the claims to attention of local, discontinuous, disqualified, illegitimate knowledges" (Foucault, in Coles 1991, p. 110) in order to recover some sense of the power struggles that have silenced them. In social psychology we find the well-known studies of Gilligan (1982), and Belenky, Clinchy, Goldberger, and Tarule (1986), which attribute distinctive styles of moral discourse to women, ones that have been trivialized and in other ways discredited by a privileged masculine form of reasoning. In linguistics, anthropology, and sociology

there is a steadily evolving literature exploring the display and reproduction of dominant and subordinate status in talk (e.g., Lakoff 1990;
Thorne, Kramarae, and Henley 1983), a literature that puts power at the
forefront despite the aforementioned problems that accompany much
conversation analysis. Also well known are feminist analyses of "wom-
en's ailments," such as anorexia and "hysteria" in the last century,
which reformulate these conditions as women's ways of raising problems through the distinctively feminine language of body (e.g., Bordo
1989). And the current boom in cultural studies (see, for example,
Grossberg, Nelson, and Treichler 1992) is tied to a new interest in how
"the people" evade or resist dominant ideologies through their participation in popular pleasures. As Ibarra and Kitsuse observe, the theme of
"resistance from below" runs through British studies of popular culture,
where (for example) the idea that members of youth subcultures make
claims through "fashion statements" is by now a familiar one.

   What is of interest to us in these diverse studies is their commitment
to read the activities of these groups as marginalized, i.e., depoliticized
ways of raising problems. As well, they share an assumption that the
form of these activities is related in some way to the specific conditions
of oppression experienced by each group. In every case, the effect of the
analysis is to *reinstate these inaudible speakers as claimants*, thereby re-
politicizing their talk. This is done in the belief that the ways problems
are raised, including the ways they are ignored or trivialized, are members' achievements, which can and should be studied. In what follows I
shall suggest that the social problems theorist can learn much about
marginalization from these other perspectives. The salient research
questions are two: (1) How have some ways of talking problems (making
claims) emerged as privileged or normative, as others have been
eclipsed or silenced? (2) What do these processes reveal about power
and how it operates?[8]

II. The Poststructuralist Vision: All Talk Makes a Claim

   For an adequate understanding of marginalization as process, there is
no better place to turn than to the approaches that place marginalization
at the top of their theoretical agendas. I refer here to poststructuralism
and to some variants of feminist theorizing. While these perspectives are
not in agreement in all respects,[9] they do come together around their
common interest in'subjugated knowledges"—ways of saying and
knowing that have been silenced or discredited by dominant discourses
and practices. In what follows I want to explore several of their insights,
in order to indicate what should interest social problems theorists in

them, and how they make a difference to the social problems research agenda.

At the heart of the poststructuralist vision is a reconceptualization of *power*. Formerly understood as "owned" by elite groups (classes) and individuals (kings), power in a contemporary milieu is understood to exist in a host of microsites all across the social landscape as the struggle over meaning. Following the later Foucault, poststructuralists argue that if power "resides" anywhere, it is in the dominant discourses of the day. Thus power is displaced from the activities of politicians and interest groups to language, that is, to the routine encounters between those who artfully represent and reproduce the era's dominant discourses and those whose accounts of the world have been marginalized or silenced by them.

It is important to see that the Foucauldian reconceptualization of power does not work to destroy politics, but rather to politicize all talk. Because power is located at the level of saying and knowing, it infuses all, not just some, aspects of social life. "All talk is a text" means that all talk promotes a preferred account of the world, one that necessarily disqualifies other accounts. In short, *all* talk makes a claim—though not all ways of making claims will be equally valued.

The implications of this relentlessly politicized vision of social life could not be more radical for the constructionist approach to social problems. Its most important result is to undermine the very basis of social problems study as the analysis of a distinct class of phenomena, by undermining (or deconstructing) the empirical distinction between activities that make claims and those which do not. By recommending that we read all talk as a text, poststructuralism has taken the very feature of *social problems* talk that makes it special, according to the social problems theorist—its rhetorical or claims-making character—and has installed it as the characteristic feature of *all* talk.

I commented earlier on the gradual trend within the social problems li erature to widen the net of what constitutes claims-making; perhaps social problems theorists too would in time arrive at the conclusion that all talk makes a claim. At present, however, the trend moves forward in empirical, piecemeal fashion, so that first one area of social life, then another, is "discovered" to harbor claims-making activities, or social problems talk. There remain, by implication, some kinds of talk that *don't* make claims (for example, see Ibarra and Kitsuse).

The position that social problems theorists and researchers are edging up to—"Read *all* talk as a claim"—is asserted as a matter of theoretical election by poststructuralists and some schools of feminist thought. I remarked earlier that these approaches stand out for their willingness to take marginality seriously, and it is important to note here that it is precisely *the view from the margins* (what some feminists have called an "oppositional consciousness" and the "standpoint of the other") that reads claims-making (the contesting of meaning) as *the* important feature of interaction/talk. Moreover, their insights suggest that it is only from the standpoint of the powerful (from the perspective of dominant discourses) that "some" people *do not* appear to be engaged in claims-making (or to be taking moral stances), and that "some" social worlds *do not* appear to harbor "recognizable" social problems talk.

The point, of course, is Recognizable to whom? The value of the view from the margins is precisely its recognition that the "absence" of social problems talk in some situations is an achieved invisibility or marginalization—in short, a discursive accomplishment whose structure and workings can be studied. If people are always and everywhere raising matters of concern to themselves, then we can ask in what sites and with what discursive resources can talk's readability as claims-making be suppressed? Moreover, when all talk is read as making a claim, then the salient theoretical distinction is no longer between talk that makes a claim and talk that doesn't, but between the kinds of claims-making styles that are "readable at a glance," and those whose claims-making status is "unrecognized" or discredited.

It is against the background of a radically politicized landscape of meaning struggles that we can evaluate recent efforts to delimit and describe the field of social problems study. The perspective we have developed out of poststructuralist insights indicates that Ibarra and Kitsuse, for example, do not go far enough when they suggest broadening "the scope of what counts as claims-making," or when they observe how "social problems discourse occurs in all manner of forums and among a wide range of persons," for these comments continue to assume that we live in a world divided into two kinds of talk (talk that makes claims and talk that doesn't) and that even though the dividing line may be shifting, social problems analysts should accept it unproblematically and let it define the boundaries of the field.

By contrast, poststructuralism implies that what counts as a claim (or an instance of social problems talk) must be a topic of inquiry, rather than a limit to be assumed; "who qualifies" as a participant in social problems discourse is a matter negotiated among members and thus a differentiating practice to be studied, not an empirical fact or property that identifies a distinct "class of phenomena." The poststructuralist insight forces us to reexamine the markers (some) communities use to identify claims and claimants, according to Ibarra and Kitsuse, and it suggests that such markers mark only those kinds of claims-making activities that achieve visibility within the terms of some dominant discourse or system of meaning. If the kinds of rhetorical figures described by these authors (loss, crisis, etc.) are the conventional ways of making claims visible as claims, then how are marginalized claims-making activities marked? What are the vernacular features of claims-making *from the underside?*

The example that follows is meant to raise some of these issues. Unlike the kinds of conversations ordinarily analyzed by social problems theorists, this exchange is not noticeably rhetorical. I will argue that this outcome is *itself* an achieved appearance: just as there are discursive practices or strategies that politicize talk, thereby putting problems *on* the agenda, so there are strategies that depoliticize talk and keep them *off*. We shall want to examine how the depoliticization (or marginalization) of some kinds of talk is achieved, and how it is resisted (if it is). In this case, I shall be suggesting that the political character of the conversation is recessed or made invisible through a collaboration that works to deny the status of claimant to one of the speakers.

III. Depoliticizing Others' Claims: An Example

The exchange analyzed below is drawn from a British study of dual-earner households and focuses on women's decisions to return to (paid) work after the birth of their first child (Brannen and Moss 1987). The authors are interested in the persistence of the "male breadwinner ideology" and accordingly, in the ways that wives' contribution to the household economy through their wages is defined. The ideology in question says, in part, that husbands are the primary earners while women's earnings "help out," i.e., are secondary to their husbands'. The study included women who, before they left the labor force, had earned both less and more than their husbands. In this transcribed conversation, the interviewer talks with a Mr. and Mrs. Dunn, whose wages are "roughly similar":

Interviewer:	How important is the money you earn to the household/family budget?
Alice Dunn:	Oh! It helps. I don't think—well, yes it would matter if I didn't work, wouldn't it, Michael? I can't say it wouldn't. I think it's quite necessary.
Interviewer:	You see it that way?
Mr. Dunn:	(interjecting) Her money does buy the extra bits and pieces.
Alice Dunn:	(answering the interviewer's question) I do and I don't. I suppose if we really put our minds to it I wouldn't have to work, would I Michael? We could manage if we wanted to if we didn't have all the little bits.

Interviewer: Do you see your money as for extras or for the basic essentials?
Alice Dunn: (starts to do sums out loud) . . . . Well, I suppose I *was* thinking of it for basic living. If I was thinking of it *now* I suppose we could manage. I was thinking of it—
Mr. Dunn: (interjecting) We were without it for ten months!
Alice Dunn: (continuing) In my mind I was thinking we probably couldn't manage without it. I was sort of thinking about it I suppose—looking at your wage—I suppose we would have been really pushed wouldn't we? But I suppose I can't say that now. I suppose it's for luxuries and going on holidays and things—
Mr. Dunn: (interjecting) We don't spend a great deal. We don't smoke and we don't drink. We only have a car and a certain other person.
Alice Dunn: (with an air of finality) Yes, I suppose it is for luxuries! (Brannen and Moss 1987, p. 89)

In their discussion, the authors make a number of insightful comments regarding the way that the meaning of Mrs. Dunn's financial contribution is negotiated in the course of this and other conversations. They note Mrs. Dunn's initial tendency to define her wages as important, and how by the end of the excerpt, they have been firmly redefined as secondary (expendable, "for luxuries"), thus reaffirming the husband's role as primary breadwinner in accordance with the gendered division of labor prescribed by the dominant ideology. Their interest is largely in the substance of the talk.

Our interest, by contrast, is in this exchange as a site of (suppressed or marginalized) claims-making activity—in particular, in the discursive practices that succeed in keeping the issue raised by Mrs. Dunn (how to evaluate her contribution) off the conversational agenda. We should note at the outset that although poststructuralists and feminists alike would read this conversation as a site of claims-making activities, the passage displays none of the vernacular markers of social problems talk generally identified by social problems researchers. The conversation does not take place in an institutional setting (a courtroom, a doctor's office) nor is there present a professional claims-maker whose business it is to enforce a privileged version of "the problem" (e.g., as in Darrough 1990). Neither does husband or wife attempt to compare their family economy to the "family in the large"—a sign, for authors like Gubrium and Holstein (1990, pp. 61–70), that speakers agree *that* they have a problem, even as they disagree on its particular type. There is no "troubles-telling" of the sort that either Emerson and Messenger, or Jefferson and Lee describe; there is not even a discernible "problem proposal" (Maynard 1988, p. 319) that can be honored (or not) by one of the parties. And finally, though we hear indignation from the husband, we do not hear the sound of moral stances being taken as Ibarra and Kitsuse describe them: Nowhere does Mr. Dunn employ a "rhetoric of loss," for example, to inveigh against the demise of the good old-fashioned family; there are no "crisis motifs" apparent (see Ibarra and Kitsuse). In short, this stretch of talk does not look like social problems talk, for there are none of the "distinctive but conventional ways of speaking and reasoning that obtain whenever persons qualify as participants in social problems discourse" (Ibarra and Kitsuse) and it is probable that on these grounds, Ibarra and Kitsuse, among others, would disqualify it as a site of claims-making.

In contrast, the mandate of poststructuralism as I have developed it here invites us to read this exchange as any other, that is, as a *political* encounter centered in rhetoric and negotiation. It invites us, in other words, to challenge this disqualification by reading the talk as a marginalization, not an absence, of claims-making. In this case we shall want to examine how such marginalization is achieved, and how it is resisted (if it is).

To say that the conversation remains finally apolitical is to say that Mrs. Dunn is never able to seriously contest her husband's account of the familial division of labor. In particular, she is unable to formulate her resistance in a way that obliges Mr. Dunn to read it as a claim; as a result, "an intersubjective agreement that there is a 'problem' is never achieved" (Maynard 1988, p. 319). What might have shaped up as a dispute (claim, counterclaim) becomes in short order a descriptive collaboration, in which Mrs. Dunn is repositioned not as a claimant, but as an incompetent describer who tries to "get it right" over the course of the conversation ("Well, I suppose I *was* thinking of it . . . . If I was thinking of it *now*," etc.)—that is, one whose first description of herself as a equal contributor ("I think it's [her wage] quite necessary") is revealed as incorrect and then replaced by a more accurate one ("Yes, I suppose it is for luxuries!"). At the moment she is successfully constructed as an incompetent describer, her status as a claimant—one who raises a problem—is defused.

The politicizing of this exchange—the road not taken—might have occurred in several ways. Mrs. Dunn might have contested her husband's account by presenting herself as the victim of male oppression (one whose husband refuses to give her her due) and in response, Mr. Dunn might have come on as the champion of old-fashioned family values, both forms of rhetoric that work to up the moral ante of the talk (see Ibarra and Kitsuse). Or the interviewer, instead of retaining a neutral role, might have intervened in a therapeutic mode, and begun to engage the couple in the sort of categorizing work described by Gubrium and Holstein—say, by suggesting that the "Dunns' problem" around Mrs. Dunn's earnings was probably of *this* sort, rather than *that*.

But none of these scenarios occurs; the conventional account of the familial division of labor (as articulated by Mr. Dunn) never surfaces as a bone of contention. Because Mrs. Dunn is unable to halt the reformulation of her status from potential counterclaimant to "poor describer"— and indeed collaborates in it—her initial challenge to the dominant framework of meaning is rapidly absorbed back into it. As the producer of mere comments and incompetent descriptions, not claims (speech that must be heeded), Mrs. Dunn is herself effectively depoliticized, so that what she has to say is read as making no difference to the order of things.

The discursive subordination of Mrs. Dunn as a claimant is accomplished, of course, in the interactional situation. Here we are on the terrain of the conversation analyst, who would point out how Mr. Dunn's talk displays many of the features associated with the dominant "masculine" style: He interrupts Mrs. Dunn three times, a turn-taking violation disproportionately practiced by the more powerful speaker; he asserts his views in direct fashion, while his wife ruminates, equivocates, and couches her views as opinions: "I do and I don't," "I was thinking" (five times), "I suppose" (eight times). Furthermore, only Mrs. Dunn personalizes her utterances by using her husband's name (twice), and she employs three tag-questions ("Wouldn't it Michael?"), both features of subordinate talk oriented to producing the speaker as "poor wee me" (Zwarun, in Mackie 1991, p. 188).

But for the poststructuralist, marginalization is not adequately explained by referring to these kinds of linguistic practices and techniques alone. In addition, speakers are empowered by their ability to access and strategically deploy the dominant discourses of the day (as any speaker who has exploited the prestigious rhetoric of scientific sociology will readily acknowledge). This point represents a shift away from the interactional setting to the cultural repertoire of discourses that speakers invoke as resources for their interactional encounters. And while such discourses are employed in the interaction setting, it is important to remember that they are *collective* representations of reality—that is to say, they are social, not individual, facts. Mr. Dunn's disempowerment of his wife, then, is not simply a matter of the linguistic methods he employs (interruption, and so on), it is also a matter of his ability to invoke a dominant discourse (here, of the patriarchal family), which validates his account of the familial division of labor and empowers him as a speaker in crucial ways.

These considerations shed some light on the question of what it means to produce a readable or intelligible claim. A useful contribution is provided by the British researchers, whose theoretical interest in marginalized subjects requires them to "take women's accounts seriously" (Brannen and Moss 1987, p. 12)—in our terms, to read their utterances as claims, albeit failed ones. The researchers also note that silence and ambiguity are frequently the responses of women who are asked about their own contribution to the family economy. By instructing us to read these "muted responses" as interesting findings in themselves rather than as methodological obstacles (i.e., as unsuccessful claims rather than coding problems) the authors restore the talk's political character. Moreover, they imply that silence, contradiction, and so on are, we might say, the conventional vernacular markers of marginalized claims, or claims-making "from the underside."[10] Here we have the idea that the claims-making styles of subordinate groups will display distinctive, describable features, for those who are able to see and hear them. I return to this point in Section IV.

The British researchers then turn to why these "muted responses" fail as claims. They observe: "What is striking about these [women's] accounts is the absence of a clearly and confidently articulated set of codes" with which to talk about their concerns (in this case their economic contribution to the household). Here they suggest an important insight into the discursive basis of claims-making: For a comment to be heard as a claim, it must be able to draw on "a clearly and confidently articulated code" with which to talk about X. Thus the features of individual utterances (silence, ambiguity), as well as their fate (whether they will be intelligible as claims or not), are explicitly tied to the availability of discourses or "codes" at the macrolevel. This means that a claim is not just a comment: to make a claim is to be heard to be articulating an already available conventional discourse or account of the world, and to be marshalling it as a position or stance.[11] A claim relies on an authoritative discourse to give it moral and political force *as* a claim. By contrast, talk that is grounded in fragmented or marginalized discourses (or ones unavailable to the community of speakers) cannot be formulated as a recognizable stance or position, and is read as idiosyncratic or personal comment, having no political force.[12]

In the case at hand, Mr. Dunn is able to draw on the dominant discourse of the domestic patriarchal family. A large nexus of taken-for-granted beliefs about marriage, gender, and child-rearing enshrined as commonsense, its most salient feature for our purposes here is a set of paired assumptions concerning what husbands do (primary breadwinning; "helping out" at home) and what wives do (primary mother-work; "helping out" economically). Borrowing Schutz's insight, we may say that such dominant discourses are typifications that furnish the individual with categories for the ordering of reality. Such categories are shared, public formulations, and it is Mr. Dunn's ability to draw on them that gives his talk readability as a claim. For example, we the readers, the interviewer, and both Dunns are able to hear Mr. Dunn's comment "We were without it [his wife's income] for ten months" as the claim (or partisan position) "I support this family" because "everybody knows" that if they did without her income, it must have been expendable.

By contrast, an alternative discourse that might ground Mrs. Dunn's resistance as a counterclaim is not available, at least for her, as a resource upon which to draw: Her world provides no social rhetoric of equality or of women's rights—no *other way* of describing her economic role outside the dominant category of one who "helps out." In the absence of an alternative formulation, her talk is not heard as a position or stance, and is readily silenced or defused as incompetence. In sum, it is the availability of an alternative discourse (e.g., of equality) in a community's cultural repertoire—as well as the speaker's ability to marshall it in talk—that differentiates the fully articulated claim from the sound of inchoate resistance (silence, ambiguity). Insofar as Mrs. Dunn's concerns are excluded by the dominant discourse, her plight is like that of other marginalized speakers. Describing the problems of the oppressed, the novelist Gabriel Garcia Marquez has stated: "[O]ur crucial problem has been a lack of conventional means to render our lives believable. This, my friends, is the crux of our solitude" (Marquez, in Hartsock 1990, p. 25). The "means" the oppressed lack is language, not dollars or armies, and Marquez's point is that exclusionary practices are discursive at root.

There are several important implications to be drawn from this example. The first has to do with the way we understand power. Under the auspices of a poststructuralist, feminist reading of this conversation, we have asked how the denial of one of the speakers as a claimant—as the poser of a problem—is achieved. We are now in a position to see that it is the power of the dominant discourse (here, of the domestic patriarchal family)—not the interactional power of Mr. Dunn—that undermines her talk as a claim. Mrs. Dunn's ability to construct her talk as a (counter)claim (to problematize the received account as voiced by her husband) is very much constrained by the terms of the dominant discourse (the "code"), which hegemonically limits her way of knowing and speaking about her work to the categories available within the existing framework (mother-work and secondary earning). The capacity of powerful dominant discourses to ward off or preclude challenges to their fundamental assumptions or categories, and to conceal their exclusionary practices, is a favorite theme of Foucault's: In our example this power is displayed in the fact that Mrs. Dunn's resistance to the dominant discourse never attains the status of challenge, and is rapidly absorbed back into the dominant framework of meaning.[13]

The first point, then, is that the exercise of power in this situation is not adequately depicted as an oppressive interaction between a dominant husband and a resistant, yet finally subordinate wife; nor can Mrs. Dunn's prospects for raising a successful problem-proposal around the contribution of her work, or for renegotiating its meaning, be assessed by considering the *interactional* order alone. Instead, we have here a more complex collaboration between the speakers and the dominant discourse upon which they draw to make sense of the world ("what everybody knows" about family life). This discourse not only limits what kinds of claims can be made substantively—what kinds of moral stances can be taken—but also *whether* counterclaims and claimants are likely to emerge at all. Power is indeed at work in this situation, but, as Holstein has noted in connection with gender, it is not adequately conceptualized as a variable that predetermines talk (Holstein 1987). Instead, power is a matter of discourses, and it is exercised by speakers who deploy them as conversational resources to argue for preferred versions of social reality (or indeed to prevent a struggle over meaning from ever emerging). This point follows directly from Foucault's insistence that power is located first in the dominant discourses of the day, and only secondly in those who artfully use them.

The second point to note in connection with this example is the extraordinary hegemonic power of *commonsense* discourses—descriptions of reality that "go without saying." Like other discourses, they provide members with preferred ways to know and talk about the world. What sets everyday or commonsense discourses apart from others, however, is their extraordinary power to eclipse competing accounts of reality, and it has not escaped feminist scholars that some discourses, notably those of the domestic family and biological discourses of sexual difference, lie at the heart of Western culture and are perceived, accordingly, as unchallengeable, natural orders. Their unusual moral authority lies precisely in the fact that they are taken by "everyone" to be beyond dispute: As the way the world (allegedly) goes round, and ought to go round, they are accepted as objective truths outside human intervention. In contrast to professional discourses, they are more thoroughly naturalized. That is, they marginalize *other* ways of knowing and saying more completely.[14]

Professional discourses, however, make claims about the world that tend to be both less inclusive of social life and also more arguable. Thus, for example, Gale Miller notes how in exchanges between unemployed clients and staff members in a government work incentive program, clients will often be able to counter the staff member's descriptions of "the problem" "by pointing to aspects of everyday life that are deemphasized and left out of [bureaucratic discourse]" (1991, p. 10). By

contrast, the difficulty Mrs. Dunn has in countering the dominant discourse of family invoked by her husband is precisely the problem she
(and any other member) has in imagining and describing the world in
ways outside the conventional channels. This outcome is not a personal
failure of Mrs. Dunn's, but rather a testimony to the comparatively
greater hegemonic power of the commonsense discourse of family to
silence difference. Unlike the clients in the WIN program that Miller
describes, Mrs. Dunn is never able to articulate "what has been left out"
of the received framework to the point of raising a counterclaim. In
short, to say that commonsense discourses have greater hegemonic
power than professional ones is to say that they exclude "what they
leave out" more effectively.

Two consequences follow from the fact that commonsense accounts of
the world are so securely installed as "natural" orders: (1) Members, like
Mrs. Dunn, will find resisting or challenging them (i.e., voicing an alternative discourse) more difficult, and (2) social problems theorists will be
less likely to see routine everyday conversations, such as the Dunns', as
sites of social problems talk, for it is precisely at these sites that the
political character of the encounter, as a struggle between claimants, is
most thoroughly concealed. Here is where the poststructuralist research
agenda parts company from that of the social problems theorist: For
while the latter, taking the apolitical character of the talk at face value,
would likely find such sites of no interest (i.e., not sites of claims-
making), the poststructuralist, by contrast, will home in on them as sites
where the power of dominant discourses to silence resistance and to
mask the achieved character of this outcome is greatest, because it is the
most perfectly hidden.

The division of interaction into political and apolitical types, which
most social problems theorists appear to take for granted, is no doubt at
the heart of their tendency to focus on institutional claims-making activities or on well-marked encounters between partisan interest groups in
the public sphere, for it is these kinds of encounters (e.g., between
ordinary citizens and parole officers, or between pro– and anti–gay
rights groups) that are most easily readable as claims-making activities.
But for the poststructuralist, these are only the most obvious sites of
conversational politics. By focusing only or primarily on meaning struggles in these sites, the theorist risks leaving intact "the regions where the
logic of exclusion disguises its operations more completely" (Kamuf
1990, p. 106).[15]

As I argued earlier, the force of the poststructuralist perspective as I
have developed it here is to challenge this division. Social problems
theorists appear to treat it as a natural feature of the world, rather than
as an achievement whose workings they must analyze. While this per-

spective allows them to mark off for themselves a distinct field of study (with a mandate to study social problems talk, rather than *all* talk) it also means that they will miss (i.e., read as not political) a whole range of interaction whose political character as an exchange of claims is marginalized (rendered invisible, denied, concealed). Moreover, it blinds them to an important insight about discursive power: Power is exercised not only in the reality struggles between claims-makers, but also in sites where these struggles have been silenced.

If, as the poststructuralist argues, *all* talk involves struggles over meaning, then instead of a division between political and nonpolitical talk, we must posit a continuum, at one end of which are claims-making activities that are easily readable as such, and at the other, those which are marginalized (primarily because the status of claimant is refused or concealed). Moreover, *where* a given exchange will fall on this continuum is not a natural feature of talk, but an achievement that will depend on members' artful use of discursive resources and strategies. This view recognizes that the hegemonic power of particular discourses and speakers to exclude or silence counterclaims (competing accounts of the world) will vary, and that a speaker's ability to voice alternative accounts in given situations—to resist or contest dominant meanings—will range from the confident articulation of partisan positions and counterpositions (over abortion, nuclear power, and so on) to the inchoate styles of resistance such as that of Mrs. Dunn, in whose comments a claim is barely audible. But whether resistance emerges as a fully developed counterclaim or is marginalized to the point of inaudibility, the poststructuralist perspective will read speakers as on all occasions *negotiating* what the order of things is, and how it should be.

This is the bottom-line assumption that gives poststructuralism the edge over other perspectives when it comes to theorizing marginality. It is the source of its appeal for feminists as well. In this connection then, it may be useful to briefly compare poststructuralist and ethnomethodological perspectives in order to assess their relative contributions to the analysis of marginalization. As I have emphasized, ethnomethodologists must broaden their conception of members' methods and resources to include large-scale discourses that influence the ways interaction is accomplished, but do not have their origin there—and they must do so in a way that does not reduce speakers to the puppets of these macro-level forces.[16] An exclusive focus on the "interaction order" as conversation analysts understand this term (that is, on turn-taking, and other features stemming from the Sacks-Schegloff corpus) will never tell us, for example, why a chat about finances between working-class women at the laundromat is discredited as "gossip," while the same matters taken up in the legislature are valorized as "debate," whatever

other linguistic similarities these two exchanges display. Nor will broadening their analysis to include these social facts require the eth-
nomethodologist to step outside the realm of members' knowledge, for
members are demonstrably aware of these differences and orient to
them in their own talk. Members (tacitly) recognize these social facts as
important components of marginality;[17] so then should conversation
analysts. In contrast, the appeal of poststructuralism for feminists lies
partly in its willingness to recognize how dominant discourses (or "ideologies") have been able, historically and at present, to depoliticize whole
styles of saying and knowing, and whole communities of speakers.

Beyond this, there is a second difference. As I noted in Section I, an
important strength of the ethnomethodological approach is its commitment to agency, that is, to a strong version of members as artful reality
constructors. Each interaction is understood as the opportunity for the
situational accomplishment of the phenomenon at hand; the Dunns, for
example, are seen as jointly accomplishing dominance and subordination in the course of their talk. Thus, it is important to reiterate that from
this perspective, the features of the exchange (violations of turn-taking
order, and so on) are not understood as a *result* of differential power (or
gender), but rather as an instance of power *enacted*. If power is understood as the ability to have one's position heard, then Mr. Dunn interac-
tionally achieves this, while Mrs. Dunn does not.[18]

This way of understanding the issue brings into relief an important
difference between ethnomethodological and poststructural assumptions about the nature of action. For where the conversation analyst sees
Mrs. Dunn as actively accomplishing her subordination, the poststructuralist would see her as actively (albeit ineffectively) resisting or contesting it. By declaring that *all* interaction is essentially about struggles
over meaning, the poststructuralist transforms the documents of Mrs.
Dunn's subordination (her silences, her tag-questions) into evidence of
her resistance. In short, ethnomethodology formulates actors as *constructors of order*; the poststructuralist reads them as *constructors of power
and resistance*.

This is a difference at the level of theoretical assumptions, not an
empirical matter. And in the move from order-constructor to contester,
the poststructuralist gives the concept of action/speech a political spin
that amounts to a more proactive conception of agency than is possible
under the ethnomethodological agenda. For the poststructuralist, talk is
not just work (in the ethnomethodological sense of an achievement), it is
adversarial work. Whether it succeeds or fails in its claim, talk promotes
its version of the world against some other: Every apparently settled
order conceals a reality struggle. The appeal of this position for members
of marginalized groups is obvious, and the poststructuralist's radically

politicized assumptions about the nature of action has made it an important drawing card for feminist scholars and activists. As Nancy Fraser remarks in her assessment of the utility of the poststructuralist approach for feminism, "even under conditions of subordination . . . . conflict and contestation are an important part of the story" (Fraser 1992, p. 54).

IV. Claims-Making from the Underside

I have suggested to this point that the poststructuralist's relentless politicizing of interaction opens up new areas of interest for the sociologists of social problems, by drawing their attention to those conversational sites and practices that recess the political character of talk. Our analysis of the Dunns' conversation is meant to highlight the discursive strategies Mr. Dunn employs that work to depoliticize the conversation by, in effect, depoliticizing his wife (i.e., by "refusing" to formulate her talk as a counterclaim to the dominant framework of meaning).

The silencing of potential claims-making activities or problem proposals as "just talk"—talk that makes no difference—is a fate that may befall not only subordinate individuals, like Mrs. Dunn, but also whole groups, whose typical ways of raising concerns come to be discredited or excluded by dominant or privileged claims-making styles. Consider, for example, *gossip*, originally a term referring to a child's male "godsib," now used to refer to the idle chatter of "old women" (Rysman 1977). Insights from feminist thought would invite us to consider gossip as, perhaps, a "women's way" of talking, a historically marginalized way of discussing problems now denied (i.e., "unrecognizable") as a claims-making style at all.

One of our concerns as theorists will be in how the marginalization of certain claims-making styles has been achieved,[19] and the example of gossip reminds us that their present status has a social history that can be traced. The marginalization of styles and speakers is not a creation of interactants in the course of their talk, except concretely. Instead, it is the outcome of historical processes that, in the case of gossip, saw male discourses of rationality and generality in the public sphere become the privileged standard of serious political exchange, against which the female, home-centered, personal, and anecdotal exchange would come to be discredited as "nothing but gossip," i.e., no "real" contest of viewpoints, no "real" expression of moral stances, no "real" negotiation of troubles—only idle chatter about who beats who in the neighborhood, who cannot make ends meet and why, and so on. From the standpoint of the dominant discourse of public-sphere discussion and argument then, *gossip* is a term which silences a local, anecdotal, and feminine style of claims-making by denying its character as "real" social problems talk. Its history, we suspect, is intimately bound into the major event of the early modern era—the cultural separation of the world of male, paid work (the public sphere) from the female world of family and unpaid work (the private sphere), and the inferior status that was ascribed to the latter.[20]

We take it that it is just this kind of moral discourse that Ibarra and Kitsuse mean to alert us to, when they discuss claims-making styles we may overlook if we take state- and media-sponsored styles as the standard (see Ibarra and Kitsuse on "subcultural style" and on "rapping"). *Our* point however—the poststructuralist point—is that it is not enough to note that these are "unique" or "local" ways of commenting on the world; we must recognize in addition that their distinctive features are the products of a marginalizing or discrediting process.[21] Gossip, I have argued, (like "black English") is not a neutral term describing a simply local way of talking problems; it is a term for *inadequate* talk. The term *gossip* is thus an expression of power, and it is applied as a way of discrediting one style of claims-making from the perspective of another, historically privileged one. And as a *style*, it is marked by that history of discredit. This is only to say that an inventory of claims-making styles will be no more than an inventory unless we examine the relationship between style and power. Some ways of making claims are more authoritative than other ways, and an important strategy for retaining privilege will be to deny other styles (such as gossip) the status of claims-making activities at all.

V. Underdog Skills: Managing the Readability of Claims

The relationship between style and power becomes clearer when we see how historically marginalized styles can be adopted by subordinate groups as *strategies* of influence. Such groups may use "underdog" styles (e.g., rapping) to press their claims, whatever the topic, and this may include masking (suppressing, concealing) their readability *as* claims in the first place, since overt claims-making talk (framed as loss, crisis, etc., as Ibarra and Kitsuse point out) is conventionally identifiable by all as a contest of viewpoints (that is, as *political*) and thus inevitably brings the struggle for power into the open. Accordingly, underdogs may use particular styles to raise a concern while recessing its contentious appearance—perhaps, by *avoiding* the very rhetorics Ibarra and Kitsuse describe. Damning with faint praise, for example, or kidding might be theorized as a style of claims-making used by subordinate speakers (wives, children, employees, colonized peoples) when pressing a claim with a superior group. Like rapping or gossip, these are styles that can artfully be used by speakers when they wish to make a claim without overtly appearing to do so; in such cases "the peace is kept" precisely because the matter of a problem (e.g., "Whitey's oppression of ghetto youth") never surfaces in an unambiguous or accusatory way.[22]

This does not mean that claims-making is absent, from the theorist's point of view, but only that people know that overt, "readable-at-a-glance" social problems talk is recognizably contentious, that it involves moral positions and the conflict of viewpoints, and that knowing this, people raise problems *as problems* only when they feel they can afford to. I am suggesting here that underdogs are skilled in playing—in managing—the readability of their claims. Recessing the political character of one's talk by making it appear, ambiguously, as kidding or only music (that is, as harmless) can be a protective strategy of use to individuals and groups who speak from a position of structural inequality in the system. Part of the difference between an established civil rights organization and a rap group is that one can afford to take a partisan position on matters of concern and be seen to do so, while the other, more vulnerable, may expediently adopt a style not so unambiguously readable as a claim. Thus underdogs are always able to depoliticize their talk by playing off the possibility that it is really something else ("only music").[23] The artfulness of underdog styles, then, cannot be fully appreciated until this strategy is recognized as a feature of their marginalized position (or history); and the artful manipulation of talk's ambiguity— now you see a claim, now you don't—is part of the appearance-work that marginalized speakers are skilled in.

In the foregoing I have begun to consider the ways historically/culturally marginalized styles of claims-making may be strategically taken up by individuals in microsettings. I have suggested that some groups have learned to exploit a marginalized claims-making style—in effect, a legacy of subordination—by turning it into a strategy for achieving specific conversational ends. Thus the strategic use of different claims-making styles, from "just gossip" or kidding, to the openly accusatory styles favored by protest movements, is also a careful manipulation of talk's degree of politicality. The artful use of such styles displays a concerted orientation to the political consequences of framing a claim in this way, rather than that.

The main point, then, is that claims-making styles are systematically related to power; to ignore this is to reduce the artful, concerted manipulation of the political tenor of talk to accident or incompetence. The political status of talk (whether it is or it isn't a claim) is not a natural feature of the world, but a discursive accomplishment; by using strategies that are available to them in the cultural repertoire, speakers are able to endow their talk with a political character, to mask that character, or to deny it in the talk of others. In this way, some talk is *produced* as "social problems talk" and some is not.

The concept of underdog skills—power from the underside—has received some attention in other theoretical quarters and is of real importance to social problems theorists. Almost a decade ago the sociologist Jean Lipman-Blumen introduced the term "micromanipulation" to describe the techniques of power used by subordinate groups to survive, and to exert influence, "in a world fashioned by the dominant group's definitions, rules, rewards and punishments" (Lipman-Blumen 1984, p. 30). According to Lipman-Blumen, members of low-power groups (notably women and children) spend many years "learning the underside of power relationships, including the techniques of micromanipulation," while members of dominant groups (here, adult males) are able, in general, to assert their demands directly ("macromanipulation"). While Lipman-Blumen's discussion of micromanipulation does not focus exclusively on discursive strategies, students of social problems will find much of interest in her brief discussion:

> Restricted to micromanipulation, women, as well as other powerless groups, become well versed in interpreting the unspoken intentions, even the body language, of the powerful. They learn to anticipate their governors' behaviour, to evoke as well as smother pleasure, anger, joy and bafflement in their rulers, to charm, to outsmart, even to dangle the powerful over the abyss of desire and anguish. By the various interpersonal strategies of micromanipulation, women have learned to sway and change, circumvent, and subvert the decisions of the powerful to which they seemingly have agreed. They know when to observe the rules the dominant group has created. Women have also mastered how to "obey without obeying" those rules they find overly repressive. When necessary they cooperate with men to maintain the mirage of male control. (p. 30)

Micromanipulation, then, is the way of the fox, not the lion (p. 31). Some of these techniques might include playing the fool (thus creating the appearance of acquiescence or unseriousness, e.g., the "dumb blonde," the Uncle Tom) and strategies of withholding (of love, sex, or conversation; the "silent treatment"). In a similar vein Haraway observes that the knowledges of the dominated are "'savvy to modes of denial' including repression, forgetting, and disappearing" (Haraway, in Hartsock 1990, p. 30). For our purposes, the key to all such strategies is the way actors learn to manipulate the political appearance of their practices; underdogs are especially attentive to talk's politicality because they *have* to be. Like rap musicians who can depoliticize their comments on the world by framing them as "only music," the underdogs Lipman-Blumen discusses have learned to use micromanipulative techniques to raise problems that contest the dominant order of things without overtly appearing to do so.

Related insights into the workings of power from the underside can be found in the work of such very different writers as the French philosopher de Certeau, who differentiates between "tactics" and "strategies" much as Lipman-Blumen does between micro- and macromanipulation (de Certeau 1984; esp. Ch. III), and the American historian Robert Darnton, whose reading of French peasant folk-tales (e.g., Tom Thumb/Le Petit Poucet) emphasizes the hero's survival by the use of his wits—"the only defence," says Darnton, "of the 'little people' against the rapacity of the big" (1984, p. 42).[24]

In calling these strategies, these authors all make the assumption that power, no matter how unequally distributed, is always a negotiation—a two-way street—but that the negotiating styles of under- and topdogs are likely to be different. In short, they all imply that the ways claims are shaped (their styles) will be related to the power distribution in the community, though not in mechanical ways. Unlike Ibarra and Kitsuse, for example, who mention such styles (e.g., the comic approach) but do not see them as the ways power or the lack of it can be inflected, the feminist scholars, de Certeau, Darnton, and others are very clear that certain describable ways of raising matters of concern are not merely "subcultural" styles but *subordinate* ones (see Houston and Kramarae 1991 and Troemel-Ploetz 1991). A tactic, says de Certeau," is determined by the absence [*sic*] of power just as a strategy is organized by the postulation of power," and likens the use of tactics to the art of the Sophists who, according to Aristotle, adopted "procedures . . . . which perverted the order of truth" (1984, p. 38).

Once again it is important to remember that in labeling these styles "subordinate," I do not argue that members of subordinate groups will everywhere and always talk like this. Maynard is quite right to conclude that this is *not* the way power and speech are related (1988, p. 317). Although some feminist scholars seem to hold that literary style, for example, will "reflect" the oppositional consciousness of their oppressed authors in a direct way, there is no simple correspondence between talk and consciousness, knowledge, or social conditions. Underdog strategies are learned and deployed by underdog groups, but they may also be used by topdogs who find themselves in underdog situations (e.g., males working for female bosses) as well as by topdogs in topdog situations who may resort to underdog styles to soften the blow when dealing with subordinates (as, for example, when the boss raises an employee's problem of poor work habits with a joke, instead of making the claim in a more direct confrontational way). In principle, these styles are available in the cultural repertoire to all competent members as part of their tacit knowledge (that is, as resources not topics); whether they are deployed and by whom is an empirical matter. We readily acknowledge the importance of the ethnomethodological insistence on the artfulness of members, as any theorist must who adopts the concept of "strategy."[25] Nevertheless, such strategies are born out of hierarchical systems; they bear the marks of power and members orient to that fact in their use.[26]

VI. Conclusions

In this paper I have taken Ibarra and Kitsuse's recent programmatic statement on social problems analysis as an occasion to consider the phenomenon of marginalized social problems talk. In the final section I want to summarize the major contribution the poststructuralist perspective makes to a constructionist sociology of social problems. It has to do with power.

Poststructuralism's most important contribution is to invite systematic consideration of marginalized (or invisible) claims-making activities, an area to which sociologists of social problems have given little sustained attention. Instead they have focused on talk that is "readable at a glance" as social problems talk. Despite their recognition of gray areas, marginal cases, and so on, most social problems theorists agree in practice that social problems talk, as claims-making activity, is identifiable as a distinct class of activity and it is this they should study. Here they hold that whether a remark is a claim or not can be decided by appealing to *members' decisions* on the matter (much as Spector and Kitsuse do when they decide that the disruptive student's eccentric diatribe on the post office in Eastern religions class is not a claim; Spector and Kitsuse [1977] 1987, pp. 80–81). The sociologist says, in effect: Members didn't grant it status as a claim, so we have no interest in it; if they had, it would have been another story. Like many other social problems theorists, Spector and Kitsuse treat the "fact" that this was not a claim as a feature of the natural order—it is or it isn't—rather than as a members' achievement to be analyzed. But in taking this tack, they have adopted a members' gloss as their own. As a result, they close themselves off from a systematic look at claims-making styles in their less visible forms.[27]

By contrast, the later Foucault and the poststructuralists have put marginalized ways of saying and knowing in the spotlight. By raising the issue of marginalized claims-making styles, poststructuralism makes it possible for the social problems theorist to draw on a diverse body of work in feminist literary theory, cultural studies, and elsewhere, which all display an interest in power from the underside. Some scholars argue that oppressed groups are structurally restricted to marginalized discursive styles and are fated never to be heard; others suggest that "underdog" styles become part of the cultural lore, to be used by both dominant and subordinate groups, but always in the (tacit) knowledge that their use carries a legacy of discredit.[28] Both lines of thought are fruitful directions for the sociologists of social problems to pursue.

Above all, the poststructuralist approach emphasizes (discursive) power, and serves as a reminder to the social problems theorist that speakers are attentive to the political consequences of their different claims-making styles. The difference this point makes to the analysis of claims-making can be readily seen if we consider Ibarra and Kitsuse's brief discussion of the comic style. According to these authors, "comic styles represent interesting problems of claim-readability inasmuch as the esthetic imperative of making a good joke can come into conflict with the practical goal of building a constituency." Here the writers make reference to the fact that a claim in the comic style, if it is good comedy, runs the risk of being read as no claim at all ("just a joke"). In short, comedy mutes the political appearance of a claim. For Ibarra and Kitsuse, this "problem" is treated as something interesting, but incidental—an unintended consequence, as it were, of the use of the comic style. I have argued instead that this "problem" (i.e., the utterance's ambiguity) is an important feature of the member's discursive strategy, and that underdogs in particular (children, employees, wives—like the King's fool) will be drawn to such equivocal or muted ways of voicing their concerns as protective strategies. Furthermore, studies in other fields of scholarship suggest that this is only one in a large repertoire of underdog strategies for use in the conversational politics of everyday life. At the macrolevel, the relevant research question is: Which claims-making styles have been privileged, which marginalized? And at the microlevel: How are they used as strategies (in what situations, and by whom)? Questions like these can form the foundation of a politics of social problems talk.

In sum, the view from the margins tells us that apparently settled accounts of the world are never entirely settled, that dominant discourses are always being contested, whether as clearly visible confrontations between claimants and counterclaimants, or as "depoliticized" encounters between claimants whose status as claimants has been defused. In either case, exclusion is a member's (discursive) practice, and thus a legitimate object of study, i.e., one that does not require the theorist to rewrite or "correct" the member's agenda. From its inception the field of social problems study has made an important place for questions of power and injustice. We should not like to see these concerns abandoned. Poststructuralist insights into marginalization show us one way to bring power back in.

Acknowledgments

The author gratefully acknowledges the editors' valuable comments and suggestions on an earlier draft of this paper.

Notes

1. See Haraway's (1988) discussion of "situated knowledges." A widely known study of marginalized knowledges from a feminist perspective is *Women's Ways of Knowing* (Belenky et al. 1986). For a thorough review of the issue of "epistemic standpoints" (and the standpoint of science), see Harding (1986, esp. Chs. 6 and 7).

2. The most widespread example of marginalization within conventional sociology is the persistent debunking of commonsense knowledge and terminology in favor of the allegedly more precise and accurate concepts and terms of professional social science. Comparisons between commonsense and sociological discourse are a perennial feature of introductory textbooks, usually in an attempt to entice novice students into a greater interest in how the world "really" is.

3. It is important to remember that I am speaking here of the marginalization or "invisibility" of *ways of talking,* not social conditions (or "unconstructed problems").

4. Although Smith's work de-emphasizes the independence of members' mundane formulations, and highlights instead the degree to which their accounts of troubles or problems (e.g., the accounts of mothers) are colonized almost from the start by official state-sponsored categories (Smith 1987).

5. Maynard (1988) provides a good summary of the implications of new language studies for social problems analysis, but inexplicably omits any discussion of Foucault.

6. Exceptions are Pfohl and Gordon's (1986) deconstructionist reading of the history of social science discourse in deviance and criminology, and the work of Dorothy Smith and Alison Griffith on school children, in Smith (1987).

7. See in this connection Fraser's (1992) discussion of French discourse theories.

8. These questions are much the same as those identified by Joan W. Scott as salient for feminist theory; I have adapted her formulation to a social problems context (Scott 1990, p. 135).

9. For an example of feminist criticism that rejects Foucault but is very much interested in marginalization, see Hartsock (1990). And for a consideration of why feminists should reject structuralism for poststructuralism, see Fraser (1992).

10. See in this connection Etter-Lewis's discussion of omission, euphemism, and indirect speech ("keeping quiet"), and other related papers in this special issue entitled *Women Speaking from Silence* (1991, p. 434).

11.   Here we are suggesting that discourses offer a way of hearing "mere comments" as claims. Thus, for example, prolifers will claim, "Abortion is [a case of] murder." Similarly, the complaints of native peoples are elevated to claims once they are hitched to recognizable discourses of "distinct societies," or "guardians of the Earth."

12.   This consideration suggests a different take on the theme of "private troubles and public problems," which crops up frequently in the feminist literature. Feminists usually argue that getting women's private troubles recognized as public problems is a matter of recognizing that they are shared concerns (thus addressing the issue of isolation), and of successfully placing them on a *political* agenda. The discursive reformulation of the issue implied here is that a (private, personal) utterance becomes a readable claim (a public problem) when it becomes empowered by an authoritative discourse.

13.   In this connection see Coles's discussion of the normalizing of Hercule Barbin's difference, and Foucault's remark that this is the "first form of subjection" characteristic of Western thought (in Coles 1991, pp. 102–3.

14.   For an analysis of the resilience of one such commonsense discourse, the social rhetoric of the harmonious family, see L. Miller (1990).

15.   In this passage Kamuf is, in fact, berating some feminist scholars (not social problems theorists) for restricting their analysis of women's exclusion to institutional power; nevertheless, the argument as a whole is relevant to the field of social problems studies.

16.   Here again, the work of Dorothy Smith and Alison Griffith on mothers and the school system is exemplary.

17.   As studies of members' creative "code switching" show. See Houston and Kramerae (1991, pp. 395–96) for a brief discussion of this phenomenon.

18.   This point I owe to Jim Holstein.

19.   Unlike some feminist scholars, my primary concern here is not to resuscitate marginalized styles in order to argue that they should be revalued. The immediate goal is to understand the *process* of marginalization, and second, to analyze members' artful *use* of historically marginalized claims-making styles.

20.   This conjecture is supported by the fact that social control in the premodern world is largely informal, and that gossip, which threatens the individual's good reputation, is an important social curb in a small world. For a discussion of the feminization and demise of informal strategies of social control, see L. Miller (1987).

21.   See in this connection Hartsock's discussion of the characteristic features of fiction produced by writers who are members of marginal groups (Hartsock 1990). For a discussion of the tendency to read the political out of the analysis by treating discursive styles as "different" (rather than super/subordinate), see Troemel-Ploetz (1991).

22.   On this reading, the wives interviewed by Brannen and Moss use silence, contradiction, and so forth as strategies of influence over their (structurally more powerful) husbands while minimizing the risk of open conflict. However, Mrs. Dunn's strategy, in this exchange at least, does not seem to shift the status quo in any way. For an elaboration of this idea, see the discussion of micromanipulation (below).

23.   This is of course a risky strategy, since it can also be used by members of powerful groups to *dismiss* the claims of subordinates (as Mr. Dunn does to his wife). Hebdige's (1979) well-known study of the ways entrenched interests neutralize the resistance of youth subcultures shows how real this risk is.

24.   Darnton's essay offers a number of other suggestive insights into power from the underside, including the idea that the "view from below" can detect "no discernible morality" in the dominant system (feudalism, in Darnton's context), and that underdog strategies, such as those of Le Petit Poucet or Jack-and-the-Beanstalk, represent holding strategies or orientations to the system, rather than resistance to it. Danton also argues a cultural thesis on the French character: specifically, that the French are still trying to "outwit the system" rather than to change it, that this characteristic orientation to the world sets them apart from the Germans and the British, and that it is reflected in distinctive French versions of these widespread folk-tales. Another case study of peasant strategies of power from the underside—this time from within the social problems literature—is found in Brown 1987.

25.   There are other theoretical perspectives (e.g., rational-choice theory) that occasionally employ the concept of "strategy." However, they are usually interested in locating predictors of action, and so violate the ethnomethodological insight we want to retain (and without which the notion of strategy is emptied of value), that is, that strategies are always *situated* accomplishments, which will require us to consult interaction. Writers like Darnton and de Certeau preserve a sense of situated accomplishment, in the notion of "wits"; presumably, one can only live by one's wits if one is finely attuned to the shifting demands of the situation. But these theorists ascribe "wits" disproportionately to underdogs, on the assumption that underdogs have few other power resources at their disposal. This sets them apart from ethnomethodologists, for whom "wits" (artfulness) is an essential feature of all members, regardless of their position in the social hierarchy. In general, I would argue that the affinities between the now popular concept of strategy and the older ethnomethodological concept of artfulness invite a more systematic look, and that some approaches that employ the concept of strategy (e.g., social historians of women and the family; see Anderson 1980, Ch. 4) owe a debt to ethnomethodological insights that they fail to recognize.

26.   I use the term *orient* deliberately here, to indicate that members will use underdog styles (humor, gossip, and so forth) without *conscious* awareness of their status as marginalized. Nevertheless, this social fact is part of their tacit knowledge; if a comment is described as "just gossip," "everyone knows" that this label acts to discredit it as something to be taken seriously.

27.   This is partly rectified in Ibarra and Kitsuse's later formulation (this volume), wherein they take up the question of different claims-making styles.

28.   It is important to remember that a "legacy of discredit" is not inherent in a style of claims-making; it is entirely likely that some styles will shed their marginal status over time, much as the subcultural symbols of resistance Hebdige describes (e.g., punk fashions) lose their legacy of discredit as they are taken up—commercialized and sanitized—by the mainstream (Hebdige 1979).

References

Andersen, Michael. 1980. *Approaches to the History of the Western Family, 1500–1914.* London: Macmillan.
Belenky, Mary Field, Blythe McVicker Clinchy, Nancy Rule Goldberger, and Jill Mattuck Tarule. 1986. *Women's Ways of Knowing: The Development of Self, Voice and Mind.* New York: Basic Books.

Bordo, Susan R. 1989. "The Body and the Reproduction of Femininity: A Feminist Appropriation of Foucault." Pp. 13–33 in *Gender/Body/Knowledge: Feminist Reconstructions of Being and Knowing*, edited by Alison M. Jaggar and Susan R. Bordo. New Brunswick and London: Rutgers University Press.

Brannen, Julia and Peter Moss. 1987. "Dual Earner Households: Women's Financial Contribution After the Birth of the First Child." Pp. 75–95 in *Give and Take in Families: Studies in Resource Distribution*, edited by Julia Brannen and Gail Wilson. London: Allen and Unwin.

Brown, Julie V. 1987. "Peasant Survival Strategies in Late Imperial Russia: The Social Uses of the Mental Hospital." *Social Problems* 34:311–29.

Coles, Romand. 1991. "Foucault's Dialogical Artistic Ethos." *Theory, Culture and Society* 8:99–120.

Darnton, Robert. 1984. "Peasants Tell Tales: The Meaning of Mother Goose." Pp. 9–72 in *The Great Cat Massacre and Other Episodes in French Cultural History*, by Robert Darnton. New York: Basic Books.

Darrough, William D. 1990. "Neutralizing Resistance: Probation Work as Rhetoric." Pp. 163–87 in *Perspectives on Social Problems*, Vol. 2, edited by G. Miller and J. A. Holstein. Greenwich, CT: JAI Press.

Davies, Bronwyn. 1989. *Frogs and Snails and Feminist Tales: Preschool Children and Gender.* Sydney: Allen and Unwin.

de Certeau, Michel. 1984. *The Practice of Everyday Life.* Berkeley and Los Angeles: University of California Press.

Emerson, Robert M. and Sheldon L. Messinger. 1977. "The Micro-Politics of Trouble." *Social Problems* 25:121–35.

Etter-Lewis, Gwendolyn. 1991. "Standing Up and Speaking Out: African American Women's Narrative Legacy." *Discourse and Society* 2:425–37. (Special issue entitled Women Speaking from Silence.)

Featherstone, Mike. 1992. "The Heroic Life and Everyday Life." *Theory, Culture and Society* 9:159–82.

Foucault, Michel. 1979. *Discipline and Punish: The Birth of the Prison.* New York: Vintage.

Fraser, Nancy. 1992. "The Uses and Abuses of French Discourse Theories for Feminist Politics." *Theory, Culture and Society* 9:51–71.

Gilligan, Carol. 1982. *In A Different Voice.* Cambridge, MA: Harvard University Press.

Griffith, Alison I. and Dorothy E. Smith. 1991. "What Did You Do in School Today?" Pp. 3–24 in *Perspectives on Social Problems*, Vol. 2, edited by G. Miller and J. A. Holstein, Greenwich, CT: JAI Press.

Grossberg, Lawrence, Cary Nelson, and Paula Treichler (eds.). 1992. *Cultural Studies.* New York and London: Routledge, Chapman and Hall.

Gubrium, Jaber F. and James A. Holstein. 1990. *What Is Family?* Mountainview, CA: Mayfield.

Haraway, Donna. 1988. "Situated Knowledges: The Science Question in Feminism and the Privilege of Partial Perspective." *Feminist Studies* 14:575–99.

Harding, Sandra. 1986. *The Science Question in Feminism.* Ithaca and London: Cornell University Press.

Hartsock, Nancy. 1990. "Postmodernism and Political Change: Issues for Feminist Theory." *Cultural Critique* 13:15–33.

Hebdige, Dick. 1979. *Subculture: The Meaning of Style.* London and New York: Methuen.
Holstein, James A. 1987. "Producing Gender Effects on Involuntary Mental Hospitalization." *Social Problems* 34:141–55.
Houston, Marsha and Cheris Kramarae (eds.). 1991. *Women Speaking from Silence.* (Special issue of *Discourse and Society,* Vol. 2.)
Jefferson, Gail and John R. E. Lee. 1981. "The Rejection of Advice: Managing the Problematic Convergence of 'Troubles-Telling' and a 'Service Encounter'." *Journal of Pragmatics* 5:399–422.
Kamuf, Peggy. 1990. "Replacing Feminist Criticism." Pp. 105–11 in *Conflicts in Feminism,* edited by Marianne Hirsch and Evelyn Fox Keller. New York and London: Routledge.
Lakoff, Robin Tolmach. 1990. *Talking Power: The Politics of Language.* New York: Basic Books.
Lipman-Blumen, Jean. 1984. *Gender Roles and Power.* Englewood Cliffs, NJ: Prentice-Hall.
Mackie, Marlene. 1991. *Gender Relations in Canada.* Toronto and Vancouver: Butterworths.
Maynard, Douglas W. 1988. "Language, Interaction and Social Problems." *Social Problems* 35:311–34.
Miller, Gale. 1991. *Enforcing the Work Ethic.* Albany, NY: SUNY Press.
Miller, Leslie J. 1987. "Uneasy Alliance: Women as Agents of Social Control." *Canadian Journal of Sociology* 12:345–61.
———. 1990. "Family Violence and the Rhetoric of Harmony." *British Journal of Sociology* 41:263–88.
Pfohl, Stephen and Avery Gordon. 1986. "Criminological Displacements: A Sociological Deconstruction." *Social Problems* 33:94–113.
Rysman, Alexander. 1977. "How the 'Gossip' Became a Woman." *Journal of Communication* 27:176–80.
Scott, Joan W. 1990. "Deconstructing Equality-Versus-Difference: Or, the Uses of Poststructuralist Theory for Feminism." Pp. 134–48 in *Conflicts in Feminism,* edited by Marianne Hirsch and Evelyn Fox Keller. New York and London: Routledge.
Smith, Dorothy E. 1987. *The Everyday World as Problematic: A Feminist Sociology.* Toronto: University of Toronto Press.
Spector, Malcolm and John I. Kitsuse. [1977] 1987. *Constructing Social Problems.* Hawthorne, NY: Aldine de Gruyter.
Thorne, Barrie, Cheris Kramarae, and Nancy Henley (eds.). 1983. *Language, Gender and Society.* Cambridge, MA: Newbury House.
Troemel-Ploetz, Senta. 1991. "Selling the Apolitical." Review of Tannen, Deborah, *You Just Don't Understand. Discourse and Society* 2:489–502.

9

Social Constructionism in Critical Feminist Theory and Research

Michal M. McCall

Social constructionism in sociology is not limited to the "social constructionist perspective on social problems." It also includes the so-called
labeling theory of deviance, the case study tradition in fieldwork research, and symbolic interactionism, the conceptual framework most
fieldworkers have used. Sociologists have studied the social construction of social problems and deviance, but also careers and work routines,
communities, drug overdoses, art, scientific facts, and more.

Two major problems have plagued this kind of work. The first problem is made up of positivist sociologists' questions about the "generalizability" of findings based on fieldwork studies of one or a few cases,
along with the traditional fieldworkers' response. The problematic response is that comparative analyses of communities, occupations, and
other forms of social organization and natural histories of social problems, deviance, and other social processes are valid ways of generalizing
from single cases. For example, in one of the methodological chapters of
his *Sociological Work*, Becker said:

> In a natural-history analysis of [a] process we strip away the historical
> uniqueness of a number of instances of the same phenomenon, leaving as
> our result the generic steps in the process—those steps that would always
> occur if the same result were to be found. Similarly, in a case study of
> social structure we strip away what is historically unique and concentrate
> on the generic properties of the group, viewed as an example of a particu-
> lar kind of structure. For instance, one might study a prison or school with
> a view to discovering what the characteristic statuses and forms of interac-
> tion are in an institution in which one class of participants is present
> involuntarily. The result would be a model that might also be applied to
> other institutions having that characteristic, such as mental hospitals.
> . . . . Every case study allows us to make generalizations about the rela-
> tions of the various phenomena studied. But, as has often been pointed

out, one case is after all only one case. . . . . [However,] the problem is not
a real one if we take a long-term view of the development of theory. Each
study can develop the role of a different set of conditions or variables as
these are found to vary in the setting of the study. Over a series of studies,
the comparison of variations in conditions and consequences can provide
a highly differential theory of the phenomenon under study. (1977, pp. 82–
84)

The second problem is this: Symbolic interactionists have typically
studied the social construction of meanings independent of specific economic and political forms of organization. Because we have customarily
worked comparatively, taking our examples from and intending that our
generalizations be applied to societies as diverse as the Trobriand Is-
lands and the United States (see Becker 1973, for example), our analyses
have been "essentially *non-structural* and *ahistorical*," as Steven Spitzer
put it (1975, p. 638).

In extreme cases, our inattention to the social structures within which
people construct meanings or to the social conditions people construct
as meaningful and/or problematic, has led us to claim "value neutrality,"
a claim that is increasingly problematic in this postpositivist period
when many human scientists conceptualize knowledge as inherently
ideological. For example, in their classic statement of the social constructionist view of social problems, Spector and Kitsuse ([1977] 1987)
claimed a value-neutral or "noncommittal" stance toward "social conditions." This allowed them to avoid questions I think they should have
asked. For example, Are there morally repugnant structures of domination and oppression in our society, which people define as social problems?

> We are interested in constructing a theory of claims-making activities, not
> a theory of conditions. Thus, the significance of objective conditions for us
> is *the assertions made about them*, not the validity of those assertions as
> judged from some independent standpoint, as for example, that of a scien-
> tist. To guard against the tendency to slip back into an analysis of the
> condition, we assert that even the existence of the condition itself is irrele-
> vant to and outside of our analysis. We are not concerned whether or not
> the imputed condition exists. (p. 76)

Feminist social constructionists have not had these two problems in
their critical feminist theory and practice of feminist fieldwork. They
have not had to argue about "generalizability" because they have not
submerged their research in the positivist discourse on methodologies
and methods. For years, symbolic interactionist field-workers did just
that. By agreeing to compare the fieldwork design to the experimental
and survey designs in social science—and arguing that fieldwork was
"almost as good"—we forced ourselves to measure our work against the

goals of the positivist designs, including external validity or generalizability. Even as we argued that we were interested in cases, not variables (Blumer 1969), we turned our cases into variables by "stripping away" what was historically and structurally unique about them and concentrating on their "generic properties."

From the beginning, critical feminist theorists and fieldworkers understood their project as an alternative to and a critique of positivism. They rejected positivist social scientists' strict separation of the observer and the observed, the knower and the known, and its privileging of observers' interpretations of reality. As Margaret Andersen puts it:

> Variable analysis presumes a single voice—the voice of the dominant group. Their experiences define what variables are significant for study, what their indicators are, and what their presumed relationships are. As Blumer pointed out, variable analysis cannot account for the process of interpretation, but even more specifically for our purposes, variable analysis cannot account for the multiple interpretations of reality that we must begin to see if we are to include those who have previously been excluded. It too easily assumes that there is a single interpretation of reality. (1987, p. 18)

Critical feminist theorists and fieldworkers have also rejected the positivist social science practice of "holding constant" the ongoing contexts of human events in order to generalize about or "universalize" them (DuBois 1983; Reinharz 1983). Instead of stripping away the historical uniqueness of a case in order to generalize from it, critical feminist researchers represent the historical and structural implications of each case they study by embedding it in the context of the world political economy.

Furthermore, their stance toward problematic social conditions is not "noncommittal"; it is openly ideological and praxis oriented (Lather 1986). Research, theorizing, teaching—all are aspects of their feminism, which is "a politics directed at changing existing power relations between women and men in society" (Weedon 1987, p. 1). As we reconsider the social constructionist perspective in sociology, I suggest we consider critical feminist theorists' and researchers' solutions to the problems that have plagued us. More than that, I suggest we think about adopting them.

Feminist Constructionism

Feminist constructionism developed independently of the social constructionism of symbolic interactionists, out of the politics and epistemology of critical feminist theory. Critical feminist theory shares with other critical theories an emphasis on the historically specific, economic, and political structures within which people construct the meanings they use to organize their conduct. As Jaggar put it, critical feminists theorize knowledge and other meanings, like deviance and social problems, as social and practical constructs that are "historically determined by the prevailing mode of production [and] support the interests of the ruling class" (Jaggar 1983, pp. 358–59).

However, critical feminist theorists also take people's lived experiences seriously. Most would agree that paying attention to the histories, perceptions and conceptions, the lived experience of oppression, and the resistances of subordinate people "is the central agenda for feminist social science and scholarship" (DuBois 1983, p.108). Most would also agree it is the only way to produce "liberatory knowledge, crafted with the goal of human liberation" (Amott and Matthaei 1991, p. 6).

This dual emphasis on structure and agency has allowed critical feminists to research and theorize the "extent, the dimensions, the forms and causes" (Meis 1983, p. 125) of racial-ethnic, class, and gender privilege in the United States, but also the extent, dimensions, and forms of resistance to institutionalized oppressions. Refusing to see racial-ethnic men and women, working-class people, and middle-class white women as "victims" they have discovered a whole range of resistances, including "refusals to work, slowing the pace of work, organizing unions, and armed rebellions" (Amott and Matthaei 1991, p. 145), "creating spheres of influence" in schools, churches, and communities, "sustaining . . . . independent consciousness[es] as . . . . sphere[s] of freedom" (Collins 1990, pp. 141–43), and constituting their households and extended families as "cultures of resistance" (Glenn 1986, p. 192).

A distinct practice of feminist fieldwork has grown up around the dual emphasis on structure and agency in critical feminist theory. Looking for resistances instead of victims—Bookman and Morgen (1988) call this "empowerment"—is one of its goals. Another, overarching goal is research *for*, not *on* or *about* marginalized people. This has meant giving middle-class white women, racial-ethnic people, and working-class people voice and/or visibility in scholarly literatures. It has also meant choosing research questions that marginalized people want answers to, not questions whose answers can be used to control or exploit them, or questions that merely further researchers' own careers.

Doing research *for* the subjects of research has also meant treating them with respect: encouraging them to tell their own stories in their own words and in their own ways (see Reissman 1987 on listening to anecdotal and narrative stories), and trying not to overwhelm their interpretations of their experience with scientific explanations. In this way, feminist fieldwork is different than traditional fieldwork, "in which interpretations [were] assumed to be about others who [were] absent, rather than about those who are present and can comment upon them" (Krieger 1991, p. 17).

To some feminist fieldworkers, doing research *for* the subjects of research has also included "transformation" (Weiler 1987). All people have the capacity to make meaning of their lives and to resist oppression, even though the capacity to understand and to resist is influenced by class, racial-ethnic, and gender positions. Feminist fieldworkers committed to transformation try to help the people they study understand their lives structurally and locate productive sites for struggle against their oppression. Savage (1988) called this "neighborliness," after the praxis of educational and pastoral workers in poor villages and neighborhoods in Latin America, and defined it as critical analyses of structures of oppression "for the sake of another who has been marginalized" (p. 11). More recently, other feminist field-workers have redefined the goal again; to them, doing research *for* marginalized people means fieldworkers should avoid speaking for the subjects of their research and should, instead, create spaces in which people can speak for themselves (Lather 1991) and/or "make meaningful contributions to their own well-being and not serve as objects of investigation" (Benmayor 1991, p. 160).

In the 1970s and early 1980s, feminist research was often marked by "the innocent assumptions that gender united women more strongly than race and class divided them, and that the mere study of women fulfilled a commitment to do research" for women (Gluck and Patai 1991, p. 2). Later, "black women and other women of color confront[ed] white women about racism"; as a result, critical feminist theorists began to deconstruct "the category of gender" (Childers and hooks 1990, p. 62) and feminist field-workers began to take seriously the goal of inclusion. Now, feminist field-workers realize that excluding the experiences of working-class and racial-ethnic people from research agendas also excludes these experiences "from consideration as vital building blocks in feminist theory" (Baca Zinn, Weber Cannon, Higginbotham, and Thornton Dill 1988, p. 126).

Constructions and Conditions: An Example

Evelyn Nakano Glenn's *Issei, Nisei, War Bride: Three Generations of Japanese American Women in Domestic Service* is a good example of this kind of work. On the surface, it is not about the social construction of a social problem. But it is about the racism built into the structure of the U.S. economy, and if that's not a social problem I don't know what is. At the heart of the book are the voices of forty-six women, aged forty-one to ninety-one at the time of the study. Fifteen of the speakers are Issei women who emigrated between 1915 and 1924; nineteen speakers are Nisei women who were born in the United States between 1910 and 1940; and twelve are postwar immigrants who became war brides during the 1950s and early 1960s. All of the women are or have been domestic workers.

Mrs. Okamura, Mrs. Shinoda, Mrs. Sasaki, Mrs. Morita, Shizuko Howell, Kazuko Frankel, and the others discuss their careers in domestic service, their work routines and job conditions, their strategies for coping with demeaning work, and the ways they resist employers' attempts to control the pace and order of their work. They tell stories about defying their husbands by secretly taking jobs and stories of mothers-in-law who sent them out to work; stories about employers who follow them around and watch them work and employers who leave them alone while they work; stories of hard physical labor, low wages, and few benefits, and stories of pride in their "capacity to perform hard physical labor and to meet exacting standards" (Glenn 1986, p. 183); stories of personalistic, maternalistic, and asymmetrical relations with their employers; and stories of resistance. They also tell about their immigration and childhood experiences, their efforts to keep their families "together and to preserve family bonds in the face of racism and a stratified labor system" (p. 198), and the gender politics in their own families.

In the beginning, according to Glenn, the goals of her study were "modest":

> My intention was to collect and assemble a set of oral interviews of Japanese American women employed as domestics. In teaching and writing about women and work, I had become acutely aware of the dearth of materials documenting the day-to-day struggles of Asian American, latina, and black women working in low-status occupations, such as domestic service, the most prototypical job for racial-ethnic women. Little was known about the conditions they confronted, what they felt about their situation, or how they responded to menial employment. Accounts in which women spoke in their own words about themselves and their work seemed the best vehicle for illustrating how gender, race and class intersect to shape the lives of racial-ethnic women. (p. ix)

If she had done nothing more than meet her own initial goals, Glenn could have contributed to a comparative analysis of domestic service and thus accomplished the research goal set by traditional fieldworkers. She could have compared her case study of Japanese American women who worked as domestics in the San Francisco area with Judith Rollins's case study of African American women who worked as domestics in the

Boston area (1985), Shellee Colen's case study of Caribbean immigrant women who worked as domestics in New York City (1986), and others. The "comparison of variations in conditions and consequences" could have "provide[d] a highly differential theory of the phenomenon under study": "the prototypical job for racial ethnic women." But she didn't:

> Once started, the project took momentum and drew me along.
> Questions raised in the initial interviews led to a broadening of the study both empirically and theoretically. My new aim was to uncover the relationship between Japanese American women's experience as domestic workers during the first seventy years of the twentieth century and larger historical forces: the transformation of the economy and labor market in Northern California and the process of labor migration and settlement in that locale. (Glenn 1986, p. ix)

In other words, Glenn did as other feminist field-workers have done: She located the lived experiences of the Japanese American women she interviewed in an historically and structurally specific part of the world political economy. "The experiences of Japanese American women," she concluded, were "a microcosm of a worldwide phenomenon—the movement of people from less developed regions to fill labor demands in more advanced economic centers" (p. 11). In this worldwide process, "advanced countries (core economies) are in a position to exploit the economies of less advanced countries (peripheral economies)" (p. 13).

Labor migrants are typically drawn from countries and regions "whose economies have been disrupted and subsequent development distorted by western colonial incursions" (p. 9). What labor migrants find in the advanced countries to which they are drawn is a dual economy, made up of monopoly firms whose "size and operating procedures enable them to reduce uncertainty through control of raw materials, financing, marketing, and labor" and competitive industries whose "production processes remain competitive" and who therefore "rely on low wage labor for profits" (p. 13):

> Corresponding to this dualism in the economy is a dualism in the labor market. The primary market consists of jobs in the monopolistic sector, which are characterized by high wages, job security, promotional ladders, and bureaucratic supervision; the secondary market comprises jobs in the competitive sector, which have the opposite characteristics: low wages, insecurity, few opportunities for promotion, and arbitrary supervision. . . . . The secondary market uses the most exploitable categories: minorities, women, migrants, and youth. Of these categories, migrants are the most flexible. They can be drawn to the particular geographic areas where labor needs are greatest; they are available to work long hours because they are eager to earn money quickly and are free of personal and family

ties. According to this model, migrant labor serves as a reserve army, easily called up when production expands, and just as easily pushed out when demand contracts. (pp. 13–14)

Racism (white-skin privilege) is necessary to the creation and maintenance of dual labor markets in "advanced" economies and explains why U.S. immigrants from Europe and their children were upwardly mobile into the primary labor market whereas immigrants from Asia, Africa, the Caribbean, and Latin America have remained in the secondary labor market for generations:

> The development of a two-tiered labor system requires that groups be initially distinguishable, ethnically or in other ways. Such a system can be more easily maintained beyond the immigrant generation when groups are racially, as well as ethnically, identifiable. Because of racial distinctiveness, later cohorts of non-white immigrant groups had different labor market experiences from later cohorts of white immigrant groups. Whereas the children and grandchildren of European immigrants became dispersed throughout the occupational hierarchy, latinos, blacks and Asian Americans tended to remain at the bottom of the ladder even after several generations in the United States. (p. 11)

Gender stratification has also been part of racial-ethnic immigrant women's work experiences. As they were incorporated into the capitalist wage-labor system, "their employment was limited to a narrow set of occupations" (p. 67), in which the work

> could be fitted around family responsibilities (e.g., it was done at home, children could be taken to work, hours were flexible); it involved tasks that were an extension of women's work in the home (e.g., food preparation, laundry, and sewing); it was in a low-technology, labor-intensive field where low wages and long hours reduced competition from white women; it took place in a family-owned or ethnic enterprise where language difficulties and racial discrimination did not constitute barriers to employment. (p. 75)

Conclusion

It could be argued that Glenn produced a "natural history" of the process of labor migration and settlement not unlike symbolic interactionists' natural histories of social problems and other social constructions. Indeed, she found "striking continuities" in the process despite differences in time and place: that labor migrants can be recruited to fill labor needs in "receiving" societies because those same societies have disrupted and distorted the economies of sending societies; that receiving societies pass laws and design policies to prevent permanent settlement by labor migrants; that labor migrants typically begin as sojourners but because "they are relegated to insecure, low-wage employments, migrants often find it difficult to amass sufficient capital to go back" home; they decide to stay but capitalists and native laborers don't want them to and "at this point [overt] hostility to migrants often erupts" (Glenn 1986, pp. 9–11).

Or, it could be argued that Glenn used a "model of social structure"—world systems or dependent development theory—not unlike the models traditional field-workers intended to build and use. Glenn claimed to be filling in the missing pieces in existing studies of labor migration and settlement—women's experiences, variations in labor market segmentation over time and across locales, and the perspective of labor migrant groups on their own situation—in order to create a "more detailed and dynamic picture of labor migration and settlement" as a "necessary first step toward developing an adequate conceptual framework for understanding the way in which racial-ethnic groups are incorporated into and move within the labor system at different stages of capitalist development" (p. 18).

Both counterarguments amount to saying Glenn's work and the work of other critical feminist theorists and field-workers isn't as different from symbolic interactionist theory and traditional fieldwork practice as I have argued they are. Maybe not, but I think there are significant differences between a theory of human behavior that claims to be universal (e.g., "all human beings have selves and create the objects of their own actions") and one that claims to be an historically and structurally specific model of capitalist development, even if it claims this development is worldwide and has lasted for at least five hundred years. One theory allows its users to choose examples without regard to time and place; the other requires its users to locate examples in historical time and social structural place. In the same way, I think there are significant differences between a practice that claims to be "noncommittal" about social conditions and one that seeks to change them. One practice allows for generalization across cases after stripping them of their context; the other requires specifying the context of each case.

When critical feminist theory is coupled with feminist fieldwork like Glenn's, it becomes a "critical theory in practice" (Leonard 1990), a way of describing oppressive social structures without "reproducing them" by "diverting attention away from them" and "valorizing individuals" and their collective activities (Denzin 1991, p. 4). Critical theory in practice interrupts our traditional, social constructionist perspectives and practices. It calls into question our generic stories and our noncommittal stance, which have helped to keep alive "the myth of the individual, the myth of the helping social structure and the myth that in a free democratic society politically neutral, scientific social texts could somehow be written (p. 8). And even if these are only qualitative differences, I think they merit our attention as we reconsider our theory and practice and look for alternatives to them.

References

Amott, Teresa L. and Julie A. Matthaei. 1991. *Race, Gender and Work: A Multicultural Economic History of Women in the United States*. Boston: South End Press.

Andersen, Margaret. 1987. *Denying Difference: The Continuing Basis for Exclusion of Race and Gender in the Curriculum*. Memphis, Tennessee: Memphis State University, Center for Research on Women.

Baca Zinn, Maxine, Lynn Weber Cannon, Elizabeth Higginbotham, and Bonnie Thornton Dill. 1988. "The Costs of Exclusionary Practices in Women's Studies." Pp. 125–38 in *Reconstructing The Academy*, edited by Elizabeth Minnich, Jean O'Barr, and Rachel Rosenfeld. Chicago: University of Chicago Press.

Becker, Howard S. 1973. *Outsiders: Studies in the Sociology of Deviance*. New York: Free Press.

_____. 1977. "Social Observation and Social Case Studies." Pp. 75–86 in *Sociological Work*, by Howard S. Becker. New Brunswick, NJ: Transaction Books.

Benmayor, Rita. 1991. "Testimony, Action Research, and Empowerment: Puerto Rican Women and Popular Education." Pp. 159–74 in *Women's Words: The Feminist Practice of Oral History*, edited by Sherna Berger Bluck and Daphne Patai. New York: Routledge.

Blumer, Herbert. 1969. "Sociological Analysis and the Variable." Pp. 127–39 in *Symbolic Interactionism: Perspective and Method*, by Herbert Blumer. Berkeley: University of California Press.

Bookman, Ann and Sandra Morgen (eds.). 1988. *Women and the Politics of Empowerment*. Philadelphia: Temple University Press.

Childers, Mary and bell hooks. 1990. "A Conversation About Race and Class." Pp. 60–81 in *Conflicts in Feminism*, edited by Marianne Hirsch and Evelyn Fox Keller. New York: Routledge.

Colen, Shellee. 1986. "'With Respect and Feelings': Voices of West Indian Child Care and Domestic Workers in New York City." Pp. 46–70 in *All American Women*, edited by Johnnetta B. Cole. New York: Free Press.

Collins, Patricia Hill. 1990. *Black Feminist Thought: Knowledge, Consciousness, and the Politics of Empowerment*. New York: HarperCollins Academic.

Denzin, Norman K. 1991. "Deconstructing the Biographical Method." Unpublished manuscript prepared for the American Educational Research Association meetings in Chicago, Illinois, April.

DuBois, Barbara. 1983. "Passionate Scholarship: Notes on Values, Knowing and Method in Feminist Social Science." Pp. 105–16 in *Theories of Women's Stud-*

ies, edited by Gloria Bowles and Renate Duelli Klein. New York: Routledge & Kegan Paul.

Glenn, Evelyn Nakano. 1986. *Issei, Nisei, Warbride: Three Generations of Japanese American Women in Domestic Service*. Philadelphia: Temple University Press.

Gluck, Sherna Berger and Daphne Patai. 1991. "Introduction." Pp. 1–5 in *Women's Words: The Feminist Practice of Oral History*, edited by Sherna Berger Gluck and Daphne Patai. New York: Routledge.

Jaggar, Alison. 1983. "Feminist Politics and Epistemology." Pp. 353–94 in *Feminist Politics and Human Nature*, by Alison Jaggar. Totowa, NJ: Rowman and Allenheld.

Krieger, Susan. 1991. *Social Science and the Self: Personal Essays on an Art Form*. New Brunswick, NJ: Rutgers University Press.

Lather, Patti. 1986. "Research as Praxis." *Harvard Educational Review* 56:257–77.

———. 1991. *Getting Smart: Feminist Research and Pedagogy With/in the Postmodern*. New York: Routledge.

Leonard, Stephen. 1990. *Critical Theory in Political Practice*. Princeton, NJ: Princeton University Press.

Meis, Maria. 1983. "Towards a Methodology for Feminist Research." Pp. 117–39 in *Theories of Women's Studies*, edited by Gloria Bowles and Renate Duelli Klein. New York: Routledge & Kegan Paul.

Reinharz, Shulamit. 1983. "Experiential Analysis: A Contribution to Feminist Research." Pp. 162–91 in *Theories of Women's Studies*, edited by Gloria Bowles and Renate Duelli Klein. New York: Routledge & Kegan Paul.

Reissman, Catherine Kohler. 1987. "When Gender Is Not Enough: Women Interviewing Women." *Gender and Society* 1:172–207.

Rollins, Judith. 1985. *Between Women: Domestics and Their Employers*. Philadelphia: Temple University Press.

Savage, Mary. 1988. "Can Ethnographic Narrative Be a Neighborly Act?" *Anthropology and Education Quarterly* 19:3–19.

Spector, Malcolm and John Kitsuse. [1977] 1987. *Constructing Social Problems*. Hawthorne, New York: Aldine de Gruyter.

Spitzer, Steven. 1975. "Toward a Marian Theory of Deviance." *Social Problems* 22:638–51.

Weedon Chris. 1987. *Feminist Practice and Poststructuralist Theory*. New York: Basil Blackwell.

Weiler, Kathleen. 1987. *Women Teaching for Change: Gender, Class and Power*. South Hadley, MA: Bergin and Garvey.

10

Cultural Theory, Social Construction, and Social Problems

Herman Gray

Introduction

I want to use the appearance of the Ibarra and Kitsuse essay (in this volume) to raise the following questions: What is it that social constructionist theory is being asked to do in the Ibarra and Kitsuse reformulation? Why is this being asked of social constructionism now? What are the historical, intellectual, and institutional conditions that stimulate such a reformulation on the one hand and enable (or prevent) social constructionism to respond to such demands on the other? Finally, what are the political and theoretical consequences of these demands for social theory, social problems, and social constructionism? I raise these issues at the outset so that they might provoke, inform, and frame my reflections and responses to the Ibarra and Kitsuse's essay.

I situate my reflections on Ibarra and Kitsuse reformulations in the context of recent developments in cultural theory, especially theories of representations (particularly in the areas of literary theory, film studies, and popular culture), poststructuralism, cultural studies, feminist theories, theories of multiculturalism, studies of diasporic and subaltern peoples (including African American studies, Chicano studies, postcolonial discourse). Most significantly, I am interested in the crisis for social (and sociological?) theory that these theoretical developments have produced. In significant ways, they have called into question the totalizing and hegemonic stance of theories, paradigms, and master narratives (including social and sociological theory) that propose to explain broad universes of social reality as well as the unified Western male subject position from which social reality is constituted and narrated (Pfohl 1985; Pfohl and Gordon 1986).

The most insightful of these conceptual developments, cultural studies, for example, emphasize the centrality and semiautonomy of representations (including theoretical narratives produced by social science) as a site of intellectual inquiry and political struggle (Hall 1982, 1985, 1990; Lipsitz 1989, 1990; Ryan 1988). In this view culture is not simply an artifact or effect of structural and material practices, but is deeply integral to and constitutive of social and material life. Culture and systems of representation figure significantly into how social reality is constituted and organized. This position does not privilege representation and culture so much as it recognizes and attempts to theorize the complex relationship between representation and material life in the context of popular culture and contemporary modes of communication.

This is an important insight for the Ibarra and Kitsuse project both theoretically and politically. For it signals, and indeed often challenges, the constructions and relations of traditional intellectual boundaries. Many of the recent theoretical insights explicitly critique the often invisible but consequential relations of power inscribed in theoretical (and disciplinary) constructions of the social world and social production of knowledge (Pfohl 1985).

My concern then is to indicate how the reformulations and refinements suggested by Ibarra and Kitsuse are engaged with (and perhaps emblematic) of these developments in cultural theory. I want to consider the extent to which the reformulations and modifications suggested by Ibarra and Kitsuse represent a vantage point, within sociology at least, from which to engage these developments. And finally I shall try to indicate some of the conceptual, disciplinary, and political problems and possibilities stimulated by the Ibarra and Kitsuse reformulations.

Social Constructionism and the Discourse of Social Problems

The constructionist approach to social problems is built on an edifice of theoretical traditions that critically signaled among other things the socially constructed nature of the social world and therefore the centrality of representation and meaning (Hazelrigg 1986). The initial appearance of the work of Kitsuse and Spector, Blumer, Becker, and their students disturbed the dominant sociological conceptions of social problems with respect to empirical research and social theory's relationship to the social world that it purported to study and represent (Becker 1963; Blumer 1971; Kitsuse and Cicourel 1963; Spector and Kitsuse [1977] 1987). By emphasizing the socially constructed nature of both the members' activities and those of sociological experts, early social constructionist interventions in the sociology of social problems produced lively debates about the position of sociologists, the dominance of objectivist approaches, and the role and consequences (for members and sociological experts) of sociological theory in the operation and representation of the social world (Hazelrigg 1986). With its initial disturbance, this second and third generation of social constructionists effectively displaced the hegemony of functionalist and objectivist paradigms of social problems. Constructionism subsequently guided several generations of social problems researchers through the paradigmatic shifts in the reconstitution of social problems as a subfield and object of sociological investigation. Ibarra and Kitsuse's most recent attempt to rethink social constructionism and address the central tensions, confusions, and criticism within the approach continues this project.

The Ibarra and Kitsuse reformulation is not just occasioned, however, by debates within sociology over the salience, logic, and continuing relevance of social constructionism, but also by challenges and developments outside the discipline of sociology and the theory of social constructionism. Theoretically, for instance, the current period is characterized by the proliferation of competing claims for and about social problems emanating from critical legal theory, literary criticism, feminist theory, and cultural studies. Notable works from these perspectives examine AIDS and the representation of homosexuals, IV drug users, and minorities as deviants in science fiction and horror films (Guererro 1990), the struggles over bilingualism as public vs. private issues (Flores and Yudice 1990), and the representation of black males as menace in political discourse and film (Rogin 1990). These studies of representation are relevant for social constructionism because increasingly they are sites of multidisciplinary explorations of politics, culture, and representation (what Ibarra and Kitsuse identify as vernacular resources). They use practices and expressions such as fictional literature, language, film, and other popular expressions to examine the representation of issues that have been seen, at least by sociologists, as the province of the sociology of social problems. As George Lipsitz points out, these are struggles over representation in both a political and intellectual sense; more importantly they are struggles waged in culture (Lipsitz 1989).[1] With Ibarra and Kitsuse's decided shift to the terrain of culture and representation, social constructionism too has engaged this multiple sense of struggle in and over representation.

By drawing on these ways of knowing and representing the complexities of the social world, recent theoretical interventions such as cultural studies have placed different forms of knowledge and sites of practice on the agenda of that which sociologists must consider if we are to study the meanings and activities of members. Of course, this means that sociology's claims to a unique approach to the study of social problems is increasingly open to challenge. It is significant that discourse theory, interpretive and textual analysis (literary and linguistic), and cultural studies (film and popular culture) either directly or indirectly inform the Ibarra and Kitsuse concern with meaning and representation (Gitlin 1989; Lipsitz 1990).[2] The very existence of these theoretical approaches and Ibarra and Kitsuse's identification of vernacular resources as the object of the study of social problems compels constructionists to engage, elaborate, and extend its insights into the area of culture, especially representation, discourse, texts, and ideology.

The contemporary sociological discourse on social problems has also been stimulated by social and political developments outside the academy. Among these I would include the new social circuits and configurations of capitalist transformation and representation (Davis 1991; Jameson 1990). These shifting configurations present us with new sites and ways of representing social life, as well as transformations in the very practices and representations of social life, especially with respect to gender, race, sexuality, and identity.

Discourses, organizations, interest groups, and members outside the academy continue, often vigorously, to contest scientific, academic, and professional claims about social problems. This mobilization and intensification, especially its politicalization (debates over AIDS, abortion, sexual identity, political correctness, affirmative action, tenured radicals, the university), heighten the tensions and expand the sites within which the academic, theoretical, political, and practical struggles over representation are waged (Kitsuse 1980).[3] As Ibarra and Kitsuse note, this no doubt is the stuff of a social constructionist view of social problems. However, I want to go further and suggest that sociologists and social constructionists are deeply implicated in these activities and debates, but not just as dispassionate and neutral observers or experts or even political partisans. Rather, it seems to me that the very nature of the sociological (and intellectual) enterprise is implicated in these activities since they are struggles in as well as over representation.

For sociology in general and social constructionism in particular, this is an especially opportune if not paradoxical moment, one where new discursive connections, articulations, contingencies, and realignments are possible, or one where existing relations of power/knowledge are simply reconfigured (Foucault 1980). In this regard, I am persuaded by Pfohl and Gordon's (1986) desire for a more radical move, that is, to see this moment of potential (re)articulation in terms of the critical possibilities that it presents for illuminating the relations of power inscribed in traditional discursive regimes of knowledge and power. It is a moment that Cornel West (1990) has described as offering different possibilities for exploring new knowledges and relations of power, different ways of imagining, naming, representing, and knowing.

Social Constructionism and Cultural Theory

Theoretically and rhetorically, one of the key conceptual moves in the Ibarra and Kitsuse reformulation is to reposition the objects of social problems discourse—i.e., members, the vernacular resources and expressions involved in social problems activity, sites where these activities take place, intellectual and professional practices, media, language, and rhetoric. Conceptualizing social problems in terms of culture and representation problematizes the existing constructionist conceptions of social problems in terms of the relations of power inscribed in the object/subject relations (Hazelrigg 1986; Woolgar and Pawluch 1985).

As encouraged by the recent interventions of Ibarra and Kitsuse as I am, I cannot help but think that as a theoretical project, their interventions and reformulations (especially the responses that they have engendered within the social constructionist paradigm) are related to, perhaps even emblematic of, the larger crisis of sociological theory and social problems theory (Best 1989; Hazelrigg 1985; Pfohl 1985; Schneider and Kitsuse 1984; Schneider 1985a, 1985b; Woolgar and Pawluch 1985).[4] This is especially evidenced by the extent to which their intervention and the debate it has stimulated remain bound by intellectual, professional, and epistemological positions that turn on staking and defending existing theoretical and methodological turf. Perhaps we have reached the moment when the paradigmatic status of constructionism, together with the crisis of theory (especially the shifting professional and disciplinary boundaries), fuels the need for social constructionism (and sociology) to identify new and reposition old objects of study and to modify the rules that enable a distinctive theory of social problems (Kuhn 1970). At the same time we may have also arrived at a point of discursive realignments, where strict disciplinary boundaries themselves must be rendered problematic and interrogated as narratives that disciplines and paradigms (including social constructionism) have produced about themselves (Pfohl and Gordon 1986). In either case I simply insist on calling attention to the social constructionist story, its nature, aims, and how it is privileged and operates in relationship to other stories.

Ibarra and Kitsuse's move to carve out new conceptual territory, refine and redefine methodological approaches, identify new data, and build linkages to different discourses on social problems, seems to shift more dramatically and decidedly into an area of greater multidisciplinary engagement. And yet, as their reformulations move sociology and social constructionism into greater and greater interdisciplinary dialogue, they also appear to maintain claims for the uniquely sociological dimension of what constructionism brings to the study of social problems. To be sure, sociology and social constructionism still have much to say about social problems: its negotiated and constructed character; how organizations process and organize claims; how members make, advocate for, and oppose claims; the distinction between objective conditions and claims-making activity. However, in light of theoretical developments such as cultural studies, the specific terms of these insights might also be reevaluated and rethought rather than assumed.

It is precisely the broader interdisciplinary developments in cultural theory such as cultural studies, feminism, literary theory, and minority discourse that present the greatest challenge for the strategies suggested by Ibarra and Kitsuse. With the kinds of discursive adjustments and challenges now underway in cultural theory, social constructionism can no longer remain theoretically secure with simply reconfiguring the constructionist project in terms of identifying new sources of data or increasing methodological and theoretical precision (Pfohl 1985).

Social Constructionism and Cultural Representation

What then are the theoretical possibilities for a critical cultural approach to social problems that might be mobilized from the site of social constructionism? Ibarra and Kitsuse's strategies for reconstituting a constructionist approach to social problems has culture and representation as a central feature. They suggest that social problems activities (and their theorization) be seen as a study of the language game (organized and produced by certain rules, strategies, structures), produced by members to articulate their understandings, desires, and disagreements about their social world. The stated aim of social problems theory and research in the reformulation is to describe, analyze, and theorize just how members negotiate, mobilize, and utilize these rules, structures, and resources to construct, express, and negotiate their social world. Social problems activities are the rhetorics, languages, and vernacular practices of the members, and they are expressed as different kinds of knowledges (e.g., mundane as well as expert) at various sites of social life—street corners, political rallies, and smoke-filled back rooms, courtrooms, classrooms, and television. Constructionism directs attention to the textual expressions and interpretive meanings of these representations and accounts; the processes, negotiations, and struggles they produce; and the sites where such activities take place. In a social and cultural condition such as ours where representations of our world are mass produced and circulated by large multinational culture industries, the realm of mass-mediated culture is an important social site where meanings are constantly made and negotiated and where struggles over the terms and shape of the social world are waged (Gitlin 1989).

I agree with Ibarra and Kitsuse's insistence that social constructionists develop more explicit theoretical strategies for grappling with the centrality of culture, in particular, identifying the ways that claims about social reality are produced, shaped, modified, and expressed by members at different sites of social life (especially mass media and popular culture). These are aspects of our social world about which sociology has much to offer. I think, for instance, of sociologically informed studies of literature and women's reading groups (Long 1985; Radway 1984) and studies of television as a site of negotiation and the creation of meaning (Morley 1986; Newcomb 1984; Spigel 1988). It is quite appropriate, therefore, that Ibarra and Kitsuse insist that social constructionists identify, describe, organize, and theorize about the members' categories and constructions. As the authors suggest, such theoretical injunctions, of course, put social problems theoretical practices and productions immediately onto the terrain of culture, where the language, rhetorics, constructs, and vernacular resources of members constitute expressive sites and contexts in which social problems activities take place. In such a move, culture (and social problems for that matter) is neither static nor simply an artifact or effect of a separate material practice. It is always in the making and it is the means through which and resource over which we struggle to make sense of and organize our social world.

By shifting the focus of constructionist theory to culture and representations, an entire body of literature, practices, and strategies of critical interrogation are available to students of social problems. Insights can be gained into the claims of members and the ways that such claims are shaped, organized, selected, registered, and so on by institutions, organizations, and activities. Feminist, Black, and Chicano studies of identity, experience, and the imaginary in literature, fictional television, film, popular music, and everyday life are potentially rich sites of theory and research for social constructionists (Chabram and Fregoso 1990; Guererro 1990; Lipsitz 1990; Williams 1991). In addition, from the production of culture perspective, studies of cultural organizations and industries such as the press, television, film, advertising, and popular music are rich with examples of how such organizations produce, organize, transform, and process competing claims and representations of social life (Gans 1983; Gitlin 1980, 1983; Gray 1983; Montgomery 1989; Tuchman 1983). These literatures are potentially rich meeting grounds for media studies, cultural studies, and social constructionism. By investigating

these sites of cultural production and interpretation social constructionists can more directly examine what people do with various kinds of
representations and constructions of the social world generated by mass
media and popular culture as well as where and how they modify and
fashion these representations and forms of knowledge into their experiences and activities as claims-making activity. Because it seeks to broad-
en its scope, social constructionism must of necessity be actively engaged with theoretical developments that offer strategies and insights
for identifying and reading the texts and practices used by members to
construct and produce meanings.

Social Constructionism and the Politics of Representation

To Ibarra and Kitsuse's move to privilege meanings and representations, I would add the relations of production and power operating in
culture and systems of representation (including intellectual and theoretical representations) as constituent of the social constructionist project (Foucault 1980). It therefore seems to me theoretically reasonable
and politically necessary to interrogate the stakes, warrants, and consequences of Ibarra and Kitsuse's call for social constructionism to enact a
theoretical performance of sorts, on the vernacular practices of members. Who benefits from such a performance or deployment of theory in
this way? At this point in history can the commitment to the accumula-
tion and refinement of knowledge proceed without a critical positioning
and interrogation of (any) theory's claims about itself?[5] As a theoretical
practice, I want to retain a critical but healthy skepticism about (any)
theory's ability to focus and method's power to discipline researchers
and theorists from privileging various kinds of claims. Given the possibilities for discursive realignments that have been revealed from the
quarters of cultural theory, minority discourse, and feminist theory, it is
important that our own theoretical practice avoid simply reconfiguring
and reinscribing the relations of power and privilege implicit in our
enterprise. If the practical projects of members operate within shifting
fields and relations of power, so too do the theoretical performances of
social constructionists.

Indeed, our power to identify and privilege theoretical knowledge or
making sense gives us access to a distinctive empowered language and
specific arenas in which that knowledge circulates and gains legitimacy
(the university, social policy, journals, books, the press). This too must
be viewed as part of the language game of social problems theory. Although Ibarra and Kitsuse's distinction between the first and second

order of signification signals this recognition, the more difficult and far thornier problem remains: How and to what end does social constructionism conceive and understand its own activity? How does social constructionism identify and theorize its own intellectual practice, as one among many, which figures into and shapes social problems, especially insofar as such practice is inscribed in (and by) professional and institutional relations of power and legitimation?

Insights from cultural studies, minority discourse, and feminist theory suggest that professionally and intellectually our stances, claims, and locations (especially in terms of race, gender, class, and sexual preference) do matter. They are central to the identification and analysis of claims and claims-making activities, especially what happens to and with such claims beyond our professional and intellectual milieu. With the decided move toward culture and representation, social constructionism faces some responsibility for self-reflection and criticism of its own practice and productions.

Social constructionism faces the challenge of naming, locating, and theorizing the relations of power and politics at work in its own theoretical practice. I therefore want to reframe as a critical and political question Ibarra and Kitsuse's call to make sense of the way that *all claims* (especially our own) about social reality are shaped and implicated in theoretical practice and the production of knowledge (Aronson 1984). The shift to culture and representation means that there is no outside position (Becker 1967; Pfohl and Gordon 1986; Pfohl 1985), even if social constructionism continues to claim one. It is still very much a narrative about the social world, a narrative that shapes, limits, frames, and influences the definition and representation of the social world including its problems and possibilities. I want to avoid conflating positivist issues of methodological neutrality, disciplined and systematic observation, and greater precision in the specification of data with the warrant to ignore constructionism's own theoretical practice and to locate it, as it were, outside the history of its own production and practice.

Theory—its conventions, practices, or productions—does not operate outside history or the social, political, and cultural relations in which it is produced, deployed, or received. The theoretical practices and performances called for by Ibarra and Kitsuse are themselves rooted in internal debates, shifting discursive alignments, and specific historical conditions. The very practice of theorizing about the vernacular resources and performances of members is a production and reading about the social world. Simply because social constructionism can name those practices (and benefit from the privileged status they occupy in the hierarchy of representation) and declare their significance and consequence at a different level (than say mundane practices) should not obscure the centrality of social constructionist practices in the social problems process. Indeed, from the view of cultural politics, one could easily figure the productions and practices of social constructionists into the process by which members negotiate, struggle over, and produce claims. By minimizing this central feature of social constructionism in relationship to the creation or production of social problems we run the risk of marginalizing one of the most significant and enduring features of the social constructionist project: namely, its concern with examining the processes by which social problems are socially created and produced.

By subjecting social constructionist practices to the same rules and conventions used to interrogate the practices of members, we might achieve a fuller, more complex sense of the formation of social problems. Figuring social constructionist practices in this way is a more radical advance than merely reconfiguring its existing terms, rules, data, and method. For example, instead of continuing to frame political and methodological issues of who the constructionist sides with—the weak, the powerful, no one—we might see such positions as contingent, conjunctural, and indeterminate rather than as given and unchanging. By exposing or interrogating the terms of our own practice through a kind of ongoing critical self-reflection, we might conceive of social problems in their formative process, taking note of the different positionalities, modalities, and registers of all groups and claims (including our own) in the social problems process. Social constructionism achieves its work (persuades, convinces, legitimates, demonstrates) through the use of rhetorics, vernaculars, resources, organizations, sites, and performances that can be interrogated according to the rules, procedures, and conventions of social constructionism. Such a position does not necessarily diminish the commitment to theory or disciplined observation so much as it enriches our conception and analysis of social problems as a process and activity. This too is very much the stuff of social problems and therefore ought to be the object of a social constructionist approach to social problems.

Acknowledgments

A different version of this paper was presented at the 1989 annual meetings of the Society for the Study of Social Problems. My thanks to Stephen Adair, Wini Breines, Michael Brown, James Holstein, Peter Ibarra, John I. Kitsuse, George Lipsitiz, and Gale Miller for their helpful comments and insights in the preparation of this paper.

Notes

1.   I am grateful to George Lipzitz for his helpful discussions and insights on this point.
2.   It is significant that Ibarra and Kitsuse's bibliography includes references to Bakhtin, Geertz, and Hebdige.
3.   For example, popular media and press coverage of the PC debate has been quite widespread and has included in-depth stories by ABC's "Nightline," PBS's "McNeil/Lehrer News Report," *Time, Newsweek, New Republic, Village Voice,* and *New York Times* among others (see Berube 1991; Bloom 1987; Goldstein 1991; *Newsweek* 1990).
4.   Here I refer to the rather lively and long debates that occurred during the Social Problems Theory Roundtable, where Ibarra and Kitsuse originally presented their paper, SSSP Annual Convention, Berkeley, California, 1989. See also exchanges by Woolgar and Pawluch, Kitsuse, Schneider, and Kitsuse and Schneider.
5.   Kitsuse and others have acknowledged and continue to acknowledge the salience of these and other explicitly political questions. They have insisted, however, that such questions are outside the theoretical and methodological project of social constructionism.

References

Aronson, Naomi. 1984. "Science as a Claims-making Activity: Implications for Social Problems Research." Pp. 1–30 in *Studies in the Sociology of Social Problems,* edited by J. Schneider and J. I. Kitsuse. Norwood, NJ: Ablex.

Becker, Howard. 1963. *Outsiders.* New York: The Free Press.

————. 1967. "Whose Side Are We On?" *Social Problems* 14:239–47.

Berube, Michael. 1991. "Public Image Limited: Political Correctness and the Media's Big Lie." *Village Voice* (June 18):31–37.

Best, Joel. 1989. *Images of Issues.* Hawthorne, NY: Aldine de Gruyter.

Bloom, Allan. 1987. *The Closing of the American Mind.* New York: Touchstone.

Blumer, Herbert. 1971. "Social Problems as Collective Behavior." *Social Problems.* 18:298–306.

Chabram, Angie and R. L. Fregoso (eds). 1990. *Cultural Studies* 4 (special issue on Chicano representations).

Davis, Mike. 1991. *City of Quartz.* London: Verso Press.

Flores, Juan and George Yudice. 1990. "Living Borders/Buscando America: Languages of Latino Self-Formation." *Social Text* 24:57–85.

Foucault, Michel. 1980. *Power/Knowledge: Selected Interviews and Other Writing, 1972–1979.* New York: Pantheon.

Gans, Herbert. 1983. "News Media, News Policy and Democracy: Research for the Future." *Journal of Communication* 33(3):174–85.

Gitlin, Todd. 1980. *The Whole World Is Watching.* Berkeley: University of California Press.

————. 1983. *Inside Prime Time.* New York: Pantheon.

————. 1989. "Postmodernism: Roots and Politics." In *Cultural Politics in Contemporary America,* edited by I. Angus and S. Jhally. New York: Routledge.

Goldstein, Richard. 1991. "The Politics of Political Correctness." *Village Voice* (June 18):39–41.

Gray, Herman. 1983. *Producing Jazz.* Philadelphia: Temple University Press.

Guererro, Edward. 1990. "AIDs as Monster in Science Fiction and Horror Films." *Journal of Popular Film and Television* 18:86–93.

Hall, Stuart. 1982. "The Discovery of Ideology: Return of the Repressed in Media Studies." Pp. 56–90 in *Culture, Society, and the Media,* edited by T. Gurevitch, T. Bennett, J. Curran, and J. Woollacott. London: Methuen.

————. 1985. "Signification, Representation, Ideology: Althusser and the Post-structuralist Debates." *Critical Studies in Mass Communication* 2:91–114.

————. 1990. "The Emergence of Cultural Studies and the Crisis of the Humanities." *October* 53:11–25.

Hazelrigg, Lawrence. 1985. "Were It Not for Words." *Social Problems* 32:234–38.

————. 1986. "Is There a Choice Between Constructionism and Objectivism? *Social Problems* 33:S1.

Jameson, Fredric. 1990. *Postmodernism or the Cultural Logic of Late Capitalism.* Durham, NC: Duke University Press.

Kitsuse, John I. 1980. "Coming Out All Over: Deviants and the Politics of Social Problems." *Social Problems* 28:1–13.

Kitsuse, John I. and Aaron Cicourel. 1963. "A Note on the Uses of Official Statistics." *Social Problems* 12:131–39.

Kuhn, Thomas. 1970. *The Structure of Scientific Revolutions.* Chicago: University of Chicago Press.

Lipsitz, George. 1989. *Time Passages.* Minneapolis: University of Minnesota Press.

————. 1990. "Listening to Learn and Learning to Listen: Popular Culture, Cultural Theory and American Studies." *American Quarterly* 42:615–37.

Long, Elizabeth. 1985. *The American Dream and the Popular Novel.* Boston: Routledge and Kegan Paul.

Montgomery, Kathryn. 1989. *Target Prime Time.* New York: Oxford University Press.

Morley, David. 1986. *Family Television.* London: Comedia.

Newcomb, Horace. 1984. "On the Dialogic Aspects of Mass Communication." *Critical Studies in Mass Communication* 1(1):34–50.

Newsweek. 1990. "Taking Offense" (December 24):48–55.

Pfohl, Stephen. 1985. "Towards a Sociological Deconstruction of Social Problems." *Social Problems* 32:228–32.

Pfohl, Stephen and Avery Gordon. 1986. "Criminological Displacements: A Sociological Deconstruction." *Social Problems* 33:S94.

Radway, Janice. 1984. *Reading the Romance: Feminism and the Representation of Women in Popular Culture.* Chapel Hill: University of North Carolina Press.

Rogin, Michael. 1990. "'Make My Day!': Spectacle as Amnesia in Imperial Politics." *Representations* 29:99–123.

Ryan, Michael. 1988. "The Politics of Film: Discourse, Psychoanalysis, Ideology."
Pp. 447–487 in *Marxism and the Interpretation of Culture*, edited by C. Nelson
and L. Grossberg. Urbana: University of Illinois Press.

Schneider, Joseph. 1985a. "Defining the Definitional Perspective on Social Problems." *Social Problems* 32:232–34.

———. 1985b. "Social Problems Theory: The Constructionist View." *Annual Review of Sociology* 11:209–29.

Schneider, Joseph and John I. Kitsuse. 1984. *Studies in the Sociology of Social
Problems*. Norwood, NJ: Ablex.

Spector, Malcolm and John I. Kitsuse. [1977] 1987. *Constructing Social Problems*.
Hawthorne, NY: Aldine de Gruyter.

Spigel, Lynn. 1988. "Television and the Home Theater." *Camera Obscura* 16:11–
46.

Tuchman, Gaye. 1983. "Consciousness Industries and the Production of Culture." *Journal of Communication* 33(3):330–42.

West, Cornel. 1990. "The New Cultural Politics of Difference." *October* 53:93–110.

Williams, Patricia. 1991. *The Alchemy of Race: Diary of Law Professor*. Cambridge,
MA: Harvard University Press.

Woolgar, Steven and D. Pawluch. 1985. "Ontological Gerrymandering: The
Anatomy of Social Problems Explanations." *Social Problems* 32:214.

11

Constructing Conditions, People, Morality, and Emotion: Expanding the Agenda of Constructionism

Donileen R. Loseke

It is obvious that the social construction tradition is alive and well. Joseph Schneider (1985) described the range and sheer magnitude of studies in this perspective; continued theoretical debates attest to the perspective's intellectual vitality. In this volume, Peter Ibarra and John Kitsuse offer a vision about the future of constructionism. I suggest that their proposed agenda could be profitably extended in two interrelated ways.

First, although constructionism has tended to focus on claims-making surrounding putative *conditions* (Spector and Kitsuse [1977] 1987) or *condition*-categories (Ibarra and Kitsuse), claims constructing such categories often simultaneously construct the types of *people* who inhabit those categories. Given this, there are "putative people" as well as "putative conditions." Constructionists might give more attention to examining this rhetorical practice of "people production."

Second, Ibarra and Kitsuse emphasize how social problem claims can be organized around *moral* themes, and I suggest that discursive productions of people-types simultaneously construct preferred *emotional orientations* and responses toward the constructed categories. Because emotions can be analyzed as "socially constructed language forms" (Perinbanayagam 1989), social problems claims might be profitably examined as members' ways of constructing moral evaluation *and* emotion.

In brief, I will argue that constructionists could maintain a radical focus on members' constitutive practices yet expand interest into the construction of people categories; and I will argue that rather than *a* social problems discourse, there are interconnected discourses that rhetorically constitute categories as residing within folk universes of morality and emotion. Although my points are related, I will begin with the production of putative people.

Constructing Putative People

If social problems claims-making were confined to situations where claims-makers and claims-hearers shared the lived experience of the condition-category and where all unique individuals in the category were biographically known others, then it would be possible for claims to merely "designate and dramatize" (Holstein and Miller 1990) the people inhabiting the category. But claims-makers and hearers in our complex, media-driven, and anonymous world often do not experience the lived reality of the condition-category, nor are all, most, or even some category inhabitants biographically known others. Given that the condition-category and the people in the category can be unknown in lived reality, claims construct types of conditions and types of people. Thus, there is the interactional process of constructing particular individuals as types of people (e.g., Holstein 1992), *and* there is the social problems claims-making process of rhetorically producing people-type categories. The extent to which category inhabitants are biographically unknown others is the extent to which constructing people-types is integral to the process of constructing condition-types.

As noted by Holstein and Miller (1990), in commonsense reasoning, social problems are constructed as "harmful conditions." Therefore, every social problems condition-category is inhabited by a *victim*. While harm might be to nonhumans (such as the environment, the economy, or nature), my interest is in those condition-categories constructed as containing human victims, be they current social members (such as crime victims, the unemployed, or persons without medical care), potential social members (prolife constructions), or future social members (such as in claims about environmental ruin, economic collapse, and nuclear annihilation). Second, Holstein and Miller also note that in commonsense reasoning every social problem condition-category is inhabited by a *victimizer* who is the causal agent of harm. While such causal agents might be vague and impersonal (capitalism, the system, racism), victimizers often are personified (the politician, the greedy capitalist, the sexist).

Critically, if a victim were only a person harmed by a condition, and if a victimizer were only the causal agent of harm, then constructing a condition would require merely "naming" the persons harmed by it and the persons responsible for it. Yet within folk reasoning, victims and victimizers are membership categorizations (Sacks 1972; Holstein and Miller 1990); they are labels for *types* of persons. Hence, a victim is more than a person experiencing harm. Within commonsense reasoning, a victim is a person judged as *not responsible* for creating the harm experienced (Holstein and Miller 1990). Likewise, within folk reasoning, a victimizer is more than a causal agent of harm. Victimizer rather is a label for a person judged to have *chosen* to do harm, and one judged as *intending* to do harm (McHugh 1970). In brief, assigning responsibility, intent, and choice is an interactional accomplishment in producing particular people as types of people (Holstein and Miller 1990), *and* it is a claims-making activity when victim and victimizer types of people are rhetorically produced by claims-making activities.

Interactional victim-contests (Holstein and Miller 1990) and victimizer-contests (Maynard 1984) also have parallels in the production of people-types. Are "the poor"—a category of person—in that category because of their own failure or because of social failure? Does the "battered woman" type of person choose to remain within the condition called "wife abuse," or is she trapped through no fault of her own? Is the "drug dealer" type of person a victimizer or a "victim of poverty?" Are ghetto apartment building owners "greedy landlords" or just "regular folk" struggling to pay taxes and maintenance costs? When such contests over people-types occur in claims-making, there are possible consequences for condition-categories associated with people-categories. For example, condition-categories can be constructed as social problems only if the persons in these conditions are constructed as victims who are not responsible for their placement in these categories (Holstein and Miller 1990). Hence, a "counterrhetorical strategy" is that of shifting attention from condition-categories to people-categories. In addition, such rhetorical contests constructing people-types can influence the shape and naming of condition-categories. If the drug dealer type of person is constructed as a victimizer who chooses and intends to do harm, then "drug dealers" is a logical condition-category. But if this type of person is rather constructed as a victim of poverty then "poverty" commonsensically becomes the associated condition-category.

My first points are that claims-making constructing putative people can be examined as a "language game" (Wittgenstein 1958), and that such constructions can be an important activity in constructing condition-categories. My second point is related: Claims producing putative people caste these types as residing within particular moral universes, which simultaneously constructs such persons as residing within particular universes of "sympathy-worthiness" or "condemnation-worthiness." Social problem discourse is the interrelated languages of morality and emotion; constructing morality and emotion can be examined as claims-making activities.

Constructing Morality and Emotion

Most clearly, social problems discourse is moral talk (Ibarra and Kitsuse); it is "talk that evaluates and judges; that creates, reinforces, and
challenges moral meanings" (Schneider 1984a, p. 182). In addition, within folk reasoning, constructing morality simultaneously constructs preferred emotional orientations. Therefore, social problems discourse can
be examined as *emotions* talk.

First, claims constructing victim and victimizer people-categories
place these people in distinct folk universes of *morality*. In commonsense
reasoning, a victim is a person who is "absolved from responsibility in
creating harm" (Holstein and Miller 1990), a victim is "innocent" and
hence "moral." Conversely, within folk reasoning, victimizers choose
and intend to create harm. Such a person is "immoral" (Douglas 1970).
Second, constructing moral or immoral types of persons simultaneously
constructs preferred *emotional* orientations. Within folk reasoning, a
moral person unjustly harmed deserves "compassion and concern"
(Holstein and Miller 1990); within such reasoning this person deserves
"sympathy" and its behavioral expression of "help" (Clark 1987). Also
within folk reasoning, an immoral person who creates harm deserves
the emotional response of "condemnation" and its behavioral expression of "punishment" (Douglas 1970; McHugh 1970). Hence, commonsense reasoning links morality with expectable emotional and behavioral
responses.

At the interactional level, categorizations of particular people as victims or victimizers involve multiple and situated evaluations. In the case
of evaluating sympathy-worthiness (Clark 1987), for example, "in what
may be a split second a potential sympathizer considers the moral
worthiness of the other, the sympathy-worthiness of the other's plight,
the other's complicity in the plight and one's own situation relative
to the other's" (p. 297). Likewise, placement of particular individuals
into the people-category of victimizer is situated and complex because
"members of our society do not, in fact, find it easy to agree on what is
right and wrong, moral and immoral, in concrete situations" (Douglas
1970, p. 15). In brief, assigning victim and victimizer status to particular
individuals depends upon situated evaluations of conditions (Has harm
been done?) *and* people (Are the persons experiencing the harm moral?
Are the persons causing the harm immoral?).

This interactional process of assigning particular individuals to
people-categories of victim and victimizer has its parallel in social problems claims-making. Claims construct condition-categories as harmful;
claims construct victim-categories as containing a moral type of person;

claims construct victimizer-categories as containing an immoral type of person. My point is that social problems construction of people-categories places these person-types within particular moral universes, which simultaneously places them within particular universes of sympathy-worthiness or condemnation-worthiness. Within folk reasoning, constructing morality simultaneously constructs preferred emotional orientations.

Because evaluations of conditions and persons, morality and emotion are commonsensically related, counterrhetorical strategies surrounding a condition-category can be organized around constructing morality or immorality, sympathy-worthiness or condemnation-worthiness of persons *in* the category. The most obvious example is the condition-category of "AIDS." When this category was constructed as inhabited by homosexual-type people, intravenous drug user–type people, and Haitian immigrant–type people, there was little concern among heterosexual, middle-class Americans. Within heterosexual, middle-class folk reasoning, such types of persons can be constructed as complicit in creating the harm they experience and, hence, as not victims and therefore as persons not sympathy-worthy, and thus as persons not deserving help. Middle-class, heterosexual concern about the condition-category of "AIDS" increased when this category was constructed as inhabited by sympathy-worthy types of people: heterosexual-type people, baby-type people, women-type people, and hemophiliac-type people. In brief, dramatizing the victim status of person-types dramatizes their morality, dramatizing their morality dramatizes their sympathy-worthiness. In the same way, rhetorically dramatizing the choice and intent of victimizers dramatizes immorality, immorality is associated with the emotional response of condemnation, and this supports the behavioral responses of punishment and control. So, for example, punitive laws surrounding the condition-category of "drunk driving" emerged simultaneously with the construction of the "drunk driver" as a type of person characterized by hedonism and wanton disregard for others (Gusfield 1981).

I am suggesting here that emotions are analyzable as "socially constructed language forms" (Perinbanayagam 1989). Within such a casting, emotions discourses are linguistic cultural resources available for members to situationally use in evaluating, labeling, expressing, and managing putative internal states. Such vocabularies are claims-making activities. Indeed, emotions claims-making is similar to claims-making for the cultural category of "social problems." Activities in both are historically and culturally embedded, both activities reflect power and politics (Denzin 1990), and both reflect the particular and local concerns of claims-makers (McCarthy 1989). Although psychiatrists, counselors, advice book writers, and clergy are the most obvious emotions claims-makers (McCarthy 1989), social problems claims-makers also construct emotions when they rhetorically produce categories of people. Claims construct ways to "think" and to "feel" about people-categories.

Most clearly, this is a sociology of knowledge approach to emotions and morality. It is about how social problems claims construct categories as inhabiting various folk universes of morality and emotion; it is about how emotions and morality are discourses and claims-making activities. Outside the constructionist perspective there are myriad questions about relationships among such claims and cognition, situated appraisals, and lived feelings; within the constructionist perspective there are questions about how emotions and moral discourses are interrelated rhetorics of social problems claims.

Expanding the Constructionist Agenda

My points here were quite straightforward: If constructionists are to examine the "full range of definitional activities" (Schneider 1984b, p. viii), then constructing putative people and constructing these people in ways placing them within one or another folk universe of morality and emotion might reasonably be examined as claims-making activity.

My call to focus explicit attention on the creation of putative people is merely a call to bring into the foreground of study something often left in the background. For example, I am emphasizing that Joseph Gusfield's book, *The Culture of Public Problems: Drinking-Driving and the Symbolic Order* (1981), is as much about the people-category of "drunk driver" as it is about the condition-category of "drunk driving"; I am noting that claims constructing the person-category of the "battered woman" are a critical component of claims constructing the condition-category of "wife abuse" (Loseke 1992). There are three potential benefits to bringing this study of people- categories into sharper focus.

First, just as claims-making surrounding condition-categories is important for "subsequent social and political activity" (Schneider 1984b, p. xix) so, too, is claims-making about the types of people inhabiting these categories. Most clearly, the construction of people-types is consequential for the subsequent official interactional production of people. Social services are organized for specific types of people; organizational rules, methods of service delivery, and worker understandings reflect and perpetuate these constructed images (Loseke 1992; Miller 1991). More subtly, given the complexity of our world, members often are asked to evaluate and respond to some anonymous and unknown others as victims, and to evaluate and respond to unknown others as victimizers. The extent to which unique people in condition-categories are unknown in lived reality is the extent to which people-type constructions are practically important since members' cognitive understandings, moral evaluations, emotional responses, and behavioral expressions can be based only on these constructions.

Second, examining the rhetorical production of people-categories takes seriously the often inextricably tied package of social problems claims linking person-type and condition-type. This is critical in our postmodern world where social problems claims to the general public can come in the form of magazine articles, political slogans, mass mailings, and television talk shows, docudramas, and movies of the week. Condition-categories on such stages of social problems construction often are represented by individual stories of persons in the categories. Hence, "Willie Horton" symbolizes a type of person and a type of condition; characters in the television movie, *The Burning Bed,* symbolize the condition-category of "wife abuse"; "Adam Walsh" symbolizes the condition-category of "missing children." In such claims, condition-type and person-type are all but interchangeable; the condition-category is collapsed into victim and/or victimizer person-categories.

Third and finally, attention to the production of people categories is necessary for theoretical consistency within constructionism. While there is ongoing concern about the problems of objectivism in claims about condition-categories, there should be similar concern about objectivism in person-categories. After all, since putative people exist only within putative conditions, deconstructing conditions should involve deconstructing the inhabitants of those conditions.

In brief, I have argued that constructionists might profitably maintain a radical focus on members' constitutive practices while expanding attention to the rhetorical production of people-categories. I have also argued that while Ibarra and Kitsuse emphasize that social problems talk is moral talk, such discourse also constructs preferred *emotional* orientations toward constructed categories. Because morality and emotion are associated in folk knowledge, constructionists might begin to examine how emotions discourse is a language of social problems claims.

Adding a study of emotions discourse to constructionism is methodologically compatible with the perspective because emotion, like morality, is found in language. Furthermore, examining relationships among folk categories of social problems, emotions, and morality recognizes a defining characteristic of claims-making in postmodern times. In particular, observers have noted how claims about social problems are being made to "increasingly jaded audiences" (Best 1990), who daily see on their televisions the images of "troubled, pained, dying, starving, mutilated persons" (Denzin 1990, p. 105), and who feel increasing ambivalence toward unknown others (Weigert and Franks 1989). Within such a world, logic and cognition are relativized and in their place is emotion consciousness: What members "feel" is judged as more important than what members "think" (McCarthy 1989). It makes sense that claims about social problems categories made by and for members in such a world would use rhetorics organized around emotional themes. So, criticisms that constructionists have paid too much attention to claims made in the political sphere (Ibarra and Kitsuse) might be paralleled by comments that constructionists have privileged cognition and rationality at the expense of examining discourses of emotion.

Most clearly, my remarks about emotions discourse in social problems claims are exploratory. First, while I have drawn from a field called the sociology of emotions, this perspective is historically very new and does not contain a vast catalog of insights pertaining directly to the languages of social problems claims. So, for example, there are examinations of claims-making in the construction of emotions such as the feelings and expressions of love (Oakes 1989), anger (Sterns and Sterns 1986), ambivalence (Weigert and Franks 1989), jealousy (Clanton 1989), or bodily and emotional control (Elias 1978), but there are primarily only calls to undertake such examinations for the social categories of "victim" (Holstein and Miller 1990) and "victimizer" (Douglas 1970). Likewise, within the constructionist perspective on social problems, attention to emotions discourse has been narrowly centered on examining "horror stories" in mass media claims (e.g., Best 1990; Johnson 1989). General questions about relationships among cognitive, moral, and emotions themes in social problems discourse remain largely unexplored.

Finally, my remarks are exploratory because attending to members' ways of constructing emotions no doubt would require constructionists to stop privileging word-bound language and to begin developing methods for examining *visual images* as claims. In our postmodern world it might be that visual images do not merely *"alter* a claim" (Ibarra and Kitsuse); such images might *be* the claim. Stated otherwise, if a picture is worth a thousand words, a visual image organized around emotional themes might be worth a thousand word-bound claims. Because constructing such images is claims-making activity, deconstructing such images is sociological activity.

In summary, it is the right historical time to expand the constructionists' agenda in order to examine the rhetorical production of people-types and the production of these types as residing within particular folk universes of morality *and* emotion. The rhetorical production of conditions, people, morality, and emotion can be interrelated claims-making activities; the languages of morality and emotions can be the interdependent discourses of social problem construction.

Acknowledgments

As usual, I am greatly indebted to James Holstein and Gale Miller for their comments, recommendations, and encouragement.

References

Best, J. 1990. *Threatened Children: Rhetoric and Concern About Child-Victims.* Chicago: University of Chicago Press.

Clanton, G. 1989. "Jealousy in American Culture." Pp. 179–96 in *The Sociology of Emotions: Original Essays and Research Papers,* edited by D. Franks and E. D. McCarthy. Greenwich, CT: JAI Press.

Clark, C. 1987. "Sympathy Biography and Sympathy Margin." *American Journal of Sociology* 92:290–321.

Denzin, N. 1990. "On Understanding Emotion: The Interpretive-Cultural Agenda." Pp. 85–116 in *Research Agendas in the Sociology of Emotions,* edited by T. Kemper. Albany: State University of New York Press.

Douglas, J. D. 1970. "Deviance and Respectability: The Social Construction of Moral Meanings. Pp. 3–30 in *Deviance and Respectability: The Social Construction of Moral Meanings,* edited by J. D. Douglas. New York: Basic Books.

Elias, N. 1978. *The Civilizing Process, Vol. 1, The History of Manners.* New York: Urizen.

Gusfield, J. R. 1981. *The Culture of Public Problems: Drinking-Driving and the Symbolic Order.* Chicago: University of Chicago Press.

Holstein, J. A. 1992. "Producing People: Descriptive Practice in Human Service Work." Pp. 23–40 in *Current Research on Occupations and Professions,* edited by G. Miller. Greenwich, CT: JAI Press.

Holstein, J. A. and G. Miller. 1990. "Rethinking Victimization: An Interaction Approach to Victimology." *Symbolic Interaction* 13:103–22.

Johnson, J. M. 1989. "Horror Stories and the Construction of Child Abuse." Pp. 5–19 in *Images of Issues: Typifying Contemporary Social Problems,* edited by J. Best. Hawthorne, NY: Aldine de Gruyter.

Loseke, D. R. 1992. *The Battered Woman and Shelters: The Social Construction of Wife Abuse.* Albany: State University of New York Press.

Maynard, D. W. 1984. *Inside Plea Bargaining: The Language of Negotiation.* New York: Plenum Press.

McCarthy, E. D. 1989. "Emotions are Social Things: An Essay in the Sociology of Emotions." Pp. 51–72 in *The Sociology of Emotions: Original Essays and Research Papers,* edited by D. D. Franks and E. D. McCarthy. Greenwich, CT: JAI Press.

McHugh, P. 1970. "A Common-Sense Conception of Deviance." Pp. 61–88 in *Deviance and Respectability: The Social Construction of Moral Meanings,* edited by J. D. Douglas. New York: Basic Books.

Miller, G. 1991. *Enforcing the Work Ethic: Rhetoric and Everyday Life in a Work Incentive Program.* Albany: State University of New York Press.

Oakes, G. 1989. "Eros and Modernity: Georg Simmel on Love." Pp. 229–48 in *The Sociology of Emotions: Original Essays and Research Papers,* edited by D. D. Franks and E. D. McCarthy. Greenwich, CT: JAI Press.

Perinbanayagam, R. S. 1989. "Signifying Emotions." Pp. 73–94 in *The Sociology of Emotions: Original Essays and Research Papers,* edited by D. D. Franks and E. D. McCarthy. Greenwich, CT: JAI Press.

Sacks, H. 1972. "On the Analyzability of Stories by Children." Pp. 329–45 in *Directions in Sociolinguistics: The Ethnography of Communication,* edited by J. J. Gumperz and D. Hymes. New York: Holt, Rinehart & Winston.

Schneider, J. 1984a. "Morality, Social Problems, and Everyday Life." Pp. 180–206 in *Studies in the Sociology of Social Problems,* edited by J. W. Schneider and J. I. Kitsuse. Norwood, NJ: Ablex.

———. 1984b. "Introduction." Pp. vii–xx in *Studies in the Sociology of Social Problems,* edited by J. W. Schneider and J. I. Kitsuse. Norwood, NJ: Ablex.

———. 1985. "Social Problems Theory: The Constructionist View." Pp. 209–29 in *Annual Review of Sociology,* edited by R. Turner. Palo Alto, CA: Annual Reviews.

Spector, M. and J. I. Kitsuse. [1977] 1987. *Constructing Social Problems.* Hawthorne, NY: Aldine de Gruyter.

Sterns, C. Z. and P. N. Sterns. 1986. *Anger: The Struggle for Emotional Control in America's History.* Chicago: University of Chicago Press.

Weigert, A. and D. D. Franks. 1989. "Ambivalence: A Touchstone of the Modern Temper." Pp. 205–28 in *The Sociology of Emotions: Original Essays and Research Papers,* edited by D. D. Franks and E. D. McCarthy. Greenwich, CT: JAI Press.

Wittgenstein, Ludwig. 1958. *The Blue and Brown Books.* New York: Harper Colophon.

Index

Abortion issue, 27–28
Academia setting, 50–51
Acquired immunodeficiency syndrome (AIDS), 116–118
AIDS (acquired immunodeficiency syndrome), 116–118
Alzheimer's disease movement, 59–60, 63–64
Analytic constructionism, 71–72, 74–75
Analytic topics, 91–93
Antipatterning, 41
Attitude of scientific theorizing, 93–94
Attitudes, multiplicity of, 93–95
Audience, 56–58

Battered woman collective representation, 138–139
Bracketing, 30, 99–100
Bricoleur, 94–95

Calamity, rhetoric of, 30, 37
Civic style, 46, 48
Claims-making
  commonsense discourses and, 165, 166
  depoliticizing, 162
  exchange of, 159–160
  managing readability of, 170–174
  marginalization and, 160–161, 162
  membership and, 25
  muted responses and, 163–164
  politicizing, 161–162
  poststructuralism and, 166–169
  power and, 164–165
  producing readable, 162–163
  professional discourses and, 165–166
  referential aspects of, 30
  silencing potential, 169
Claims-making styles (See also specific types)
  condition-categories and, shift from, 38–39

Constructing Social Problems and, 120
  definition of, 31
  marginalization of, 169–170
  power and, 170–174
  rhetorical analysis and, 45–49
  settings and, 49–51
  social constructionism and, 45
Collective representations, 133–134, 138–139, 162
Comic style, 47
Commonsense discourses, 165, 166
Condition-categories
  bracketing of, 99–100
  claims-making styles and, shift to, 38–39
  rhetorical idioms and, 32–33
  "Vernacular Constituents of Moral Discourse" and, 26–29, 120
Constructing Social Problems (See CSP)
Construction, 84
Constructionism (See also specific types)
  definition of, 70
  ethnomethodology and, 84–85
  social problems theory and, 83–85
Construction of reflexivity, 76–78
Constructivism (See Constructionism)
Contextual constructionism
  ontological gerrymandering and, 7–8
  perspective of, 118–119
  strict constructionism and, 8
Contrast structures, 137
Counterrhetoric of hysteria, 42
Counterrhetoric of insincerity, 41–42
Counterrhetorics (See also specific types)
  definition of, 30–31
  rhetorical analysis and, 38–43
  unsympathetic, 41–43
CSP (Constructing Social Problems) (Spector and Kitsuse)
  claims-making styles and, 120
  emendation of, 70, 78–79

217

Morality, 210–212
Moral representation, 46–47
Motifs (*See also* specific types)
  definition of, 31
  examples of, 43
  identical, 44
  rhetorical analysis and, 43–44
  social problems and, 44
  symbolic currency of, 44
Mundane, 61–63
Mundane labeling theory, 10
Mundane ontology, 25
Muted responses, 163–164

Natural attitude, 22–23, 93–95
Naturalism, 64–66
Naturalizing, 39

Objectivism, 74–75
Objectivist constructionism
  Constructing Social Problems and,
    74–76
  description of, 70–71
  reflexive responses and, 74–76
  strict constructionism and, 114
Ontological gerrymandering
  Constructing Social Problems and, 69,
    120
  contextual constructionism and, 7–
    8
  social constructionism and, 3, 7–9,
    199
  social problems and, 8–9
  strict constructionism and, 114–115

Perspectivizing, 40
Policing juveniles, 12–13
Political correctness, 51
Political representation, 200–202
Positivism, 182–183
Poststructuralism
  claims-making and, 166–169
  marginalization and, 156–159, 174–
    176
  power and, 157
  social problems and, 157–159
Power
  claims-making and, 164–165
  claims-making styles and, 170–174
  gossip and, 170
  poststructuralism and, 157

Practical project, 25–26
Private sphere, 44
Professional discourses, 165–166
Psychiatric testimony, 141–143
Publicity, 58–59
Public problems, 44 (*See also* Social
    problems)
Putative conditions
  ambiguity of, 74
  Constructing Social Problems and,
    23–24
  social problems and, 4
  "Vernacular Constituents of Moral
    Discourse" and, 23–24, 26, 74
Putative people, 208–209

Reflexive constructionism, 76–78
Reflexivity, 13, 69–70, 74–76 (*See also*
    Construction of reflexivity)
Rhetoric, 30
Rhetorical analysis
  claims-making styles and, 45–49
  counterrhetorics and, 38–43
  definition of, 29–30
  motifs and, 43–44
  rhetorical idioms and, 31–38
  settings and, 49–51
Rhetorical idioms (*See also* specific
    types)
  condition-categories and, 32–33
  definition of, 30
  function of, 31–32
  rhetorical analysis and, 31–38
Rhetorician, 58–61
Rhetoric of calamity, 30, 37
Rhetoric of endangerment, 35–36
Rhetoric of entitlement, 34–35
Rhetoric of loss, 30, 33–34
Rhetoric of unreason, 30, 36

Satanism, 110–111, 116–117, 119
Scientific style, 45–47
Selective relativism, 75
Sense of agency
  audience and, 56–58
  membership and, 63–64
  mundane and, 61–63
  rhetorician and, 58–61
  vernacular tone and, 61–64
Settings (*See also* specific types)
  claims-making styles and, 49–51